DAVID LAWRENCE

The King of White-Collar Boxing

A MEMOIR

▲
Rain Mountain Press
New York City

First Printing May 2012

The King of White Collar Boxing
Copyright 2012 © by David Lawrence

Some names have been changed to protect the privacy of individuals.

ISBN: 0-9834783-3-1

Rain Mountain Press
www.rainmountainpress.com

An excerpt from this memoir appeared in *Boxing Scene*

"Snow Scenes in Jail" appeared in *Fullosia Press*

Printed By: Publishers Graphics, Carol Stream, IL

Design: Sarah McElwain
cover photo: Abel, Atlantic City, 1992

Library of Congress Cataloging-in-Publication Data

Lawrence, David, 1947-
  The king of white collar boxing / David Lawrence.
    p. cm.
  ISBN 978-0-9834783-3-1 (pbk. : alk. paper) 1. Lawrence, David, 1947- 2. Boxers (Sports)--United States--Biography. 3. Boxing--United States. I. Title.
  GV1132.L357A3 2011
  796.83092--dc23
  [B]
                    2011042461

Thanks to Lauren
for staying with me despite my
changes and disappointments

David in front of his Rolls
Royce at the old Gleason's Gym
near Madison Square Garden in
the 1980s.

1

I'M SPARRING WITH LIOR. I'm his coach. He's paying me thirty dollars for the lesson. He's not even my weight class. He weighs thirty pounds more than me. He's a lot stronger than I am. He's built like a fire pump. He's less than half my age and benches three hundred pounds. But this is boxing, not weightlifting.

He's not supposed to hit me in the head. I'm not even supposed to be in the ring boxing, due to head injuries. I was never very good at following doctors' orders. My EEG report said that I had localized slowing of my brain waves. I suppose that meant that I had some sort of brain damage. I don't know. I like the idea of being brain damaged. It is dramatic. Call me a jar labeled "Schmuckers." I spread myself out. I stick to taking chances. I lick the knife. I read the bread crumbs fallen from the toast as if they were tea leaves. Sometimes I don't know who I am. Other times I am whomever my behavior defines. I am my interpretation of my own actions. Indeed, I am defined by my deeds. Or perhaps I am that vast shifting, sometimes dishonest, plain of self-interpretation.

Lior bashes me in the head anyway. He's no neurologist. I loop an uppercut into his nose and he starts bleeding. We stop. I apologize. I didn't mean it. I'm the one who wasn't supposed to be hit. I was only trying to slow him down. I didn't want to go home with a bruise and get killed by my wife to whom I had promised I wouldn't step in the ring again. She worries about me. I am her psychology project. That's nice. I like her attention but it can be constricting.

My sparring with Lior is all in good fun. We get along. We go back into my office to chat. Lior's a twenty-five year old stockbroker who's trying to get into shape. I enjoy talking to him. I am a chatterbox. Half the boxing lessons I give are social. We gossip. I help the guys with their girlfriend problems. I help the girls with their boyfriend problems. I am a boxing social worker, a counselor. I help myself by relating to a captive audience. I have lived long enough to become wise. It's August 2006 and I am nearly sixty years old. Wow. Death is at hand. Come and get me. I can fight.

How many lifetimes have I lived? How many times have I wandered between my left and my right, my love and my hate, lost in the ambivalence of an aging neurotic from the baby boomer era? I am from the love generation that was supposed to save the world. Instead we failed to define it. We assumed. We assumed that love was simple and that violence was ipso facto negative rather than the first step towards ending violence. We did not know that avoiding the responsibility of war could result in our pacifism killing millions of people in Cambodia and Vietnam. We were good-hearted but ideological and self-destructive. We called ourselves the "love generation" but hated anyone who didn't share in our hippy values. Anyone who rebelled against the military industrial complex was labeled intelligent rather than naïve and self-destructive. We didn't understand that violence could be more curative of violence than passivity. We didn't know that a stalemate of nuclear bombs prevented the use of them. We didn't think that disarmament could lead to war.

Courage involves the bad public relations of aggressivity. Let love die because love kills. Ooh, but we do get deep or confused. I have a lot to say. I box. It keeps me simple, honest, sincere.

I started boxing at Gleason's Gym in New York City in 1985. During the sixties I had gone through a phase of being a peacenik wearing puka beads, going to poetry readings and chanting Om. Then I became a businessman whose idea of violent exercise was tennis. I thought boxing would put me back in touch with my teenage years when I used to get into fights. I hated violence and the loud screechiness of emotional street fights but I somehow missed dominating another kid. Boxing became the substitute for the ugliness of neighborhood brawls.

A couple of years later Gleason's moved to Brooklyn and I followed it. It is the oldest and the most famous boxing gym in the world. It was once referred to as the Sorbonne of Boxing, which I liked. After all I had gotten a Ph.D. in Literature from City University Graduate Center in 1976. I was part of the literary "cognoscenti."

My current office at Gleason's is cluttered and stuffed like a breadbox. The other day a mouse ran across my floor. I'm not afraid of mice. I thought its patter was rather charming. Back at my old office at 120 Wall Street where I was a businessman the custodial staff would have sent in the mouse patrol with rodent killing equipment. Now I don't even know if I'll bother to report the mouse to the owner of the gym, Bruce Silverglade. Let the mouse rule. I had a whole team of them when I lived at the halfway house.

I was once the Chairman and CEO of my own insurance brokerage, Allied Programs Corp. We occupied the entire twenty-sixth floor at 120 Wall Street. I had a private office in the corner with a huge tree-lined terrace hanging over the East River. My staff used to jokingly call my office "The Shrine." The walls were filled with pictures and magazine articles about my boxing career. There was not much to say about my business career. The idea of making a lot of money wasn't theatrical. It was nice but it wasn't thrilling. I was successful but I wasn't big like Donald Trump. Unlike my dalliance with boxing, my insurance career wasn't newsworthy. I wore Armani suits and Cartier watches. I hid my Rolex because it was too crass, tacky.

The office, the money, the prestige are all gone. But the same magazine articles, plus stray new ones, now cover my walls at Gleason's Gym—*People Magazine, New York Magazine, Men's Journal, American Health,* etc. Only my walls are smaller. I share 150 square feet with the world super bantamweight kickboxing champion, Devon Cormack and his sister, the female world boxing featherweight champion, Alicia "Slick" Ashley. Their belts are on Devon's desk. The only championship belt I have is from the Rapper's Federation Fights. What a joke. I fought Kurtis Blow. Not exactly world class caliber. But at least it's something and I'm strangely proud of it.

"There's a sign that the gym is closing early tomorrow," Lior says. "What's up with that?"

"They're shooting a scene from *Law & Order*. Bruce said I could be in it but I don't know," I said.

"Are you kidding? Do it. It's who you are. An actor. A coach. That's what all your students like about you," Lior said.

"It's only extra work."

"Does it pay?"

"One hundred and forty bucks."

"Hey, that's almost five lessons."

He was right. I only got thirty dollars a lesson.

"What the heck. I'll do *Law & Order*," I told Lior.

Later I told Bruce that I'd take the part and thanked him profusely.

That night I asked my wife if I should be an extra on *Law & Order*.

"How much does it pay?" she asked.

"One hundred and forty dollars," I told her.

"Take it," she said. "I'm proud of you. You're working so hard."

I kissed her on the cheek. She was proud of me. When I bought her a hundred thousand dollar diamond ring in 1985, she seemed less happy with me than she did at this moment. I thought of the Beatles song, "Can't Buy Me Love." It's all in the effort. Sometimes.

That's one of the beauties of being one of the have-nots. Every little thing I did for her now thrilled her. The poor whine about having nothing but they get love for next to nothing. Every little thing they do impresses. Not much is expected. Everything is a gift or a surprise. My wife was just happy to see me trying. And I was happy to see her happy that I was trying. Not that we hadn't had our rough times when we were adjusting to our marriage and our child. But now was different. Age had mellowed us. We let things slide. We felt like young newlyweds saving for our first apartment.

I guess my wife thought all those millions in the past came easy. In some ways they did. Money was meaningless. I now liked being a working stiff more than I liked being a millionaire. Even food tastes better. When I laid out twenty bucks at a diner it was more meaningful than using my old house charge at Le Cirque. I was finding truth in struggling. I liked being poor. I was an idiot. Was I crazy? Maybe.

According to the doctors I am brain damaged. I discovered this through acting. When I lost my business, I tried to get rich and famous by becoming a movie star. I wanted to earn back everything I had lost. I played in underground films that never made it to the screen.

While taking classes at Weist-Barron Studios I discovered that I couldn't memorize my lines. I mean it could have been my age — I was in my fifties. Or it could have been because I was bipolar. Or it could have been the stress of having lost my business. Or it could have been all of that plus having been punched in the head thousands of times over a couple of decades of boxing.

Anyhow, I went to a psychologist, Joel Redfield, who gave me a battery of tests. He discovered all sorts of cognitive deficits and dysfunctions. He said I'd have to see a neurologist to discover if there was any structural damage from boxing. He suggested that I should always box with headgear. Like that would really help. He didn't know that it was illegal to box without headgear in a New York State gym anyway. Headgear merely protected fighters against cuts from head butts. It didn't reduce the impact of a concussion.

The neurologist, Dr. J. Charney, did an EEG. He discovered that the test came out abnormal with "localized slowing of the right temporal-parietal area (which) suggests an underlying structural abnormality." He told me to quit boxing immediately.

I did. But I didn't quite believe him that I was brain damaged nor did I believe the psychiatrists who say I'm bipolar. Maybe I have dementia pugilistica? Maybe I'm punch drunk. I don't even really know what dementia pugilistica means. To me it's a name, a label I can hang onto. It says something about me that I did something enthusiastically enough to get hurt. That I'm the kind of guy who lays it all on the line for whatever his goal is. That's not much. But when you're looking around for who you are, it's something. It gives me an outline I can bounce against. I don't float free towards insanity.

My feelings about Bruce's offer to be in *Law & Order* changed the next day. The idea of sitting around the gym for hours being an "extra" was awful. I had things I wanted to do. There were poems to be written. I had been writing most of my life. I had a few hundred poems published. I was a poet. Not that I liked poets. Most of them were wimps. They displayed their superficial sensitivity to avoid being more deeply sensitive; they hid behind their soft bellies. Writing was part of me. I couldn't stop it. My poetry was my communication to the next generation. It was my goodbye letter.

Besides, I wanted to see my wife early. I didn't want to get home at midnight. I called her and told her that I decided not to take the part in *Law & Order*.

"Why not? Is it because you're just an extra, not a star?" she asked.

"No. It's just that nothing's going to come of it. And I'd rather be home with you," I said.

"But you need the money."

"I know. I'll work harder during the week," I said.

"All right," she said. "It will be nice to see you early."

"You too," I said and hung up. I told Bruce that I decided to skip the shoot. He didn't care. Plenty of extras wanted the work.

I went back into my office and took out a sheet of paper. I started writing a poem about anything. It didn't matter. I liked the process not the commentary. I liked to be engaged in creation. I didn't care what I created.

I was happy to be in my office. I didn't belong in the outside world. I wasn't really part of it. I had fallen from grace. I had bailed out of Wall Street. I had done a two-year bid at Schuylkill Federal Prison Camp. Would I end up a bum on the streets? Would I go back into business again and regain my wealth? Maybe I'd teach poetry at a university. Maybe I'd return to active boxing. No, I couldn't. No one would give me a license at my age with my messed up EEG.

I was a surprise. I didn't know what shadow was rising to meet me or falling behind me. It was fun to walk in my footsteps. I was a happy guy. No matter what.

•••

It was 1986 and I was happy to see Sam bleeding. I liked
Sam but I didn't like what he represented—the proliferat-
ing field of corporate lawyers. They possessed the laws, the
rules, the regulations. Their shit didn't stink. My chest still
hurt from the punch he gave me when we sparred a couple of months ago. It was a lousy punch, a thud more than
a snap. But Sam weighed over two hundred pounds and his
fist cracked my sternum. I think. I never got it x-rayed. I
was no wuss. I didn't need any doctors. I couldn't laugh or
cough for weeks.

Chuck was sparring with Sam. I liked watching Chuck
master him. Chuck was a six-foot tall, one hundred and
forty pound black man who moved like Sugar Ray Robinson. He lived in Harlem and used to spar with businessmen to pick up extra money. Later his picture appeared in
a book of people with unusual occupations.

Men are killers. It's built into the tips of their penises.
I had spent the sixties trying to get in touch with my feminine side. Now I wanted to embrace my masculine side.
Sam had all-American blond hair. He had played high
school football. He was rah rah, and all that. He caught a
straight right and his nose bled red droplets onto the spotted canvas. I thought of Jackson Pollock splattering paint
in the hopes of immortality. I thought of Sam getting his
nose busted up in the hopes of discovering his own mor-
tality. Hell, what was I thinking? I was the only one in the
gym who'd even heard of Jackson Pollock.

When Suzanne Berlin first showed up at Gleason's
Gym in March of '86, I didn't pay her much mind. I had
figured she was working for some local newspaper. Ever

since I started boxing I was used to being interviewed by small time presses. Everyone wanted to know why a millionaire would box. It was a sport for poor people like polo was for the rich. I had no idea Suzanne was a big-time reporter. She was wearing khaki pants and a flight jacket. There was a friendly purple mole on her right cheek. She was foreign, cute. I was standing on the ring apron with her, watching Sam bleed.

"I'm a reporter," she said with a German accent.

"That's nice," I said.

I had started boxing at Gleason's about a year ago. I was still working out there even though I was now training two nights a week at the New York Athletic Club for the Wall Street Charities Fight, which was a much-ballyhooed tournament for brokers. All my respect went to Gleason's. I was in awe of its hallowed tradition of pain. The New York Athletic Club was some sort of white-collar crap. It was the kind of place George Plimpton might go to, a salt and pepper cartoon of violence. A little blood sprinkled here and there. There were no blacks or Puerto Ricans fighting for their lives there. It was like an all-white glee club. I wasn't afraid of the New York Athletic Club and without fear there wasn't any religion. There was something sacred about pain.

"Is his nose hurt?" Suzanne asked about Sam.

"His nose bleeds all the time," I said. "Don't worry about him." I figured because she was a woman she'd be upset.

"It's not my nose," she said. "Why should I care?" She was German. I forgot that her culture's etiology was the gas chamber. What was a bloody nose to a person who came from a country that did scientific experiments on twins? The Nazis used to throw naked children in snowdrifts and time how long it took them to freeze to death.

"I'm doing an article for *People Magazine* about Yuppie boxing," she added. "I'd like you to be in it."

She said it just like that. Like *People Magazine* wasn't the biggest deal in the world. Like I wouldn't be knocked over with joy to get a write-up there. Like I wouldn't want my fifteen minutes of Warhol fame. But one thing really bothered me about what she said. "I'm no Yuppie," I said. I hated Yuppies.

"What do you mean? Aren't you rich, young, and upwardly mobile?" She must have seen my chauffeured Rolls Royce waiting outside the gym.

"I'm not young for boxing," I said. "I'm thirty-eight already."

"But you're young to be so rich."

"Maybe. But I'm not upwardly mobile. I'm the CEO of my own insurance brokerage. I'm not a striver." I smiled. This was an upper class distinction. Like knowing the difference between a French Cabernet and a Merlot. Like knowing the distinction between discreet, clear diamonds and hazy bling. I hoped she'd understand. I didn't mean to be a snob. I took pride in a little wit. It wasn't for effect like Oscar Wilde. I didn't want to escape from myself. I was always trying to define who I was.

"So you don't want to be in *People Magazine*."

Of course I wanted to be in *People Magazine*. "I just don't want to be called a Yuppie," I said.

I had only been boxing a year. I had played tennis for twenty years and here I was getting so much attention as a neophyte boxer. For my tennis, I never got more than one line in the *New York Times*.

"I'll try not to call you a Yuppie," she said.

"I don't care," I said. *People Magazine*. Wow.

●●●

On the surface, the reason I got involved with boxing related to my wife's making me give up my motorcycles. On a deeper level there was this tribal thing. I wanted to defeat enemies. Boxing was a forbidden planet. It was filled with ethnic lower classes. I was separated from the poor by my position. I thought they might have some secret I wanted to hear. A sacred truth I could write a poem about. I used to teach English at Hunter College. Poetry was my way out of death. If someone read my poems in the future, I would live forever. But I hadn't written anything in a long while.

One morning in May 1985, I was fiddling around with my motorcycles in the garage at my summer home in West Hampton. I loved my early morning rides. I felt reckless, free.

My neighbors were all upscale schmucks. I looked at the happy families around me and I wanted to puke. They reminded me of myself. Boys with toys, girls with wardrobes. I spent many joyous mornings sneaking out of the house to go over to the professional motocross track. I was starting my Yamaha up when I saw my wife, Lauren, and my son, Graham, coming into the garage. They were never up this early. Graham was seven years old. He wore little jeans and his hair in a Beatles cut. He was adorable. He had done some work for Ford Modeling Agency but my wife made him quit when she got worried that it would interfere with his schoolwork. Give the woman her due. She was no stage mother. She wanted what was best for him.

Graham was crying when he came into the garage.

"Daddy, you're going to die," he said.

He looked so sad. I patted his head. What was he talking about? I wasn't dying.

"Did you hear?" Lauren asked, all teary-eyed.

"Hear what?" I asked.

"Our driver, Jerry. He died in a motorcycle crash!"

"Don't die, Daddy."

I was stunned. Jerry had only been driving for us a couple of years. I was sad to hear that he had died. He was a wild, cool kid. He had told me he was getting a motorcycle. I wasn't listening. I did not stop to consider that it would end in his death.

In a way Jerry's death made me jealous. He actually rode his motorcycle to a grave. That took balls. I didn't have his guts. I was still trying to get the nerve to jump a bump on the motocross track. And there he was, courageously dead. He outdid me.

"You better get rid of those bikes before you kill yourself. You owe it to your son," Lauren said.

"You owe me daddy," Graham shrieked.

Lauren didn't want me to kill myself? That was nice. But you don't take away a man's courage in the face of death. I was a gladiator. I'd show her. I'd do something that would really blow her away.

"Then I'm taking up boxing. I'm going to fight at Madison Square Garden," I said.

I didn't know where that came from. I had never wanted to box before. I had never even attended a fight. I figured the image of me slugging it out like some mad African in the ring would drive Lauren crazy. I didn't want to annoy her. Yet it somehow tickled me. Love is a sadistic, erotic field of action. I wanted to see if I could get her to respond. Putting her on edge was like arousing her. I wanted to stick pins of wakefulness in her. I wanted her to love me uncomfortably.

"Good," she said. "Take up boxing."

Good. But it didn't really matter that I would have to give up the dirt bikes. I wasn't going anywhere with them anyhow. I was scared to jump the bigger bumps on the racetrack. At least maybe I'd have the balls to fight. I did some street fighting when I was a troubled teen. I once split a kid's head open. Screw it! I was ready to roll my testosterone around like craps in Atlantic City, to prove that I was the man. Not that I had anything against women. I just wasn't one. I was from Mars, not Venus. I was Iron David.

Who was I kidding? I was brought up with a Jewish golden spoon up my ass. There was a bar mitzvah in my rectum. I was a golden Torah. When I became a success in business, I attended museum soirees and charity functions in an Armani tuxedo. You could meet me at book parties or boutique openings. My picture appeared in the society pages of magazines. I was aristocratic like a gentleman horse breeder. If someone told you that I planned to become a professional prizefighter, you would have laughed. Remember this was before white-collar people and women started joining boxing gyms.

I really wasn't the boxing type. I was not war torn Bosnia. I was a small postal district out west.

2

IT WAS A FRISKY day in October 1985. I had never boxed before. I decided I would give it a try. The sun bobbed and weaved behind the clouds. My brother, Pete, was with me. He was two years older than me. He worked with me at my company, Allied Programs Corp. I also asked a nerdy, unathletic employee, Marty Banks to come along. He was barely hanging onto his job and seized any opportunity to get into my good graces. I felt bad for the guy and was looking for a reason to keep him on board.

We turned on Sixth Avenue and Thirtieth Street and walked over to Gleason's Gym. It was right near Madison Square Garden. I had called all the Y's and none of them gave boxing lessons. It was too dangerous. We had to try a professional gym. We walked inside and I felt like we were in the shadow land of the fight game. Sweat, grunts, gulps, shouts. The rat-a-tat-tat of speed bags. The thuds of heavy bags. Ropes skipping. The sound of punches landing on headgear. The scent of hurt. A trickle of fear. I felt like I was enrolling in the University of Pain.

We lined up at the desk at the front of the gym like schoolboys waiting for cookies at the commissary in camp. Ira Becker, the owner, a skinny little guy in his sixties with a punch-drunk face, was standing behind the desk. His partner Bruce Silverglade, a former business executive, was talking with an Hispanic fighter. Bruce didn't look like a fighter but Ira's nose was all over his face and you could see that he put in his time in the ring. He wore his nose proudly. Injuries are trophies in an arena where manliness is the highest virtue. It's like getting a long sentence in jail. Something you can be proud of. I'd later find out that everyone in jail looked down on short-termers the way boxers scoffed at straight noses. There are private societies in the world with their own values and rules.

"What do you want?" Ira said, gruffly. There was a flicker of a smile hiding in the corner of his mouth. He was wondering what three stiffs like us were doing in his gym.

"We want to take boxing lessons, sir. We heard you teach businessmen." I almost choked on the words. I sounded like a jerk.

"We can teach anyone who wants to learn."

"I play tennis."

"That's not a sport. Give it up."

I was thinking, no way I was giving up tennis. I was a tournament player. I had dedicated thousands of hours to playing and getting coached to be as good as I was. The old coot had to be kidding, thinking I would quit tennis. I just came here to Gleason's to dabble in boxing and to get my wife back for making me dump my motorcycles. Of course, I wasn't totally closed-minded. Maybe I'd cut my tennis down to three times a week. Box twice. That's as far as I was going to go.

"Hector Roca," Ira shouted out. A wiry, Panamanian in his late thirties came over from the back of the gym. He had an Afro, brown Hispanic skin and gold fronts on his teeth. Three gold chains and a pharaoh's head hung down from his neck like he was a rapper. He looked like Lionel Richie. He would one day be a famous trainer and train twenty world champions. Not yet. There were inky, faded tattoos on his arms.

"Hector. Five o'clock tomorrow. You train these guys," Ira said.

"I don't know if we'll be free then," I said.

"Take it or leave it," Ira said.

Hector looked over at us. He must have been wondering what he was going to do with three losers. It was embarrassing to teach guys who looked like such wusses. But poor people have a nose for money. Hector could smell us coming. Yeah, it would be worth his while to teach us after all.

"Dues are thirty bucks a month. Trainer's five dollars an hour," Ira said.

What a joke. A tennis lesson was sixty dollars an hour plus court time. Five dollars? Hector must have been thinking these guys were good for ten. He went to the back of the gym to coach some fighters on the heavy bag. He didn't say, nice meeting you or anything. He figured he was doing us a favor just to talk to us. In his world we were lower than the file clerks in my office. I felt like I had dropped to the bottom of a well and didn't have to deal with the snobs on the patios of the polo parties of the upper class. I had escaped from the delicate limitations of my breeding. I was a thoroughbred who looked over the fence and saw that he had a chance to play with the work-horses. I could get that damn pesky jockey off my back.

I looked around the gym and watched the crooked noses bobbing in and out of the shadows. I was in the land of lepers. The fighters were rejects. They were indicted by their own violent tendencies. You'd think they'd rise up and attack the world that put them here. But they were too busy punching each other. For the amusement of the world. For its entertainment. For a payday. I was an outsider. But for some reason I was drawn to the lepers. I wanted to be one of them. To share their violent disease. To be amputated.

We made our escape from the zombie-land of sweating torsos and went out the door into the land of light. We were blinded by the day and the busy people rushing down the streets from appointment to appointment to earn more and more. I already felt there was something nobler inside the gym than out on the street. Some ancient gladiatorial spirit. Some riddle about life and death. Some larger stakes. Call me romantic. Call me full of shit. But I felt like I was onto something.

"I can't wait to tell my kids that I'm a Gleason's fighter," Banks said.

"You're not yet," I said.

"I don't know if it's for me," my brother said.

Me? I felt like I had found a new home. The gym was a hat to keep the rain off my face. Or it was a magic hat filled with rabbits.

3

WHEN PETE, BANKS and I went back to Gleason's, Hector told us to practice in the back between rows of lockers. I think he was embarrassed to have anyone see us. We were jokes in a foreign language. He wanted us hidden. He had us line up and throw jabs. Step, jab, step, jab. Back and forth between the lockers.

"Do this until I come back," he said.

He left us there walking and jabbing for fifteen minutes. Banks' balance wasn't too good and he kept knocking into the lockers. We felt like fools. Hector wasn't paying any attention to us. He came back and showed us the one-two, left, right, left, right. He taught us to turn our wrists as we snapped the punches out and then went away again. Twenty minutes later he came back.

"That's enough for today. Ten dollars each," he said.

Ira had said five. But I wasn't going to bitch about an extra five dollars. I was too afraid. Besides, boxing was the cheapest workout in the city. Next to jogging.

There was one broken down shower. We got in and out quickly. Afraid of shower rape. But no one started in with us. No one noticed us. We weren't threatening. In the land of gladiators you were measured by your boxing skills. We had none. Therefore, we were not measured. We did not exist. We were invisible men, Liquid Paper. Not even worth beating up. Not worth raping. It would have been an embarrassment to hurt such weaklings. We hadn't earned the right to be murdered.

•••

I was standing in front of Gleason's, talking with a few homeless guys at six o'clock in the morning. Dressed in torn and filthy clothes, they struggled out of their cardboard box caves, their grizzled faces lit up by the morning sun like stale milk. I never knew their names but we'd become friends. They were homeless but I had found a home. These guys never begged me for money. They never rattled their cups in front of me. Even though I showed up there in a Rolls Royce, they acted like I was one of them. I had a way of fitting in with people different from me. I was a chameleon. They were embarrassed to hit up on a friend. It didn't matter that I was rich. I forgot that I was a millionaire. They forgot that I was a millionaire. I wanted to be one of the boys. I treated them like equals. I showed them respect. I was probably the only rich man in America who looked up to them. I felt more alive chatting with them and drinking coffee while they drank beer than I did at a boardroom on Wall Street. I realized that I'd rather eat a stale donut than yellow fin tuna.

Hector showed up a couple of minutes later. His pharaoh gold medallion glowed in the sun like a pyramid at dawn. It went with his gold teeth. He was wearing an old

Adidas sweat suit. The gym used to open at eleven o'clock. I had made a deal with the owner, Ira, for a hundred dollars a week extra, to open the gym early so I could train before work. I also raised Hector to thirty dollars a lesson to get him to come in on time and because I was embarrassed to pay him less. Trainers in other sports like tennis and golf made at least twice that.

My brother and Banks struggled into the gym with crusted sleep hanging out of their eyelashes. The strands of hair on Banks' balding head didn't look like they'd been washed. He had dandruff on his bald spot. It was disgusting.

Then Chuck, a thin, tall black guy, showed up. Hector had invited him down to spar with us. He told us to give Chuck ten dollars each for sparring. I had to give him ten for el cheapo Banks.

We had never sparred before. I got to go first. I was frightened but excited. Chuck threw some light jabs at my headgear. I thought I was getting brain damage. I had no frame of reference for getting hit. I had no idea how many millions of punches it took to get punch drunk. But I didn't want to be walking around on my heels, dribbling saliva from my mouth, telling everyone that I was once a contender. I had never thought about brain damage when I was drinking a lot of vodka or snorting cocaine. I guess it was because there was nothing dramatic about substance abuse. It was slow and disgusting. Boxing was theatrical. It captured the imagination. It worried the subconscious. It itched. The rest of the round, Chuck chased me around, smiling, like it was a big joke. Buzz! The bell rang. My first sparring session was over. Three lousy minutes and I was tired. I hardly landed a punch on Chuck. He didn't even try to hit me. He just tapped my headgear.

My brother was next. He gagged on his mouthpiece. Hector told him to box without it. Chuck wasn't going to hit him anyhow. Pete threw some good jabs. He was bigger than I was. Better coordinated. Chuck threw one light jab near Pete's face. He winced, turned red and closed his eyes. You'd think he had been hit by a thunderous, right hand cross. He tried to jump out of the ring and Hector threw him back in. My brother flinched whenever Chuck went near him. He was scared to death of him. When the bell rang, Pete sneaked out of the ring and whispered to me, "Where am I?" He was worried that he was hurt even though Chuck had pulled all his punches.

Banks' turn came. He went into the ring like a happy punching bag. Banks was in lousy shape. His belly hung over his gray gym shorts. With his headgear on and his bald spot on top he looked like Friar Tuck. He bounced around the ring, laughing whenever Chuck tapped him on the headgear, thinking it was fun. He didn't care much if he got hurt. His life was a mess. His wife had left him and he couldn't even afford to pay for heating in his apartment. He blew most of his paycheck on peep shows and massage parlors. His work stank. I was getting ready to fire him when he sucked up to me and started boxing.

After Gleason's we all walked back to the office. We were no longer virgins. We had sparred. We were really fighters. At least I thought I was a fighter. Banks was too out of shape and my brother couldn't even suck on his mouthpiece without choking.

"Why should I get hit?" my brother asked.

Real boxers didn't ask that question. "We want to get hit," I thought. Or a voice in my head said we wanted to get hit.

A few weeks later I was down at the gym watching Sam Allen spar with Chuck. Sam was the securities lawyer I mentioned earlier. Suzanne Berlin would later include him in the *People Magazine* article with me. He had played college football and loved contact. He was the kind of guy who patted your ass in the locker room and said, "Let's get them!" He was a team player. I just didn't like teams. He was a good guy. I liked him but I disliked his type, the cliché that circled around him like a fist, his profession—lawyer.

Sam outweighed Chuck by sixty pounds. But when he boxed he couldn't lay a glove on Chuck. Chuck was smooth and fast. He moved like a dancer. Sam was a brawler. He liked to stick his head in and mix it up. Chuck caught him with a straight right and gave him a bloody nose. That was the first boxing injury I had witnessed. I liked it. Hector waited until the end of the round to grab a towel and wipe the blood off Sam's nose.

It was all pretty grungy and exciting. I looked at the canvas. Bloodstains were all over the place. Not just from Sam. From all the Gleason's fighters. Splat! Sam's blood was part of the painting. The expressionistic violence was priceless. It was deep as the sacrifice of a lamb. The loveliness of wool and wounds. There was love in all these beatings. Dedication and the deep commitment to taking punishment without wimping out.

After Hector had cleaned Sam up, he told me to put on a cup and headgear and get in the ring. He told Chuck to get out and Sam to stay in. Not a pleasant prospect. I thought I was going to spar Chuck again. He would at least have taken it easy on me. Sam had a football mentality. I could be punted across the goal posts. I was nervous climbing into the ring.

"Isn't he a little big for me?" I asked.

"Don't ask stupid questions, chicken. I'm the coach," Hector said.

I was in the ring dancing around on chicken legs. I pecked at him with unconvincing lefts. I was afraid to connect. Sam jabbed at my head. Thud! I don't think he was trying to hit me hard but he had heavy hands. I felt like my brother did. I was sure I had brain damage. I was scared I would forget where I was. That I'd speak Turkish.

Hector could see my fear and looked nauseated. But not wanting to risk his big fees, he told Sam to throw easy. This gave me confidence. Afraid of Hector, I started hitting Sam harder. I started slamming him to the body. I dug hooks up under his ribs. I was having a grand old time knocking Sam around like a heavy bag. I was singing victory songs in my head when Sam stuck out his bear paw. I felt it hit me in the center of the chest like a giant shot of Novocain. I heard my sternum crack. I stopped in my tracks. Oops. Something was wrong. I was broken.

I finished the round because I was too scared not to finish. After the bell I told Hector my chest hurt.

"Go hit the bags," he said. He gave me a look of disgust.

I winced. I could hardly throw a punch. I pushed my hands out like I was an old lady holding a cane.

My brother came over all smiley. "You really showed Sam," he said, sarcastically.

I wanted to laugh at what a fool I must have looked like. But it hurt too much. The pain made me feel faint. I wanted to be tough. But I was a soft, aging businessman. What did I care about being tough? But I did. It was more important to me than being a businessman. I began to see business as a woman's sport. Something without honor and courage, filled with deception. Executives were like usurers; they made money out of nothing because they were nothing. They had no skills, no craft. I thought of how Ezra Pound hated usurers. But he was nuts. I wasn't nuts. I was pleasantly disturbed.

When I took a shower I had trouble soaping myself up. My chest really felt cracked. I kind of hoped so. Not that I liked pain but having a boxing injury was smart. You had bragging rights to your bruises. It wasn't some pretend S&M shit where you dressed in diapers and took fake beatings, degrading yourself as a sex slave at a club.

•••

A couple of weeks after my injury from Sam, my chest was still hurting me. It was probably broken but I never bothered with an x-ray. I still couldn't laugh or throw a good punch. If I sneezed or coughed I was in agony. I still worked out. Just not as hard as usual. I wanted to show Hector that I wasn't a wimp. I didn't go to a doctor because I thought only weaklings went to doctors. Besides, what could he do? Put a cast around my entire chest? Tell me not to box? I was no quitter.

4

I KIND OF suspected my brother would do this. I was sitting in my Rolls Royce with my driver Said at the wheel in front of Pete's apartment on the West Side. He lived in the Century Building with his wife and daughter. I was going to give him a lift to the gym.

"I used to be an amateur fighter myself," Said said. "It was in Egypt. Before I became a Davis Cup tennis player." Said was the driver I hired after my former driver Jerry died in the motorcycle accident. I knew him from the tennis courts. He used to be a diplomat in Egypt. His life was very up and down. He needed a job.

"Why'd you quit boxing for tennis?" I asked. I was impressed by Said. I didn't know he had been a fighter.

"Some guy beat the shit out of me in the Egyptian nationals," he said. Wow! He had been in the nationals. I was surprised that losing had made him quit. I wanted to be able to take the pain. I had big ideas for a beginner who had never even been knocked out. I thought of Bernie Spitzer, a kid on my block in East Meadow when I was growing up who never said, "I give up." Other kids would beat him to a pulp. It became a kind of neighborhood thing to beat the kid up. Every day after school some kid would throw him on a suburban lawn and jump on him or knee him in the thigh. But he held his peace. He didn't give in. When I moved from the neighborhood, I lost track of him. But I'll always remember Bernie as being beautiful. Stupid. But beautiful.

Said and I were waiting about ten minutes when I saw Pete coming out past the doormen in his pajamas and overcoat. He looked pasty like some cannoli down in Little Italy.

"I'm not feeling well. I'm dropping out of boxing. I don't like sparring. I can't sleep at night thinking about it," he said. "I choke on the mouthpiece. Besides, I have to get my daughter ready for school in the mornings."

He ran back into his building. He probably expected me to be angry. What did I care if he boxed or not? This was my journey. I was going it alone anyhow. It was personal. He was just there for the ride. I liked his company but he was hitchhiking. I didn't need him. I felt like Mahatma Gandhi wandering around with boxing gloves instead of a cane. I was an aggressive pacifist. I had found truth.

As Said and I were heading over to the gym I suddenly felt big. I had more guts than my older brother. When I was young I used to cut my arm with razor blades to show I wasn't afraid of my own blood. I could do this.

I've always been competitive. In June, I had made it to the semifinals of the New Jersey State 35 and Over Tennis Championships. I was ranked in the USTA three years in a row. Still, it was a miracle that I had gotten through the quarterfinals. I usually got knocked out of the tournament by the second round. I was a drone. Not that I was bad. I was workmanlike. I just couldn't play as well as any of the queen bees. I was too good for a weekend player but not good enough for a professional. Tennis was all about levels. I just wasn't on that level. If anything, I was middle-of-the-road. I was a fierce competitor with limited talent.

I got matched up against a tall, lanky Australian. He was a serve and volleyer. I couldn't pass him at the net, despite my topspin. I got blown away love and love. There was no way that I was good enough to be state champion. Even in a dumpy state like New Jersey. I was a quarter-finalist. A failed semi-finalist at best. I just didn't have the time to be better. I'd need to practice four hours a day to even improve my game one level. I wasn't going anywhere in tennis. My talent was a cute, diminished thing. I needed to be brilliant. I needed a sport that would be less time consuming. Maybe I could go further in boxing than I did in tennis. Why not? It seemed that boxing was less about talent than desire and the willingness to take a beating. I was willing to take a beating to win.

Too bad that my brother no longer wanted to box. I liked to hang out with him. But that was his problem, his battle with himself, not mine. We left his apartment building and Said dropped me off at the gym. Banks was there waiting for me. Anxious to win brownie points that he was still boxing. Looking out of shape in his gym shorts. He was an awkward fellow. He had told me he went to nude beaches. I felt sorry for anyone who had seen him.

"Where's your brother?" Hector asked.

"He quit," I said.

"Chicken," Hector said.

"I don't know."

Hector told us to spar together. I was too athletic and

strong for Banks. But what the hell, I'd go easy on him. When the bell rang, he came after me. Some of his clumsy punches landed. It was humiliating to get hit by a nerd like Banks. I dipped down to the side and hooked him in the kidney. I heard his organs bounce. He fell to his knees.

"Don't hit so hard," Hector yelled at me.

"I'm sorry," I said. But I wasn't. I had nothing against Banks but it felt good to knock him down. Anyhow, he had no right to punch me. He made me look bad. He didn't have the right. He was ugly and weak. I rejected him on behalf of the universe.

"Get out of the ring," Hector yelled at Banks as he struggled to his feet. "You get in, Chuck."

He figured Chuck would teach me a lesson. Chuck peppered me with long jabs and straight rights. He had longer reach than I did. But I bobbed and weaved till I worked my way to the inside and hit him with a few good body shots. I felt like a brawler. Like Joe Frazier. I couldn't even feel the punches bouncing off my head as I got inside and hit him in the ribs.

"You fight good," Chuck said when we finished.

After showering and changing I walked over to Hector and said, "I'm sorry about Banks." I didn't want Hector to be angry with me. I didn't apologize to Banks. He hadn't earned my respect. I cast him aside.

"Next time you hit your friend so hard, I'll get in there and kick your ass," Hector said.

When Banks and I got back to the office he said, "My ribs still hurt. I have to see a doctor. I can't afford it."

"I'll pay," I said. He later found out that he had blood in his urine. I was proud. Not that he was hurt but that hurting him meant that I had a good punch. Maybe a killer instinct. I was changing. I used to have false empathy for my opponents and competitors. I was becoming more honest.

Banks was becoming more honest too. He admitted that boxing was too much for him. He quit.

•••

One Saturday morning in April, my in-laws came over to my apartment in the city. My mother-in-law had a manic, high, Forest Hillsy voice. My father-in-law chewed on his words slowly like Milton Berle. They were nice people. They were comfortable like old pajamas. At the beginning I felt a little snobby towards them because they hadn't been to college. Sometimes I was a snob. Yet I hated snobs. Somehow I forgave all faults within myself.

"Come on down to Gleason's and watch me box," I said to my father-in-law, Jack. He used to box. I respected him for that. When Jack was a boy in San Francisco he trained in a gym with Jack Sharkey. He had a thick neck and huge hands. He told me he had ten amateur fights but never went pro. Who knows if it was true? Still, I was impressed.

Jack came with me to Gleason's. Hector put me in the ring with a lightweight Puerto Rican pro.

"Keep at a distance," Jack said from outside the ring.

Hector told the pro to go easy on me. But the pro landed a perfect uppercut and drove my nose up into my brain. It swelled like Rudolf the Red-Nosed Reindeer's nose. It was an early Christmas present. It was a cartoon. It felt good. Thick. Manly.

I got out of the ring and Papa Jack acted all attentive, *My poor son-in-law.*

What was all that sympathy shit? I was high on my own masculinity. I didn't like his fussing over me.

"That's a nice nose you got there," Hector said. "Go hit the bag."

The fighter on the bag next to me had a nose that went in sixty-six directions. Maybe sixty-seven. He was lean and mean, not an ounce of body fat on him. His name was Doc Novick. He was both a vet and a lawyer.

"He's nuts. He likes to get beaten up," Hector said.

"I do too," I thought. But I didn't say anything.

"He's one of Duran's regular sparring partners," Hector added.

I hoped I never ended up fighting the Doc. His nose made me dizzy. It was frightening. I think I was jealous.

"Ice your nose," my father-in-law said.

I held it at different angles so he could see the bulge.

We got in the car. I made fun of my nose like Cyrano de Bergerac. "My nose reminds me of a traffic light, round and red" and "Don't forget to stop at the nose." I told my father-in-law to watch out or, "My nose will get you."

At my apartment Lauren and her mother picked on my nose. It must have gotten hit again.

"Aren't you going to quit now? Can't you see what boxing is doing to you?" Lauren asked, icily, imitating Jackie O's voice.

"You poor dear," my mother-in-law cried and flapped her arms like an injured bird.

I looked in the mirror. My nose looked good. Like a trophy. Swollen. I was no longer cute. I was rugged. A man. With a man's nose. I was defining myself as I was beating myself up. I was sophisticated rough. I came from both worlds. I could appreciate Rudolf Nureyev and a good punch. Ballet and a bloody nose. The dance of red. Wisdom's brutal color.

"You mean you don't like my nose like this?" I asked.

"It's horrible," my mother-in-law cried.

"You used to have a small, cute nose," my wife said.

Jack smiled. He had turned me over to the women. I was no longer his problem.

Photo from an article in *Men's Journal*, which was subsequently used for subscriptions

5

HECTOR WAS MY GURU. I looked up to him even though he had never graduated from a Panamanian high school. He had been educated by life. Somehow his gold teeth made sense in his mouth. He was wearing a super thick gold chain he got from a drug dealer student of his who was now doing triple life for nine homicides. Sam, the guy who broke my chest, was hanging around the ring looking for some sparring. Hector put me in with Chuck instead. I felt safe with Chuck. I jumped all over him. I had no fear because he was now on the payroll – ten bucks to spar. I kept banging his body. It had to hurt. But he kept smiling. And I kept hitting him harder. Then I started laughing too. It was funny, me trying to hurt him so hard and him hardly feeling it. We were like kids or a cartoon where a farmer keeps killing a duck and the duck keeps staying alive.

Boxing was more honest than work. Everything in the insurance business was a rabbit punch or a foul. Brokers would ask me for insurance quotes on their properties and then give them to their regular brokers to beat the prices down. They'd hand in broker of record letters to try to take over my quotes directly from my companies. They'd hit me in the kidneys or the back of the head with snide comments and sarcastic innuendos. They climbed over my shoulders to listen in to my thoughts. They took what they could get and gave back what wasn't worth getting. My attitude had sure changed since I first walked in and thought I was in the land of the lepers. I discovered that all the dirt was on the outside. That businessmen were the untouchables. That fighters were the pure, noble recipients of damage.

When we finished, Hector put Sam in the ring with Chuck. Chuck was all over him, bloodying Sam's nose. Sam threw bombs but couldn't land clean punches on Chuck. And each time Sam missed, Chuck nailed him with a combination. I was amazed at Chuck's skill. Sam was a bear. He broke my sternum by just sticking out his paw. But he couldn't lay a glove on Chuck. That-a-boy Chuckee. Show the motherfucker up.

I wondered why Chuck didn't go pro. He had the skills. All he needed was some confidence. If I could fight like him, I'd be fighting on television. I'd be flashing who I was like a pervert in a subway station.

"Hey, Lawrence, they're having some fights over at Madison Square Garden," Sam said to me after he got out of the ring.

"Who's fighting?" I asked.

"You, me, and all the Wall Street brokers. It's some Wall Street Charities shit," he said. "Geraldo Rivera fought in it two years ago and it was on television."

I agreed to meet Tuesday night at the New York Athletic Club on 59th Street to sign up. The famous referee, Arthur

Mercante, was running it. I figured it should be a cakewalk for me. I was a Gleason's fighter. I sparred all the time. I got back into the ring to spar with Chuck again. We went to war. I was dropping overhands like hand grenades, doing better against Chuck than Sam did. It didn't make sense. I could beat Chuck. Chuck could beat Sam. Sam could kill me. It was all about styles. Or was Chuck holding back on me because I paid him ten dollars? But Sam paid him ten dollars too. Chuck should have been killing me. Maybe I was better than I thought, though I doubted it.

6

THE NEW YORK ATHLETIC CLUB was luxurious. It had none of the flavor of a boxing gym. I felt like I was at a country club. Sam and I signed up for the Charities with some Irish coach, Doherty.

"How old are you?" Doherty asked. I felt like I was nineteen.

"Thirty-eight," I said.

"That's awfully old, fella," he said. "The cut off is thirty-five years old."

"But I have to fight," I said.

"No one has to fight." He looked at me like I was a freak. "You can work out today but you'll have to speak to Mercante about being in the show."

The room was filled with preppy looking boxers. It was a prissy clean, brightly lit room with two rings laid out on mats on the floor. There were three speed bags and two heavy bags. The weights were polished, clean, and shining. It was a cocky, sure-of-itself, arrogant room. A bragging, bullying room. It was built for the kind of guys who hung out in packs drinking beer and talking bullshit. Young men capable of gangbangs. Hicks and pig fuckers camouflaged as WASPs. These guys were latent homosexuals. Circle jerks. They weren't Gleason's fighters, the real thing.

I didn't like the boxing room. But I was impressed.

Arthur Mercante came in. A trim man in his sixties, he looked like he just stepped off a yacht he didn't own. He could have been the assistant captain or the headwaiter. He led us through a bunch of namby-pamby, girly aerobic exercises. He looked like Jane Fonda's mother. Some of the guys got exhausted. What a joke!

"On Thursday we start boxing," Mercante said.

Whoo Hoo! The king had spoken. There was a fearful whisper throughout the room. A hush that went clear through to some of the toughest looking guys' bowels. A couple of farts broke loose to the left of me.

I went over to Mercante.

"Doherty told me to speak to you," I said.

"Speak," he said.

"I'm thirty-eight years old but I still want to box."

"You're too old. You'll get hurt."

"I already box at Gleason's," I said.

"Stay at Gleason's."

"Please," I said, desperate.

"No."

"I'll buy a thousand dollars worth of tickets if you let me fight," I said.

"You're in," he said. "Don't tell anyone how old you are."

"You mean it?"

"You better buy a lot of seats."

"I will."

I was floating when I changed in the locker room with Sam. I had bought in cheap. I had designer sweaters that cost that much. I would have paid Mercante ten thousand dollars. Now, I'd get to say I was a real fighter. I was a fighter in the Wall Street Charities.

Sam and I went into the shower room together.

"I want to kick some ass," Sam said.

I didn't want to kick any ass. When I thought of ass I thought of women. I pictured a field with a thousand thonged asses floating above the wheat. And all the drifting women were wearing red high-heeled shoes. Men didn't have asses. They were neuter. Like Sam. It was embarrassing. Kicking men's asses sounded like some gay shit. I believed in the romantic polarity of the sexes. Marc Antony loved Cleopatra, not Chuck. I did not identify with Venus. I came from Mars. I just wanted to prove that I had the balls to fight.

•••

A few weeks later I was back in the spic and span boxing room at the New York Athletic Club. Unlike Gleason's, everyone was white. Boxing was for the blacks and Hispanics. They fought casually, like they were breathing leather. We were dysfunctional whites. We tried too hard. We were frightened. We didn't know how to relax.

I was sparring with some skinny stockbroker who was the captain of the Villanova boxing team. He was about twenty-five years old. He was a nice, redheaded, freckled Irish kid. I liked him. I wanted to kill him. He had a perfect jab and he was sticking it in my face. I was eating it up like candy. Delicious. He couldn't hurt me. But he had fast hands. And he made me look clumsy.

I landed some good body shots whenever I got in close enough. I hurt Villanova. I knew it. I could hear the air flying out of him. We fought three rounds. It felt good fighting in front of the other charity fighters.

"You have a mean hook to the body," Villanova said after we finished.

I went over to Mercante feeling proud about myself to see if he shared my opinion.

"Not bad, not bad, son. We'll see how you do at the next practice," Mercante said.

Not bad? I was better than that. But it was okay. He hadn't kicked me off the team. Not that he would. I had pushed his button. He wanted to sell a lot of tickets. I'd be back next week.

7

I WAS SITTING in my 200 East 72nd Street dining room under a chandelier surrounded by mirrors, eating spaghetti with canned meat sauce. It was a nice apartment—neat, new, and tight. It was before we could afford a prewar apartment. My wife didn't cook. That wasn't her fault. I once told her that she should leave the cooking to professionals. We mostly ate at restaurants.

I told her about the Wall Street Charities Fights, "They're going to take place in Madison Square Garden. That place is historic. Muhammad Ali fought there."

"Just don't let anyone ruin that nose," she said.

"What's the difference?" After all, it was my face.

"You have a son to think of."

"If I get a bruise, it's not going to hurt him. He can't inherit it."

"Brain damage. You could lose everything."

"That's movie talk. No one gets brain damage," I said.

"You will. Mark my words."

"I'm the Man of La Mancha. I'm reaching out for that star. You have to take risks to make some meaning out of all

40

this meaninglessness," I said. I got up from the table and pretended I was Don Quixote dancing around the room on my donkey, singing "I am the Man of La Mancha...."

Lauren grabbed me and kissed me. "You're cute," she said.

If I was cute, she was beautiful. She had a broad forehead like Marlene Dietrich and blue eyes like a slice of glacier in the morning sun. I wanted to climb Everest. If only I weren't afraid of heights. I could see Lauren rising above me just beyond my reach. I could touch her but not know her. At these peaks of involvement I was a novice. I was too engaged with myself to really understand her. I got dizzy when I looked in her eyes. I had vertigo at those heights.

One of my friends said she looked like Marilyn Monroe. I think she was more high fashion than that. Her cheekbones were above the treeline. Her forehead was broad like Dietrich's. I was poetic about her. I'd get maniac. Lauren said she looked like Twiggy before I met her. When I met her she was one hundred pounds. Now she was one hundred and ten. I liked my women thin. I couldn't figure out what to do with the meat on the heavier ones. I liked them boney. Lauren was nicknamed "Bones" in high school. She was five-foot-five and a half. She did some modeling but she was just a bit short. I had a crush on her all these years. She unsettled me. That drew me near her. I suppose that was why we'd fight so much. We were growly puppies.

"It is the act in itself with no ulterior motive that is gratifying. It is lighting a candle in a room filled with lights," I said.

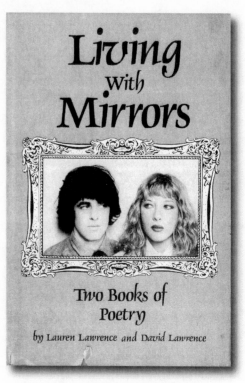

Poems by Lauren Lawrence and
David Lawrence collected from
their magazine publications,
1974

"What are you going on about now?" she asked. "You think you are a poet."

"I am. We are," I said, "Remember when we wrote *Living with Mirrors* together?"

We'd co-written and published a book of poems. We had to pay for it ourselves but most of the poems had appeared in magazines before. It was vanity. But the poems were good.

"What do you mean about a candle in a room filled with lights?" she asked.

"I have no idea," I said and giggled. I tried to kiss her but she turned her cheek flirtatiously. She sat back down at the dining room table. I sat too.

"Why are you always giggling?"

"Because life's funny."

"You're going to get lost in that giggle one day," she said. "I think you're manic depressive."

"Sticks and stones will break my bones but names will never hurt me," I answered, like a child. But it did hurt me. I didn't like being called manic depressive. I was sane and brilliant. It was like she didn't know me.

I was laughing a lot and saying things for the heck of it. I pictured Rodin's *The Thinker* breaking out of his meditative posture to ring the bell, starting the first round of a boxing match. Getting hit in the head rattles your brain and makes you think more creatively. It's a purifier. It lays waste to superficial concerns like money and clothes.

"I hate boxing," Lauren said.

"You hurt more than a punch."

"You know I'm the sweetest woman on this planet," she said.

She was. Sometimes. Still, she shouldn't have called me manic depressive. I was seeking truth. If she stood between boxing and me than she separated me from enlightenment. I had to find my way. I was Buddha on a journey to wisdom. I had to go the route in boxing. It represented the disenfranchised lower classes that I needed to embrace. I was Moses leading the poor in me to the Promised Land. Boxing was a multicultural mélange of religions. I was the inarticulate voice of an absent God.

I laughed, trying to ease the tension. But it wasn't easing. Her love for me turned angry and hard like a calcium deposit. She was a wall. I was bouncing off her surfaces. Not that I totally blamed her. She wanted a relationship. And I wanted to be moving on into love's punch. Hitchhiking on a depressive star. Even if it was a wrong star. Chasing pure ether into outer space. Why not? So I had a wife. So I loved my wife. You can't compare a relationship with a person to an affair with God. Just ask a nun. The spirit inside a boxing glove is the ability to suffer pain. Where did my wife fit in? I didn't want to see her hurt along with me.

I wanted to die doing something careless. There was nothing as beautiful as suicide. The Japanese made a cult out of seppuku. I was intoxicated with a blank mind. Suicide is a lonely thing. That's where the Arabs failed. Their suicide bombers killed everyone around them. They were into group pleasure. Orgies of pain.

Where did Lauren fit in in all this? I got amnesia at these heights. She was like waterlogged seaweed at the bottom of the sea. I wanted to float free of entanglements but always to remain within touch. I wanted to be close to her while distant. I wanted to drown with scuba gear. I wanted to wrap her around my neck and strangle myself.

Suzanne, the reporter from *People Magazine,* came with me to a training session at the New York Athletic Club.

"I'm doing an article for *People Magazine* about the Wall Street Charities featuring Sam Allen and David," Suzanne said to Mercante.

"*People Magazine.* Am I going to be in it too?" Mercante asked.

"Yes," Suzanne said.

"You can count on my full cooperation," Mercante said, slipping into his charming best. He wanted the publicity for himself and for the Wall Street Charities.

"Sam's a good fighter here," Mercante said. He then looked at me, shook his head and said, "He's not too hot."

"I'm happy with my choices," Suzanne said. I loved her for that.

Mercante couldn't get rid of me now. He needed me for the thousand dollars worth of tickets and he needed me for the *People* article. I had suddenly become the most important person in the fights. It didn't matter that I was too old for boxing or that I might get hurt.

"You're sparring with Sic Vic today," Mercante said. Sic Vic was a twenty-something-year old kid who worked as a clerk at Goldman Sachs. He was a short, stocky Hispanic with a mean sneer and tattoos up and down his arms. He was their ringer. He had twenty amateur fights and fought in the Gloves three times. He planned to turn pro after the Charities.

I belonged in the ring with him like I belonged in the ring with Marvelous Marvin Hagler. When I entered the Charities I figured I'd be fighting other CEOs. I didn't realize all the companies would be sending killers from their mailrooms. I was the only fool who sent himself.

I guess Mercante figured if he could hurt me in practice he could get rid of me and still have Suzanne write the article for *People Magazine*.

While I was getting into the ring, Sam came over to me with a worried expression on his face and said, "Move. Duck. Don't let the fucker hit you."

The bell rang. I rushed out to the center of the ring and started bouncing from foot to foot, trying to get into a position where I could throw a punch while Sic Vic was circling around me, stopping, going the other way, then reversing himself. I started following him around like a puppy dog. My hands were dropped and I was hypnotized by his dancing. My face was wide open. Then, out of nowhere, before I even threw a punch, boom bam bang. I had never tasted the canvas before. It tasted good. I was chomping on a mouthful of tart unconsciousness. I didn't feel a thing. I was napping on the mats. It was surprisingly painless. I pulled myself to my feet. I shook my head and squared off with Vic again. I was no challenge. He took it a little easier. I danced. And danced. And survived the round. During the break Mercante asked me if I was all right. I told him, "Never better." He pushed me out into the ring when the bell rang. I didn't want to look bad with Suzanne there. I bobbed and weaved, ducking punches and getting inside on Vic. I was right where I wanted to be. Up close and personal. Where I could unleash my bomb body punches. I twisted sideways to snap out a wicked hook. I figured that would bust him up good. Boom bam bang. I was on the floor again. How did it happen this time? I had been all over him. I must have gotten decked while I was winding up. Hector was always telling me, *Never look for the knockout punch. Throw punches in bunches. Forget power. Speed is power.*

I struggled to my feet and started dancing again. I was wobbly but moving fast to avoid getting decked. I wanted to survive the round. Dancing in a circle like Indians around a wagon train. Mercante had seen enough.

"Stop," he yelled. "Lawrence, get out of the ring." Then he put Villanova in against him. Vic tried to swarm all over Villanova but Villanova kept him off with his jab. It was amazing. Last week I had beaten Villanova in sparring and here he was taking on Sic Vic. Sic Vic could murder me. Who's on first? It didn't make sense. I hoped I wouldn't end up fighting Sic Vic at the Garden. He'd kill me. He'd make me look like a beginner. I was a beginner.

After practice Mercante pulled me over. I figured he was going to congratulate me for being so game and taking so much punishment. "David, I think you're a little old for boxing. Maybe you should drop out," he said.

"Think of *People Magazine*, Mr. Mercante. And the thousand dollars worth of tickets I'm buying."

"We'll see how you do at the next practice," Mercante shrugged.

Suzanne and I left the New York Athletic Club and went out to dinner at Nirvana, a tented Indian restaurant overlooking Central Park. I usually went there with my wife.

"What did Mercante say to you back in the gym?" Suzanne asked.

"He's worried that I'm too old," I said.

"That's why he puts you up against that killer, Sic Vic?" Suzanne said, sarcastically.

"I just hope Mercante doesn't kick me out of the tournament."

"He can't. Without you there's no story. Wall Street Charities would kill Mercante if *People* dropped the article. All those stock brokers on the board are dying for publicity."

The Indian waiter came over. I felt like buying Suzanne three lamb biryanis. Or taking her to the moon on a balloon made out of poori. Sometimes people come into your life that do you so much good. Why do we waste so much time with those who are dragging us down? Suzanne was my good angel. She wasn't looking for anything outside of her article and a little friendship.

●●●

I owed my father for putting me in the business world. If it weren't for him, I'd still be teaching English at Hunter College. At first I didn't want to go into the insurance business. But when the Vietnam War ended, I lost my job teaching at Hunter. All the draft dodgers dropped out of school and there was no longer room for young professors. I hated the idea of going into business. I was an academic. I had read *Death of a Salesman* and thought that there was nothing more pathetic than a salesman. I thought of Woody Allen in *Take the Money and Run*, punishing his persona by locking him in a cell with a life insurance salesman. The business majors I knew in college seemed inarticulate and jerky. That was long before MBAs became prestigious. They had no artistic depth. They didn't have my intellectual snobbery. The idea of becoming one of them was anathema. But when my father offered me a job I had no choice. There were no teaching openings anywhere. So I went to work at a place called Allied Programs Corp.

My father was a secret partner in it. His history in insurance was a bit spotted. He had lost his brokerage company back in the sixties and couldn't renew his license. He went to work for a well-known crook, Raymond Karlinsky, in Brooklyn. My dad was *persona non grata* in the business and took a low profile. In the mid-seventies, after several years with Karlinsky, who had come under investigation, my dad secretly partnered up with another businessman to form a small brokerage on the side, Allied Programs Corp. The office was a shoebox in the East Twenties. There were no other insurance offices in the neighborhood. It looked like it was going nowhere when my father started it. The small brokers didn't mind dealing with him. They'd deal with the devil if he'd give them a good price. But the larger firms didn't even know he existed.

My father, like myself, was a bad judge of character and hired some ridiculous middle-aged flunky with a toupee, Robbie Schumann, as his front man. The office was losing money. I came in reluctantly as Schumann's secretary in 1976. I took a crash course for a broker's license and quickly discovered that I had a talent for the business. My dad visited us at night and gave me a list of insurance brokers to solicit. I went out and cold-canvassed them for business. We were not exactly insurance brokers. We were wholesale brokers. We didn't do small stuff like Homeowners Policies or Auto Insurance. We did large chains of stores, real estate conglomerates, and tricky product liability accounts. Because the accounts we handled were large ticket items, the retail brokers were happy to enlist our help. They were desperate to land these accounts or to salvage them. I'd bring the paperwork back to the office and sit down with Robbie and my father to develop strategies to market them to insurance companies.

I grew accustomed to the lunches at fancy restaurants, the waiters gliding across plush carpets with silver trays balanced on their palms like feminine rhyme endings. I became spoiled. I couldn't go back to the hot-dog carts and the Chinese take-out food of the academic world. The more I took clients out to lunch, the more business I wrote.

"I wish I had gone to cooking school instead of studying literature," I said to my father. "I should have studied gastronomics."

I discussed the safe preparation of poisoned Japanese blowfish with my clients. I think I owed my business career to my ability to choose good wines and order sushi by the individual piece.

Within about eighteen months I turned a defunct company into a fifty-man operation with offices in three states. I was a rank beginner. My one skill was that I was friendly. I would listen to the brokers and sympathize with them on the difficulty of holding onto their accounts. Other wholesalers would look down their noses at brokers and act like they were doing them a favor. I could never understand this. Business was business. I was looking to write their accounts. I was thankful to be given the chance. They sensed my appreciation.

"You're a genius," my father said.

I was lucky. The competition was weak. I'd pick up an account from a broker and talk an underwriter in a company into writing it cheap. The underwriters liked me.

People liked to hang out with me. I was a smile that fell into the statistical dreariness of their careers. I awoke giggles from tight lips. We'd have a few lunches and dinners together and I'd get my deal. The underwriters joked about how little I knew about insurance while they signed multi-million dollar contracts with me. I boasted that studying insurance was something for the clerical staff; bosses should be blissfully ignorant. I had never gone to business school. This didn't faze me. I discovered that the higher you went up the ladder the less you needed to know. Details were for the assistants who did the paperwork. My job was to make deals. My ignorance was an asset.

When we started making some real money, Robbie Schumann got uppity and insisted on a third of the operation I had built. He blackmailed us about some insider wheeler-dealer games we had played. He said he'd report dad and me to the Insurance Department and the IRS and that we'd end up in jail for insurance fraud and tax evasion. I couldn't sleep for weeks. I wondered if I'd be able to defend myself in jail. I didn't want to get humped by some jailhouse queer. I didn't know how to box in those days.

Still, I was much more worried about my dad than myself. I didn't want him to get into trouble again. I owed him for giving me a job when Hunter College bounced me. He had given me all his stock. I wanted to protect him.

Then, as if God were watching over us, just before Schumann went to the Insurance Department to snitch on us, he miraculously dropped dead of a heart attack at his desk. It was a gift from the heavens. It pulled our chestnuts out of the fire. You'd think we would have been upset but Dad and I laughed in my office while the paramedics wheeled his dying carcass out, his toupee falling off and his head bobbing up and down like a blue balloon. He looked so naked and vulnerable without his wig. It was sad. I wanted to dissect him like a frog. I had liked him before he threatened us with fraud. He had thrown the first punch. If you hit me, it's my nature to want to kill you. It's funny the way you can turn against people. You imagine you're a good guy and incapable of murder. But given the right circumstances we're all capable of murder. Not really. But capable of imagining murder. It's better than being a marginal insurance broker, isn't it? No. Maybe. His wife had pushed him to grab off more of the firm. She wanted him to be big. She pressured him until he turned us into his enemies and he dropped dead of his own accord. If only his damned toupee hadn't fallen off I wouldn't have felt the slightest remorse. He had a sad cranium. For years rumors went around the industry that my dad and I had knocked him off. I didn't deny them. They gave us a little caché. I missed Schumann.

Since Schumann's death the business had grown. We were one of the largest insurance wholesalers in the U.S. We occupied an entire floor at 120 Wall Street. My private office was at the end of the corridor to the left as you entered.

By the time of the Wall Street Charities, I was making millions down on Wall Street. The insurance market was tight and all the insurance brokers were looking for good intermediaries to place their business for them. I had developed a style where I hardly had to work. I entertained my clients, amusing them, so they'd rather do business with me than anyone else. I was the court jester. Business was a drag. If they needed a new television or a trip to St.

Thomas, I'd pay for it. I once paid an underwriter's rent for a year. I bought another client a boat. I was the candy man. Their time with me was sweet. No pressure. If you can do it, do it. And it got done.

To be honest, I was more interested in sparring than work. The stakes were higher. One mistake and I could get knocked out cold. It was exciting. I didn't really care whether I sold someone an insurance policy or not. So I didn't press my clients. The lack of pressure confused them and they bought from me to fill the void left by my lack of ambition. My indifference was attractive. I was the greatest salesman who never tried.

•••

A few weeks later I was back at the New York Athletic Club and Mercante was picking out the matches for Madison Square Garden. He asked if anyone wanted to fight each other.

Three welterweights volunteered to fight me. Just what I needed. I was winning Mr. Popularity at a box-off. Everybody figured I'd be the easiest guy to fight.

Wasn't anyone scared of me? All right. Fine by me. We'll see.

But Mercante, in his infinite wisdom, decided, "Lawrence. You fight Sic Vic." That made a lot of sense. Match the oldest fighter with the toughest. Maybe he figured that Sic Vic had the skills to go easy on me. That just because he was kicking the shit out of me in training didn't mean that he was going to hurt me in the actual match when thousands of people were watching us. I looked at Vic and my legs got rubbery.

●●●

The big night of the fight was a festival to me. It was a second bar mitzvah. I was in the dressing room for the fighters who would be in the blue corner at the Felt Forum. It wasn't the Garden-Garden like I was originally expecting, but the Felt Forum at Madison Square Garden. It only held five thousand people instead of eighteen thousand. It was still so cool.

The ghosts of Sugar Ray Robinson and Jake LaMotta floated over from the big arena next door.

Sam was in the room with me talking to himself about kicking ass. Suzanne came in with a scraggly, artsy photographer. He started taking Sam's and my picture while we were sitting on a bench like we were some kind of big celebrities. I was embarrassed. I was one of the worst fighters at this event and here I had a reporter and photographer following me around like I was a world champion. What were the other fighters thinking? *Why does this shit-head rate? I could knock Lawrence out in a second. Where's my press?* I thought about Sic Vic and hoped he wouldn't make me look too bad.

Hector showed up. I would have expected him to show earlier. This was the largest moment in my life. It was a small nothing for him. He was used to working the corners of professional fighters. One day he'd become famous for handling Iran Barkley, Buddy McGirt, Arturo Gatti, and other world champions. Not to mention training Hilary Swank for *Million Dollar Baby.*

I wasn't even an amateur fighter. I was some charity shit. Still, this was my big night. I was proud as a peacock.

I didn't know if I'd ever do this again. This might be a one shot deal. Like a quick lay. Some ego-building that feels great while you're doing it but you can't wait to get away from after.

Hector wrapped my hands for me. There was something solemn about this procedure. It was a ritual that bound fighter and trainer. He didn't use the cloth hand wraps he used in the gym. He used tape and gauze. With each strip he added, my hands felt like they were becoming harder, like they were turning into cement blocks. I sensed my own power. I thought I could kill with these hands. Then Chuck showed up with an inscrutable smile. I didn't know whether he was laughing at me or proud of me. I never knew what he was thinking. I don't think he thought a hell of a lot. But he was my pal. I no longer wanted educated friends. They were a distraction. I had enough intelligence within myself to go around. Chuck was my sparring partner. That's what mattered to me. He was the guy who put in the most rounds with me to get me ready for tonight.

It was funny waiting around like I was at a doctor's office for my turn to go out and get a beating or to beat the shit out of someone. My turn came. It was time to put up or shut up. I started getting scared. Not that I'd get hurt but that I would chicken out. That I'd step into the ring and start crying. The audience would boo me. I told myself to think of it as a sparring session. I had sparred with Vic before. He had knocked me down but I wasn't afraid to stand up to him. I'd make a good showing of it and fight him whether or not he beat the shit out of me. I followed Hector and Chuck into the Felt Forum. We were a little family bouncing out for our vendetta. I put my gloves on Hector's shoulders as I followed him out. The bright lights and the fans jiggling in their seats like angry insects. It was a sellout crowd. I heard applause rising through the house as they announced my name, Awesome Lawrence. The audience liked me. They were there to cradle me if I got hurt. I wanted to show them my bruises, like they were my mother when I was a kid, and hear them say, "There. There." I looked over and saw my wife sitting next to the judges. She always managed to get the best seat in the house.

Sic Vic was standing in the red corner, sneering at me. He had that tough look of one of the grocery boys who carried your bags up from Gristedes. If he wasn't wearing boxing gloves, I might have thought he was going to knife me. When the first round began he surprised me by coming out slowly instead of jumping all over me. Hey, maybe this wasn't going to be so bad. I settled in to a nice give and take with Sic Vic. We were moving around in a kind of dance. Feeling each other out. It was nice of him to take it easy on me.

About a minute and a half into the round—bam! My feet went out from under me and I was on my ass. The ref waved Vic off as I bounced across the canvas and skidded into the ropes. *You didn't hurt me, Vic. I can take your punch. Give it to me again.* I separated myself from the ropes and got to my feet as the ref counted. You see, I wasn't crying. I wasn't begging for mercy. I didn't have to be afraid of pissing in my pants. The ref shook my gloves and let us go at each other again. But before either of us landed a punch the bell rang.

Hector was spilling water behind my neck in the corner. He pulled back the waistband of my shorts and poured some ice cubes down. I squealed. I was embarrassed that I hadn't done better. Hector was like a substitute father to me. I felt like I was fucking up in front of him.

"Keep your left up," he said. "Stick and move. Move that stupid head." Then he smacked me on the headgear to let me know that he meant business. When the bell rang, he pushed me back into the ring. I got on my bicycle. Every time Sic Vic tried to slug me I rotated off. Then I slipped in and tied him up. Pushed him off again and pedaled across the canvas. I was using the ring like a dance floor.

"You fighting like a champ," Hector said when I came back to the corner. "Smart. Using your head. Now put a little more pressure on him this time but don't get into no wars."

Now I wanted to kill Sic Vic. I wasn't going to hold back. I wanted to show Hector that I could knock him out. This was Madison Square Garden. I couldn't go out like a chump. I had heard other guys earlier in the locker room saying, "One day I'm going to tell my grandchildren about this." We were all making personal history. This would probably be the most memorable event of our lives.

I charged into the center of the ring and started swinging at Sic Vic. I threw leather like I was in a coat factory. My hands whirled around me like a dervish. I thought I'd kill Vic. But when I opened my eyes I saw that he kept ducking under my punches so that I was hitting air. One thing about hitting air – it's tiring. My arms got really heavy and he started swinging back. I was so exhausted I could hardly hit him. He landed one punch in my gut that made me feel like the spaghetti I ate at lunch was coming up through my nose. I was all tied up in the ropes, hanging from the top one like Jesus Christ on the cross. The ref stepped between us as I unpeeled myself from the ropes again. He gave me a standing eight count. I was hoping the bell would ring. It didn't. The ref let us go at each other again.

Hector yelled something.

"What?" I asked.

"Run," Hector yelled. I took off. Sic Vic was chasing after me but I was here, there and everywhere. I was a track star. I was a horse doing the steeplechase. Someone in the crowd booed. I heard laughter. I felt like I was being mocked by a large set of teeth.

Screw that, I was no coward. I had to stand my ground. I stopped running and started trading body punches with Sic Vic again. You could hear my body shots thumping against his rib cage. Then he hit me so deep that I thought he found China. I felt like rickshaws were breaking apart in my ribs. Asian faces were laughing at me. I tried to pick the pieces of reality back up with chopsticks. Nothing came together. My pain confused me. I was against the ropes again, ready to go when the bell rang. It felt like the timekeeper rang it early.

Mad applause. I clapped my gloves together. Was I part of the audience? I wasn't sure where I was when the ref dragged Vic and me to the center of the ring and held up Sic Vic's hand. What the hell? I made it. That was winning. I was champion of my own survival. A wink in a population of angry faces. They gave us both gold medals.

"Good surviving," Chuck said with his big smile when I came back to my corner.

"You got balls," Hector said. Then he slapped me across the face, "Next time you listen to directions." And he hugged me, "You did okay, Davey."

I was clogged with emotions. Fighting was like that. It put you in touch with your own fears. If you let off enough steam, you found that the tea kettle wasn't all black. It was my first real fight. I felt like a virgin who was broken. I'd never forget this night. I was thankful for it. I got beat up in an historic place, proved that I was man enough to take a beating and not quit. This was what life was all about. There is nothing more beautiful than being in touch with one's corny, clichéd masculinity. Women gloat in their sisterhood. I was entranced by my own manhood.

I went to the shower room to wash up and change. Suzanne walked in with the photographer. I was stark naked. I didn't care. I was dealing with larger issues than my dick. I had proven that I had big balls out there in the Felt Forum. I was celebrating myself. Suzanne apologized and left with the photographer. Lauren came in just after.

"What's another woman doing here when you're naked?" she asked, angrily. I suddenly felt my nakedness and put my hand over my dick. She had taken away my innocence. There was no fig leaf covering me. She was right. I shouldn't have been so careless. Not caring was a bad habit in my life.

"They're doing an article about me for *People Magazine*," I said.

"Can I be in it?" she asked, all sweetness and light, forgetting about my nudity.

"I'll ask," I said.

"You better," she said. Then she became seductive, "Are you all right, my dear? I hope he didn't hurt you." She put her arm around my shoulder. She wanted to make sure she'd get in the magazine. I can't really blame her. I wanted to be in *People Magazine* too.

"Fine," I said. "Never felt better. Madison Square Garden. Can you believe it?"

"You know, you're never boxing again," Lauren said. "I asked the judges to stop the fight. The timekeeper rang the bell early for me. I flirted with him. You should thank me for saving your life."

I hoped she was lying. But it did feel like the bell rang early. She had no right to butt in on my moment of glory. She cheapened the beating I took. I felt like going out and getting run over by a truck. "You shouldn't interfere," I said. It was as if I was a toy she moved around a game board.

"I saved your butt," she said.

"Could you wait outside while I shower?" I asked. She made me feel exposed. I didn't want her to see who I was—dirty. She was not supposed to be back here.

I showered, found a towel sitting over one of the lockers, changed, and headed out. Lauren was waiting for me in the first row of seats in the Forum. Most of the audience had already left. The workers from my office were waiting around for me. They congratulated me. I liked that. I didn't like to be babied. I wanted to escape the responsibility of owing something to the people related to you. I wanted to surround myself with strangers. No give, no take. The vast exposure of things past don't matter.

"I almost fainted when you got hit," my dad said. He

was there. My mother wasn't. She couldn't stand the thought of my getting hit. I felt bad that my father looked so pale. I always looked up to him for having fought in WWII. He had wanted me to be tough like him. Now he was whining about a couple of punches. I felt bad for him. He was getting soft; he was getting old.

"If you don't quit boxing, I'm going to shop everyday," Lauren said. She could spend big time. Thousands of dollars at one store on Madison Avenue. Then she'd move on to the next. I didn't care. I was discovering my inner being through outer punches. My face was a prayer dictated by confrontation.

"No way I'm quitting boxing," I said, confidently. I was defined by my morning sparring sessions. I loved my wife, hated my wife, loved money, hated money, loved friends, hated friends, but the only thing that was constant beneath these ambivalent dichotomies was boxing. I liked getting hurt. It made me feel closer to myself. It was as if the pain was maternal. I was rocked in the arms of my own resoluteness.

Lauren slapped me just as Hector and Chuck were walking over. I lost face letting her do that to me in front of Hector. It's not macho. Panamanians don't allow that shit. I could see he was sickened. But what was I to do? I wasn't a street thug. I'd never hit a woman.

Lauren and I left for a party the Wall Street Charities was throwing at the Fifth Avenue Grill. Said drove us over in the Rolls. Lauren looked hot. She always did. She was good-looking. And as much as she could be a pain in the ass I was happy to have a pretty blond on my arm. Not that I was that superficial. I found beauty deep. I wore dark sunglasses to look cool. I wasn't hiding any black eyes. I didn't have the honor of getting any. Most of the damage was done to my body.

Sam had won his fight. But it was closer than I thought it would be. I didn't know how anyone could stand up to him. He hit like an elephant. He came wobbling over to us with a drink in his hand and said, "I kicked some ass."

Boxing was like making an appointment with death. You pick a time and place to show up and beat the crap out of each other. The world is filled with men walking around trying to look tough. So few of them show up for a beating. And yet in the end we all can't avoid the final scrap.

Suzanne was at the party. She kissed me on the cheek. My wife gave her a dirty look.

"Great fight," Suzanne said.

"Thanks," I said, knowing that my fight was anything but great.

"Catch you at the gym to finish the interview," she said. "Mrs. Lawrence, can you come to David's office to get a picture of you for *People Magazine?*"

This was every woman's dream, being splashed across the pages of a national magazine. She had just become Suzanne's best buddy.

"Me? A picture? For *People Magazine?*" Lauren asked, as if she were flirting.

"Yes. If you can make it?"

"I'll just have to check my busy schedule," she said. She took out her appointment book and glanced at it, quickly. "Yes, I can make it."

"But you don't know when it is," Suzanne said.

"How silly of me."

"Three o'clock on Friday."

Lauren looked at her appointment book again. "That will be just fine," she said. She was like Mercante and the Board of the Wall Street Charities. All they cared about was the press. My wife wanted her picture broadcast around the world. Who didn't? Her girlfriends took minor reporters out to dinners to get into the society pages of free, unknown Upper East Side magazines. Here Lauren was about to be in *People Magazine*. Her friends would have killed for that.

America had become a nation dominated by celebrity. Movie stars pretended they had educations and made comments on political situations they knew nothing about. We all wanted to be stars. We wanted the luxury of authority without the work.

A few days later Suzanne visited me down at Gleason's Gym. I was sparring with Chuck. I was hitting him with great body shots, scooping down and lifting up under his ribs. Chuck let out *oohs* and *ahs* and leaned over to his side. I caught a juicy rib. Might have broken it. Beautiful. Chuck was walking around like a beach house on stilts. I was the wave that smashed half his foundation out from under him. He was on a slant. Something like a burrow shifting to the side from carrying too much gold in the *Treasure of the Sierra Madre*.

When I got out of the ring Suzanne said, "If you would have fought like that the other night you would have won."

"It was enough that I had the guts to show up," I said. "Mercante didn't want me fighting. No one wanted me fighting." The only one who was happy to see me fighting was Sic Vic who had a field day beating up on an old millionaire with little experience. But I figured I'd catch up with Vic in a few years. I was going to get good. I'd get him back.

"The *People* article will go to press soon. Remind your wife to come down to your office tomorrow for the photos," Suzanne said.

"Fine," I said. My wife would have taken a go-cart across the Sahara Desert to be in *People Magazine*. I didn't want to admit that I would have run across Death Valley.

"David, are you here to bullshit or to train?" Hector interrupted.

I started to hit the heavy bag. When Hector barked, I jumped. He was my pugilistic guardian. He was like a father to me. He was my lifeline to survival in boxing. When I was in the ring, he was the only one looking out for me. I was Major Tom and he was Ground Control. There is nothing closer than the relationship between a fighter and a trainer. He rubs you down, puts your mouthpiece in and out, and gives you advice in the corner at a time when you're half-scared out of your mind.

●●●

The Awards Dinner was a chance to get together with the other fighters and reminisce about the great event. It was held in a private room at the New York Athletic Club on the West Side. Mercante stood up at a podium to make a speech. "I want to give special credit to the most stubborn man I've ever met," he said. "I told him at the start that he was too old to fight. He wouldn't listen. So let's have a big round of applause." Everyone around me was smiling and applauding. So I applauded too.

"For David 'Awesome' Lawrence," Mercante finished. Me? How had I gone from nuisance to star? Was stubbornness a celebratory quality? I was surprised.

I walked up to the desk to pick up my certificate. I hadn't thought about it but I guess I must have done something special. According to my wife it was the stupidest thing I had ever done. But to me it was the touchstone that made my life meaningful. It was a test by fire. It was the reason I was on this planet. To be in touch with the roots that twisted back to my ancestors.

David with Sam Allen from a
4-page article in *People
Magazine,* 1986

8

I WAS SITTING in my office when I got a call from Suzanne, "The editor insisted on entitling the article, 'Yo Chip! Fearsome Yuppie Boxers Come Out Swinging in Gyms Coast to Coast!'"

"I thought you were going to tone down the yuppie thing," I said.

"I'm sorry. I tried," she said.

It didn't really matter. I didn't have to have things my way. I wasn't a perfectionist. I didn't dot the i's and cross the t's of my life. That's why I was so versatile. I was happy to experiment. I wasn't afraid to fail because it didn't matter to me that much if I succeeded. I didn't fall short because my goals weren't that far. I just wanted to be on the playing field. I wanted to be in the game, engaged.

At least I was going to be written up in *People Magazine*. How cool was that! And besides, I wasn't really as far from being a Yuppie as I pretended. I had all the props. The designer clothes, the two houses, the car. Maybe not the car. I had a Rolls not a Beamer. A Beamer was a Yuppie car. I hadn't owned one of those in ten years. A Rolls was a big time car. It wasn't for someone who was upwardly mobile but someone who had already arrived at the top of the heap. Furthermore, I had a driver.

Lauren and David
in an intimate
moment from *People
Magazine,* (photo by
Rob Kinmont)

9

WELL, PEOPLE MAGAZINE was finally out. And it was a doozy. Prince William was on the cover. I hated royalty, a bunch of talentless jokes. Like God. He never had to apologize.

When I opened the magazine, I was thrilled to see that there was a chunky four-page section on me and my boxing buddy, Sam Allen. And there was my wife's picture, looking wide-eyed in her own glory. At the office I got calls all day from people who had seen the article.

"Now I hope you've gotten this stupid fighting out of your system," my dad said. He was always saying fighting was stupid. He forgot that he bombed people in Italy and Germany during WWII. That sometimes fighting is the first step to freedom. That defense ratifies a good offense.

My wife called me in the office, "They took a lousy picture of me. They could have used more flattering light." Nothing was ever right for Lauren. Every glass was half-empty. But she was half-full. I was attracted to her. She was imaginary. She was beautiful. We had chemistry. She was the firefly's light that I was trying to cup in my hand. Emptiness and fullness in the same glass.

I smiled to myself when I thought of driving out to a suburban mall and walking around. All the housewives who read *People Magazine* would want to suck off my fifteen minutes of fame. Strap their legs around my star. Shine.

●●●

I was in the gym when Iran Barkley showed up. He was a middleweight contender, the toughest of the tough. I got scared looking at him. He was a real killer. Hector was training him now and we got the honor of working out with him. When I first met Barkley a few months before, I wanted to manage him. I had asked my friend Stan Gold about him. Stan was a big manager/promoter who worked with Bob Arum. The word on Stan was that he was Meyer Lansky's nephew. That's like being related to the founding fathers. And legend has it that he did two years for killing a guy in a barroom brawl. He was the real thing, a gangster. At least, I thought he was. Who knew? I liked him and respected what he knew about the boxing business.

"Should I manage Iran Barkley?" I asked Stan. I figured it couldn't be too expensive to buy Iran's contract. As tough as he was, he had lost his last couple of fights.

"Forget it," Stan said. "Iran is going to end up walking on his heels. He takes too many punches. You don't want that on your conscience."

Gee. Did gangsters have consciences? Maybe they were misrepresented in the movies. I liked Iran but I couldn't have cared if he ended up walking on his heels. That's how boxers finish. It's none of the fan's business to feel sorry for them. If they haven't taken the punches they haven't

70

earned the humility and the self-reflection of the injuries. Somehow I didn't sign Iran and a couple of months later I was surprised to find out that Stan was his new manager. So much for the code of honor among gangsters. And Iran was now kicking everyone's ass in sight. He was heading towards a championship belt. Even though Stan stole Iran from me I wasn't going to make a big deal of it. I wasn't related to Meyer Lansky. And I liked Stan anyhow.

"I have a treat for you," Hector said.

"What?" I asked.

"You're going to spar Iran Barkley this morning."

Some treat. I was going to die young. I wanted to manage the guy not fight him.

When the bell rang, I came out like a cosmetician, throwing powder puff jabs at Iran. He followed me around the ring, not throwing a punch, letting me bounce my gloves off his face. After about two minutes he got pissed at my girly punches.

"You don't start throwing man punches, I'm gonna beat your face off," he said.

My heart caught in my throat. I got dizzy and started winging punches with my eyes closed. Doing my best to hurt him so he wouldn't kill me. But he didn't feel a punch. He even let me hit him straight in the nose. No reaction. I managed to survive three rounds of hitting him. I was lucky I didn't hurt my hands.

When the fracas was over, Iran laughed and said, "You did good."

Did good? I was punching him in the face and he didn't even feel it.

The rest of the day I was bragging to everybody I met how I sparred with Iran Barkley. I told them all I thought

I could give him a fight if I had to but I was taking it easy on him out of respect. Later that day I had lunch with a friend of mine, Darrell, from A.I.G. who told me he actually fought Iran in the amateurs.

"How'd you do?" I asked.

"Got knocked out in the first round."

I wanted to say I could have gone the distance. But I just couldn't come up with such a lie. I was impressed that he had the nerve to fight him. "You're my hero, man," I said.

•••

Everyone in insurance loved golf. Middle class underwriters felt like millionaires on the course. To me golf was a game posing as a sport. There was no sweat, no passion. Caddies were a staple of the sport. They were like indentured servants. I felt bad for them. I didn't want a slave. They reminded me of shoeshine boys. I could shine my own shoes, thank you very much. Still, I had to take a caddy.

Most golfers were fat. Many were arrogant and rude to the workers. They rode around golf courses in their little carts with their beer bellies, plaid pants, and tasseled shoes. I played less than any of the underwriters. Yet I was still better than most of them. Not that I was good. I still stank. But they were a gathering of missing athleticism. After a hard day of golf, which meant getting in and out of the cart a couple of hundred times, they'd add up their dishonest scores and boast to each other in the showers. I didn't shower after golf. I mean, how much do you sweat when you're driven around a course?

This is not to say that I hated the game of golf itself, regardless of the caricatures that were attracted to it. I enjoyed hitting a long drive. It's just that I placed it in a group of games with bowling and pocket billiards.

We were big clients of American International Group Insurance and we'd often get invited to a private golf course at Morefar in Brewster, New York. I'd jog behind the golf cart and shadowbox. It was an eccentric thing to do on the most extravagant private course in the world. And the least used. Four foursomes were allowed on it a day. There were bronze statues at each tee. It was a museum. It was some Robin Leach's Lifestyles of the Rich and Famous type shit. What did golf have to do with me?

David in boxing gear on the hood of his Rolls Royce in front of The New York Stock Exchange

10

A NEW GUY, Jones, came down to the morning sparring sessions. I had never seen him before. Hector told me that he was a bike messenger who had just completed a six-year bid at Riker's Island. That was a long fuckin' time when you considered you only got two years for manslaughter. He must have killed a whole state. I had never met anyone who had been to prison before. That was a foreign country I never dreamed I'd enter. Jones was a black welterweight who moved like he knew his way around the ring. I didn't like to fight strangers but Hector threw me in the ring with him. Oh well. He can't murder me with his gloves on.

The session was going so-so. I was a little tentative. I was timid about making an ex-con angry. Believing all the folklore about prisoners being bad. And I wasn't paying Jones to spar so he had no reason to hold back. He was starting to land some good shots. I started to get my back up. I wasn't going to let him make a fool out of me. So I threw a jab, hook, uppercut, cross and then, boom, just like that I busted his nose. What a thing of beauty. That was better than closing some stupid deal for ten million dollars.

"You got heart, David," Hector said.

When a Panamanian says you got heart you got heart. I felt like a cardiologist. I was busting with self-importance. But did I believe him? Did I really think I had heart? No. I was a chicken. I didn't mix it up with Jones till he hit me. I should have initiated it. But that wasn't fair either. I never gave myself props. In my own mind I was always falling short. A real man did what my father did in the war, dropped bombs on cities. If a few explosions turned little children into singed angels, fuck it! That was war. That was glory. I always felt I didn't equal soldiers. They killed while I dawdled. I needed some other venue in which to become a man. Did I have to fight Hector "Macho" Comacho? What would make me feel worthy of my father's generation? I was brought up in a hippy generation that thought men should be delicate and sensitive like women. I rebelled against that. I didn't want to emulate women. I wanted to luxuriate in being a man. Even in being a brute, if being a brute was my nature. I was delighted when I went into the locker room and changed. I looked in the mirror. There was a bright purple ring above my left eyelid. It was a badge of courage. Not a red badge of death. A little sort of thing. A testimonial that said I was there and that I had courage.

●●●

It was spring of '86, and I was on the mini-fame junket. I was a high roller, a curiosity. I was invited on the *Phil Donahue Show*. He had contacted me after reading the *People Magazine* article.

A girl in the audience yelled out, "You're cute."

Did she mean me? I think so. Wow. I thought I was cute and I didn't think I was cute. I was both modest and conceited. Perhaps she could define me for others and myself. I hoped all of America was listening. I hoped it was subliminal. All the girls walking around hearing voices in their heads, *He's cute.*

I was on a panel of four guys and one girl. All white-collar boxers. But I was the one Donahue wanted to put under the spotlight. I was the man with the Rolls Royce. I was the superexecutive America wanted to be. I was the mistake everyone made in his or her dream lives. They showed footage of me on a large screen arriving at the gym in my Rolls Royce.

The audience loved me. But they wanted to know why a man with a Rolls Royce boxed.

"Do you box for attention?" a fat lady asked.

"Maybe," I said. "But I did it before I was getting attention." I didn't tell her that I really liked getting hit. And hitting. I was in love with the sorrow of a punch. Even when I was a child and my brother hit me I used to look to my mother for sympathy. I would fight the Jones's of the world even if there was no media attention. It just wouldn't be quite the same fun.

11

WHEN THE METROPOLITAN Games came around I signed up. This was no Wall Street Charities. These fights were the real thing. Amateur fights for inner city kids held up at Yonkers High School. These were the roughest kids from the worst neighborhoods.

I drove up with Hector and Chuck. Hector had the Panamanian flag hanging from his antenna. The car was some kind of old American Chevy. I felt cool in his heap. Like I was part of a Panamanian gang.

I think I was the only white guy at the weigh-in. Everyone was half my age and either black or Hispanic. Angry. Ready to kick butt. I was constipated. Scared shitless. I was going to die.

I was waiting about an hour when a ref came over to me, "I got some bad news."

What? Were they going to make me fight a heavyweight? I looked up at the ring. The first fight had started. Two lightweights, a black and Puerto Rican, were beating the shit out of each other.

"We have no welterweights to match you up against," he said. "We're giving you a by." I made a face. "God damn," I said. "I came all the way up here for nothing."

I was saved. It was like getting a pardon from death row. These guys made Sic Vic look friendly.

Hector argued with the ref, "Hey, let him fight in another weight class. We drove up here to fight."

I kept tapping Hector, trying to get him to shut up. I whispered to him, "Don't worry. I'll give you fifty dollars for coming up here anyhow."

The second fight started. An Italian against a black. The crowd was yelling, "Yo, Rocky."

"It's the principle, Davey," Hector said.

"Fuck the principle," I said.

I looked up at the ring. The Italian was bleeding above both eyes. Now that I didn't have to fight, I acted like a big shot and asked the ref, "When's my next fight?"

"Six days," he said. The Italian now had a bloody nose. Blood was leaking from his mouth.

"I'll be sure to be here," I said, planning to make sure I disappeared to Europe for a while. The fight was stopped on cuts. The Italian was a bloody mess. The black did a back flip in the ring. There was no way I could do a back flip. These guys were real athletes. I was Woody Allen wandering from the set of *Annie Hall* into a boxing tournament. I didn't belong here. The Italians in the audience booed. The blacks cheered.

On the way back in the car I said, "Hector, I could have gotten killed there."

"You not ready for that level."

I felt a lot better. I could accept that.

Still, I was so strict on myself that I was faulting myself for not having an opponent even though I had no control over this. But, remember, I was no perfectionist. I didn't think I could win and I wouldn't have insulted myself for getting knocked out.

It made me feel brave to admit my faults. I congratulated myself that I wasn't such a bad guy. I wouldn't have to come back for the next round. That was good. I knew my limitations. I wasn't crazy.

●●●

I built a gym with a shower right in my office on Wall Street. It wasn't big or anything but it was a nice little place to play around with weights and do some strength building. I bought dumbbells, barbells, a stationary bike, a Nordic track, a sit-up board, a bench, and a stomach cruncher. And I lined the walls with mirrors so I could do muscle poses. I figured I'd work out here a few days a week and invite underwriters over to impress them. The room, which used to be a file room, was cool, shiny, glossy, and high tech.

I loved my new gym with the innocent exuberance I had felt kissing girls when I was a teenager. Fresh air, fall sweaters, and peachy cheeks. Life was sweet. The money was pouring in. I was living a life reserved for movie stars. I had it all. *Go Awesome! Go!* I rooted myself on. I was sucked into the American Dream like I was followed around by a giant Hoover vacuum cleaner. The dust of ambition made me cough up flagrant accomplishments.

●●●

Gleason's Gym moved from West 31st Street in New York to Fulton Landing in Brooklyn. It happened in January 1987. The new location was right under the Brooklyn Bridge. I was now about to become a Brooklyn fighter. That sounded pretty tough. Except the area wasn't Bed-Stuy. It was DUMBO, right next to Brooklyn Heights.

It was a real pain in the ass to go over there. It was a longer commute. Who was I kidding? My chauffeur picked me up every morning in my Rolls Royce and I had coffee, orange juice, and a roll in the back seat on a wooden airplane tray. I was a big kahuna, a tycoon. But I was a nothing boxer. I was basically a beginner. Still, I was in the news all the time. Italian, German, Japanese, and Chinese film crews covered me. My wife said, "It's not you they're interested in. It's the Rolls Royce." I suppose that car was the only thing special about my boxing. The car was the celebrity. I was an international presence. A celebrity. It was silly. At this point I had only had one amateur fight. At the Wall Street Charities where I had the shit beat out of me by Sic Vic. Boy, the other real fighters should have hated my guts. But they didn't. They were beginning to believe my press. They began to accept me as a famous fighter. They'd tell me I looked good on television. Israel Cruz, a Puerto Rican fighter, said, "I sees you on Eyewitness News. My girl is impressed that I knows you. I got laid off you, bro." He slapped me five. I think he was a little intimidated by me. He forgot that he could kick my ass.

12

"WHAT DO YOU think about him fighting David?" Bruce asked Hector. He was trying to pair me up with a stocky-looking transit cop, Ernest Medina.

"Good match," Hector said, looking Medina up and down. Medina didn't even have any tattoos. I thought maybe I could take him.

"You wouldn't put me in over my head?" I asked Hector.

"Shut up and put out your hands so I can wrap them," he said. I sat down on the bench and held my hands out. He put pieces of gauze on them and then wrapped them in adhesive tape. He did it real professional. My hands felt strong in the tightly wrapped tape. I thought these hands could really hurt someone. I was excited.

This was my first fight in Gleason's new stadium. Bruce and Ira bought a garage down the block from the gym and turned it into a boxing arena. They had big dreams. They planned to sell the fights to television. They would sell one million hot dogs from their concession stand. They'd get *Penthouse* centerfolds to be their ring girls. It was the perfect place for me to get my boxing career going. I'd take ten or twelve amateur bouts and then go pro. I'd be the first fighter in history to turn pro at forty.

My fight at the arena would be my first bout sanctioned by the U.S. Boxing Association. The Wall Street Charities wasn't official. The Metropolitan Games didn't count because I never got to fight there. I'd rather fight at Gleason's anyhow. It was home to me and I was going to show off this time. I invited twenty people and promised them dinner after the fight at the Lighthouse Restaurant, which was around the corner from Gleason's. We were all going to celebrate my victory.

The dressing room was upstairs and overlooked the arena. Everyone looked a lot tougher than I was. Most of them were in their late teens and early twenties. They were all black or Hispanic. Like the kind of kids I'd be worried would mug me in the subway. If I rode the subway. I might have split out but I had invited a lot of guests. The dressing room was hectic with the busy flinching muscles of bragging young men. They all felt they were going to do damage. I was the only one there who felt he was going to be damaged.

There was a balcony outside the dressing room where we could look down on some of the fights going on in the ring. Guys were killing each other. A few times I found myself putting my hands over my eyes.

When my turn came, I figured screw it. I was here to fight and I was going to fight. I followed Hector down the stairs, through the audience and into the ring with my gloves on his shoulders and shadowboxed around like I was a champ. The ref recited the rules. No one ever listened to him. We touched gloves and went back to our corners. It was all so official, ritualistic.

"Let's get ready to rumble," the ref said. When that bell rang I came out of my corner like a South Bronx mugger. Not some Madison Avenue dilettante. *What time was it? It was Awesome time.* I told myself I shouldn't knock him out right away. I wanted to make it look good. I pretended it was a sparring session with Chuck and moved around the ring like it was a lesson. I landed a couple of tentative jabs. A couple of long-distance body punches. I was feeling pretty good and he wasn't doing much but sizing me up. Maybe he was scared of me. I was starting to get a little confident. I was no longer afraid. That was behind me now. I felt loose, relaxed. When I landed a beautiful uppercut, I felt like an aficionado, an artiste. It was a sophisticated punch. I was getting cockier and more arrogant like a lawyer cross-examining a gym teacher. I landed a hook to the body followed by one to the head. Then I tied Medina up before he could hit me back. I felt like dancing with him. The ref broke us up. I was Fred Astaire. I could dance on the ceiling. I stepped back but forgot to lift my hands up to protect my face. I took a step forward. He was in trouble. I could kill a bear. I was going to put him to sleep.

Bang. An overhead right rocked my temple. The torah fell from its mental shelf. I couldn't read the Hebrew. I was lost in a numb, dizzy language I didn't understand.

Boing. I was stopped dead in my tracks like a deer that had been shot. Like Bambi's mother.

Boop. I fell onto my side. Out cold like jello in a broken freezer.

Dream on. Sweet dreams are made of this. . . .

After the fight a few friends told me that I looked like a steer getting decapitated. Standing there headless for about five seconds. Then falling in a lump on my side. I felt like I had been in the Chicago slaughterhouses.

Snap. Hector put a bottle of smelling salts under my nose. My head jerked. My eyes teared. And I looked up at Hector, the referee, and Medina who were all standing around me, looking down at my right shoulder. It was in some cubistic position with the bone sticking up against the skin. It wasn't bleeding; it was just bumpy. It hurt so much that I was numb. I couldn't feel it.

They gathered my flip-flop limbs and helped me get to my feet. I was standing. Hallelujah. The crowd applauded. *Awesome! Awesome!* Like I deserved applause for getting knocked out cold in the first round. I stank. I should have been banned from boxing forever for incompetence. I made myself sick. But at the same time I was happy because I was hurt but I didn't hurt. It was like when I was a kid and I used to cut myself with razors so I'd look like I was beat up. That never hurt. It just looked cool. It was a way of getting my mother to love me. I had been knocked down before but never out. So this was what it felt like. Pretty good. What was everyone so afraid of? It was like huffing glue when I was young. I was in a kind of numb, rubbery protective coating. It hurt a lot less than the time Sam broke my chest. Getting knocked out ended the beating and the pain. It was good.

The ref told me to get my ass to the hospital. All I was thinking about was who was going to take my twenty guests to dinner? Jack Kelly, my weasely vice president, ran up to me, "I'll take you to the hospital then take everyone to dinner and pick up the bill." It seemed he was always there covering my ass. I thought he was loyal, reliable. I didn't yet know how duplicitous he was. He was my right hand man. I didn't notice his left hand picking my pocket. His corruption was right in front of my face but I didn't see it.

●●●

I was in the emergency room waiting area of New York Hospital. Walking around like some comic book character in my boxing shorts, robe, and blue sequined boxing shoes. A little girl asked her mother, "Can I take Batman home with me?"

"Stay away from that crazy man," her mother said.

I was beginning to find the whole thing very funny. My brother called my wife. He held the phone away from his ear, "I knew this would happen. He shouldn't be fighting kids. The big jerk."

"Big?" That was nice. "I wasn't big," I thought.

After about an hour the intern took me into a private room. He helped me take off my robe and looked at my shoulder.

"Pretty nasty spill you took there," he said. He probably thought I was some asshole who fell off a skateboard at a costume party.

"I got knocked out at a boxing match," I said.

"Boxers break their noses. They don't separate their shoulders," he said. "You sure you weren't skiing?"

"I don't ski when there's no snow and no mountains," I said.

"You're probably going to need an operation. Some steel pins to put your shoulder back together."

He gave me two Percodans. "I can do the operation or you can go to your own orthopedist," he said.

There was no way I was letting him operate. "I'll let you know," I said.

When I got home at about 2:00 in the morning my wife said, "I told you so. You're a dope."

"Can you put off the nagging until I feel better?" I said.

"I spoke to an orthopedist, Dr. Lieberman. He said he'll see you first thing in the morning. Now thank me."

"Thank you." Lauren had a way of resolving things. She could contact the necessary people anytime, anywhere. You couldn't hide from her. She felt the world owed her and she insisted on collecting. I envied her courage. I was afraid of confrontation.

"I told you not to fight."

I was glad I fought. I was glad I got hurt. I pictured my mother holding my head when I got hurt as a child, only she never did. She was shy around me. But I loved her all the same. I think I had an oedipal thing going on when I was young. My mom was so pretty I thought my dad would castrate me for getting close to her. I went into the bedroom and went to sleep.

●●●

Dr. Lieberman had a jovial face lost in a huge body. He never stopped smiling and he kept spitting as he talked. He would have made a good character in *Alice in Wonderland*. He had a big face like the Cheshire Cat. I nicknamed him Dr. Jowels.

"I used to be a boxer too," he said.

"Great," I said.

"But I was nothing like my dad. He had fifty-six fights. He would have gotten a title shot if he was connected. In those days you needed to be in with the mob."

Dr. Lieberman was too busy talking to examine me. He just kept yakking.

"Do you remember my dad? He was on the *Friday Night Fights* once. He was a banger all right. A little guy. You wouldn't believe it. I'm six feet four inches tall, you know," he said.

He finally got around to looking at my shoulder. He took out his tape recorder and rattled off his diagnosis. *Separated shoulder, torn ligament*s . . . He put the tape recorder down and turned to me, "I could operate and put pins in but pins can rust. Sometimes you have to take them out again. You don't want to ache in the rain, do you?"

"Of course not," I said.

"I think I can fix you up with a fiberglass splint. Wait till you see it. It's great," he said. "Someday I have to introduce you to my father. You'd love him. I took care of Mark Breland, you know. And Wilfredo Benitez."

I felt proud that both of those great fighters were from Gleason's.

He went into a closet and took out this fiberglass contraption that looked like it was part of a robot's chest.

"How long will I have to wear it?" I asked.

"Six weeks. Give or take," he said.

He strapped me into it, pushing me this way and that. I felt like I was part of a science fiction movie. I was the Terminator. Or I was one of Darth Vader's stormtroopers in *Star Wars*.

●●●

I later heard that everyone had a good time at dinner at the Lighthouse after I went off to the hospital. Kelly was there announcing that I was finished and that he was taking over as the new President of Allied Programs Corp. Hee. Hee. No one cared about my getting hurt. What the heck? Even I laughed when I heard about Kelly's joke. But I made up my mind as much as I liked Kelly, I'd have to watch out for him. A joke is a joke but he had revealed his ambitions.

●●●

Maybe my separated shoulder was good for me. I changed my focus. I worked a little harder. I paid attention to business. I began to feel I didn't need boxing anymore. Maybe I should quit. Maybe I should pay more attention to my wife. There was love beneath the crusty years of arguing. But we just couldn't or didn't want to see through the conjunctivitis. We were afraid to feel our initial attraction. It left us too exposed.

Lauren loved to shop. She'd charge up thousands of dollars every month on her credit cards. I was once walking past Chanel on Fifty-Seventh Street when I ran into Lauren. She was struggling out to the Rolls with three boxes under her arm. The Rolls followed her from one fancy boutique to the next like Said was on a leash.

"Why are you always shopping?" I said.

"I'm lonely."

Was she lonely or was she in love with clothes? Was she attracted to the sexy labels? If I spent more time with her, would she be happy? Or would she be anxious to get rid of me so she could charge up a new dress to complete herself? Had I become her excuse for her own lack of initiative and boredom? Or had I become her impetus for her spitefully buying every luxury item she could get her hands on? She passed her days lunching with her friends and shopping. Was I the inspiration or the excuse? She called herself and her crowd, "Ladies who Lunched." Was she happy with this? I first fell in love with her when she was a poet and a potential actress. I talked her out of acting because I was afraid she'd dump me. Would she rise above her rich friends?

•••

After about six weeks Dr. Lieberman took the fiberglass contraption off. He put my right arm in a lightweight cloth sling. And I went back to Gleason's to train. Hector said, "Now you a real fighter. You come back after injury." I was proud of that. I was no quitter. I couldn't move my right hand so I worked on my left jab. It had always been my weakness. Hector held the mitts. I threw straight jabs, jabs to the body, jabs to the head, low jabs that rose up to the face, high jabs that smacked down on the head, jabs that snapped back to my face, jabs that I left dangling in the heavy bag, jabs with wrist snap and jabs with a firm wrist. I was having a jab fiesta.

A few days later Dr. Lieberman took off the sling altogether. I started training again with both arms. The right was stiff as hell and it creaked as I tried to punch some life back into it. I started getting physical therapy two days a week. A trainer made me stretch these long green elastic rubber bands. I stretched like a demon, trying to improve. I couldn't wait to fight again. As I got into better shape I felt more and more like my knockout at the hands of Medina was an accident and that I could do much better. If I hadn't walked into his right hand, I might have knocked him out. After a couple of weeks I started sparring again. Hector paired me up with J.T. Murray, a classy black man in his twenties. J.T. was in the bond market but he was not sure what he wanted to do with his life. His father was an insurance agent. "Do you like insurance?" he asked me.

"It sucks," I said.

"It got you a Rolls Royce. You couldn't be doing too bad."

"I'm doing great," I said. "It still sucks."

J.T. was a stylish fighter. He looked a little like Sugar Ray Leonard. I let him hit me on the head. I couldn't feel it. My right was like a dead lox. So I was mostly jabbing at him with my left. Pop pop. Pop pop. Still, my jab sucked. You can't have everything. I had a natural hook to the body. That was something. Like Julio Cesar Chavez. I was back in the game and real as real. Realer. I was ready to take whatever punishment came my way. You could beat the shit out of me and I'd still be in your face throwing punches, bleeding. That took character. That showed I wasn't some dilettante. That showed I was true blue. Black and blue. Whatever. . . .

13

OUR INTRA-OFFICE Christmas party for 1987 was held at the City Club in the Marine Midland Bank Building a few blocks from my office. It was on the top floor overlooking all the offices that were churning out money. The downtown snobs loved it. They could get drunk in a high place. We rented a beautiful, private dining room with a bar attached to it. Our whole staff showed up, twenty-five people. Before the actual dinner, I was standing at the bar drinking with Kelly. He was drinking orange juice. He was a recovering alcoholic and didn't drink booze. He finished his juice and asked me if I could order him a screwdriver.

"I thought you're on the wagon," I said.

"Just help me out this once," he said. "I can handle it. I don't want anyone to see me ordering it, boss."

I liked being called boss. It flattered me. Silly.

Kelly continued, "I'm worried about your boxing. You could get hurt."

"I'm worried about your drinking," I said and ordered him a drink. I was neither his conscience nor his facilitator. I let him do his thing. I don't believe in interfering with the universe. I don't believe in abortion or in vitro fertilization. Let nature take care of herself. If Kelly wanted to drink, that was his progression.

After that drink, Kelly didn't care who ordered for him. He ordered three drinks at once. Within two hours he had finished eighteen drinks. He left the party to go off drinking by himself at some other bars. I knew I was in trouble.

•••

My shoulder was almost ninety percent healed and I signed up for another fight. It was April and I was back in Gleason's Arena with J.T. Murray. Instead of getting stuck with one of the killer opponents from the dressing room, we had prearranged to fight each other. There was something reassuring about fighting someone I knew. I looked around at the other thugs and breathed a sigh of relief. My last fight I ended up in the hospital. This time I just wanted to finish on my feet. I was going to fight a nice conservative fight and prove I could go the distance. My dad had said, "You got a glass temple. They hit you on top of the head and it's lights out." I wanted to prove that I could take a punch, that I was tough and that my brain cells were resilient. I had a lively mind. I wanted to bounce around filled with quick thoughts and outstanding intuitions. From the balcony I looked down at the ring. Louis "Honeyboy" Duvalle was knocking out some kid in his second amateur fight. A number of years later he would become light heavyweight champion of the world. This was my third fight. I was an old veteran. I went down to the ring. J.T. and I hardly hit each other. It was as if the fight didn't happen. I did everything to avoid contact. J.T. did his Sugar Ray Leonard imitation. Making cool moves and darting in and out like an interrupted conversation. I lasted the three rounds. I felt good and didn't care who won. My defense was good but so what? Fighting was about hurting and getting hurt. That was the romance. I pictured my friends standing around my gravesite after my death in the ring. That was cool. But even though I was likeable I didn't have many friends, just acquaintances. And I fought like a chicken tonight. The ref brought us to the middle of the ring and held up J.T.'s hand. Boy was I pissed. Not at the judges or J.T. but at myself. Why hadn't I fought harder? Just because I only had one shoulder? I could have been a winner instead of letting this turkey beat me. What turkey? He was a good fighter. And what was the difference anyhow? All I wanted to do was survive.

My fourth fight had been a "by." For my fifth fight I fought a Spanish guy named Cruz. He was about my size. Not very imposing. There was something about Spanish guys that made them really tough. It came from being so macho and bossing around their women. I didn't want to be glass jaw Joe. We traded punches.

Cruz kept me at a distance and wouldn't let me get in to brawl with him. His hands were so fast I could hardly see them as they bounced off my headgear. He didn't hurt me but he mastered me technically. I was like a windshield that was being rained on by punches. This was my fourth loss. I hadn't won a fight. At least I had finished on my feet this time. I now had a two and two record. Two down. Two up. But how many businessmen did I know who would have even gotten in the ring?

"The judge was wrong," someone in the audience yelled out. "You really won." It reminded me of the time I was bar mitzvahed with several other birthday boys and my Aunt Lily told me I was the best singer there. I was tone deaf. I felt cheated. I didn't want false praise then nor did I want it now. Maybe next time I would try a little harder.

•••

"This morning you gonna take on Buddy McGirt," Hector said to me when I arrived at the gym one morning in June. Dead silence. McGirt was the World Junior Welterweight Champion. He was about one hundred and forty pounds. I outweighed him by five or six pounds. I was a welter-weight. His absolute control and total destruction of Frankie Warren for the title was a thing of beauty. It showed a rare combination of finesse and brute power. I had seen him knock guys cold with his neat, clean, short left hook. His opponents looked like cattle whose heads had been chopped off. Like I did when Medina knocked me out. They'd stand there for a second as if nothing happened, then tumble heavily onto their sides. Dead meat. But fighting McGirt was no threat. He had nothing to prove and would take it easy on me. I wasn't worth beating up. Sparring with Buddy was a no-lose situation. If I fought well, I'd feel like a champion. If I fought poorly, well, after all, what do you expect, I was fighting world-class competition. And if I accidentally got hurt by him, it was better to sport a black eye from Buddy McGirt than some unknown amateur who thought he could become me by beating the crap out of me. I didn't want to be the whipping boy for someone else's frustrations. Nor did I want to be the golden upper class trophy in some amateur's tenement.

About 8:00 a.m. McGirt showed up. He looked surprisingly small in his street clothes; a friendly, neat little guy. Unpretentious, quiet, and dignified like an accountant or a teacher. This was typical of so many fighters. They looked nothing like sloppy, loud, bar room brawlers. Looking at him in his chinos, I thought I might be able to give him a bit of a tussle. When he went into the dressing room, I said to Hector, "He looks kind of small." Hector sneered at me like I was a jerk. Buddy came out in his boxing clothes, and I immediately saw the fluid muscular body of a trained boxer. He walked like a dancer, although he had the arm muscles of a gymnast. He jumped into the ring and started shadowboxing. Fast hands. Loose muscles. It reminded me of the time I fought Sic Vic at Madison Square Garden. I looked across the ring at Buddy shadowboxing and asked myself what the heck was I doing here? The more I asked myself that question the more I challenged myself to stay. When the bell rang, I forgot all my thoughts of running and got down to work. Buddy made no jerky moves. Everything was smooth and rhythmic. He stuck out a few light jabs, waiting for me to start punching. I threw a few punches, testing the waters, seeing if I could work with him. He slipped my punches so that my lefts grazed the side of his head like a bull passing a matador's body. He moved in and out encouraging me to pick up the pace and try to hit him. It was as if he was choreographing a boxing dance. But I was unable to find my range. Now he started tapping me with a few punches on the headgear. I moved from side to side. I didn't want to walk directly into any punches. His polished work brought me up from a potentially wild amateur level to a calm professional level. It was as if I was following behind an Olympic skier. I was learning by imitation. He was making moves that couldn't be explained verbally. When the first round ended, I had hardly been touched.

Maybe he was taking it too easy on me.

I should have taken a few punches. I should have elicited them by taking cheap shots at him. A couple of bruises would show the guys back in the office that I really did fight McGirt. I became a little less cautious in the second round. I stepped inside and started throwing some body punches. He blocked most of them with his elbows and started working on me from the body up to the side of the headgear. He didn't take any sucker punches at me. Even if I hit him with a good one. In the third and last round I went directly inside again, working the body and hooking the head. I even caught him with one uppercut. I was worried he'd be angry. But he wasn't. He remained calm. Midway through the round he caught me with a pretty good hook to the head. It was just a short tight little punch but I saw stars for a moment. I shook my head and smiled, just to let him know I was a little shaken and I'd appreciate it if he didn't take my head off. The bell rang and we tapped gloves. I didn't want it to end. Yet I couldn't wait to get into the office and tell everyone that I had just fought a world-class fighter.

As we passed the waterfront in the Rolls on the way to the office, I felt lonely. I was cut off from the world by luxury. I wanted to be out there fighting in it. I began to wonder: maybe I should have gone after Buddy a little harder. I was pretty good on the inside. If I just caught his ribs right, I might have cracked a few. I was 41 years old and should have been golfing instead of boxing, but I thought one day, maybe, maybe I could turn pro.

Later that day I was at the Duck Club lunching with Kelly and an underwriter from the Reliance Insurance Company.

"You're not going to believe the way I boxed with Buddy McGirt," I said. "I even hit him with an uppercut. And some body shots." They weren't listening. They were too busy gulping down cases of beers. They were world-class beer drinkers. I wondered what kind of talent that took. And how you could be so lacking in other skills that all you could say for yourself is, *Man, I can drink you under the table.*

The American Medical Association wanted to ban boxing. I had been hit in the head thousands of times and there wasn't any effect yet. They'd be better off banning beer. I didn't believe you could get brain damage from boxing. Even later on when all the reports said that I had been damaged, I hardly believed it.

Kelly and the underwriter offended everything noble. But then we weren't living in a noble society. I came from a generation that used to spit on Vietnam Vets for having the courage to fight their battles. A generation that lauded John Kerry for accusing his fellow soldiers of torturing Vietnamese. A generation that hated itself so much that it fought itself rather than its enemies. The last of the gladiators were confined to small rings at Gleason's Gym in a warehouse building over in Brooklyn.

14

MOST FIGHTERS LOSE a few fights and quit. But I wasn't the kind of person to be discouraged by losses. In fighting, your sincerity is measured more by injuries. So far I had a fractured chest, had been knocked down three times at the Athletic Club, twice at Madison Square Garden, and got knocked out and separated my shoulder at Gleason's Arena. Not to mention black eyes, swollen noses and bruises. I was doing pretty good. I was sincere. I was willing to lay it on the line, whatever line. Back in the dressing room at Gleason's, I was waiting to be matched up again. It was the fall of 1988, and I gave myself kudos just for showing up. The room was filled with the usual young killers. They were cursing to themselves and making angry noises. They could have played extras in movies about gang wars in the Bronx. I noticed a muscular guy about thirty years old.

"I'm Gonzalez. I ain't had no fights," he told Bruce. I didn't believe him.

"What club you fighting out of?" Hector asked.

"Times Square Boxing Gym," Gonzalez said.

"Should we put him with David?" Bruce asked Hector.

"You want to fight?" Hector asked me.

"You bet," I said. I didn't. The guy looked tough. But I didn't have the courage to say, "Not on your life."

From the first punch that Gonzalez threw I knew that he was full of shit. He had definitely fought before. He had a straight right that would have knocked me out if I didn't circle to his left and stay away from it. It was typical of fighters to lie about their experience. A novice was supposed to have had less than ten fights. I knew one guy from the gym who fought in the novice division of the Golden Gloves even though he actually had one hundred and twenty fights in Puerto Rico.

Gonzalez kept his hands up good. His shots were on target. He didn't punch past me. He snapped the punches back on point of contact and maintained his balance. He settled into his punches, using his weight. I was getting hit with a lot of shots. But no bombs. I tried to keep his jab between me and his right. I was fighting harder than my last couple of fights. I had shown that I could go the distance and I figured I could take some more chances. We were slugging back and forth pretty good. I was fighting nice nice. But nice nice wasn't enough. The bell rang. I knew I didn't do great but I thought I had a chance. Then the ref held up Gonzalez's hand. Damn! I had lost another fight. I was amassing a challenging losing record.

"David, you a rich man. You don't need to fight," Hector said. "You can get good exercise in the gym."

"I'll think about it," I said. But I wasn't going to think about quitting fighting. Did Hector think I wanted to use Gleason's like Jack LaLane's Health Club for fitness? I was no pussy gym fighter. I was going to come back and I was going to win. Fuck it! I wouldn't hold back next time. I'd kill whoever they gave me. I finally understood what those sissies were saying at the New York Athletic Club, *I'm gonna kick ass!*

●●●

It was Friday afternoon before another fight. I figured I better have a light lunch. I ate pasta with my brother.

"Why do you keep fighting?" my brother asked me.

"I have to win. It's getting embarrassing," I said. Lately, a lot of people asked me why I kept fighting.

On the way back to the office he asked, "How do you even put that mouthpiece in your mouth?" That had been his excuse for quitting.

Was that my one accomplishment?

That night I went to Gleason's. I was pissed at my lousy fight record. I didn't invite any guests this time. I didn't want to be distracted. I figured if ever I was going to go for it, tonight was the night. I didn't care what happened to me. I hadn't been knocked out in a year. Time to take some chances.

Bruce and Hector matched me against Gonzalez again. They figured at least he didn't kill me the first time. Probably safe to put us back together. That was fine by me. This time I was going to knock the son of a bitch out.

When we got up to the ring Hector said, "You lose again I don't work your corner any more."

"What are you talking about?"

"You embarrassing me," he said.

I understood. He was a famous trainer now and the

other coaches were laughing at him. But tonight I was going to kill Gonzalez. The bell rang and I didn't waste a second jumping all over him. I started shifting my weight like an ape and wading into him. My motion was all side to side, not in and out. I was Tyson or Frazier, not Ali. Each time I leaned to a side I let a thunderous body shot loose and then leaned to the other side and released another one. I smashed his nose and chin with upper cuts. He was bleeding all over his white T-shirt. It was beautiful. His face was onion purple. He was startled by my attack. His eyes looked confused and sad. The ref stepped in and gave him a standing eight count. The second he finished I jumped back in again. I could hear Gonzalez's ribs cracking as I slammed his body. I sank down into my thighs and caught him with another uppercut and he fell back against the ropes. Another standing eight count. I continued to beat the shit out of him in the second and third rounds. I was beating the fucker up for the sheer joy of it. He was the world. He was my enemy. I tasted blood and wanted more. The ref gave him another standing eight count. It was a shut out. I won by a unanimous decision.

I looked at Gonzalez's startled face. There was blood trickling down his nose. His eyes and lips were swollen. This was the same guy who beat me up last time. Now I loved him. I hugged him. He was my newfound friend. I understood why fighters were so sweet to each other after a bloody fight. Respect is magical and violence is more powerful than romance. It's better than sex. It's more emotionally involving. When the world goes up in a nuclear bang it will be like we're all getting laid for eternity. This planet is on a short fuse.

I kissed my trophy. I was singing. This was what life was all about. Nothing could be better. Chuck was there congratulating me. I took him and Hector to the Lighthouse restaurant. We were a happy little family. They had never eaten in a fancy restaurant before. I was enjoying how neatly they tried to use their knives and forks. They were playing up to me the way I played down to them. But it was really all vertical. We were on the same playing field—boxing.

•••

I was down at the gym one morning when Chuck came walking in a little late, looking down in the mouth.

"What's the matter Chuckee?" I asked.

"Lost my job."

I didn't know he worked outside of being my sparring partner. I figured he was on welfare or something.

"You have a job for me?" he asked.

I had nothing for him to do at my office. Chuck had no white-collar skills. I didn't even know if he could read or write. What could he do for me? Then it occurred to me that he could do nothing. All he'd have to do was show up. And I'd give him a weekly check, which would cover his sparring in the mornings. It was great. I wouldn't have to take his sparring money out of my pocket anymore. He'd be a corporate expense. So I hired him as a messenger. He called me "Robin Hood." He said I saved his life.

Most of the time Chuck just sat around the office kitchen looking at pictures in magazines. Sometimes he'd come down to my private office to discuss boxing. He'd often sit there with a lost expression on his face while I was trying to talk to my salesmen. I didn't have the heart to throw him out. Besides, I was proud of having Chuck for my messenger. The average messenger on Wall Street was about fifty years old and disabled. Chuck could make any other messenger eat his messages. I wondered if I should start a boxing tournament for Wall Street messengers. As time passed Chuck became lazier and lazier. There was so little for him to do. He must have been feeling a little useless so to convince himself of his worth he asked me to give him a more challenging job.

"Can I be an underwriter?" he asked me.

Chuck had no chance of ever being an underwriter. I loved him but he had no education. No social graces. And a vacancy in his eyes that made him look like a dummy. I could picture him like Charlie McCarthy sitting on Edgar Bergan's lap. Not that he was really a dummy. For all I knew, he had a high IQ. Not that it mattered. I didn't like him for his intelligence. I liked him for his companionship. He was a buddy. I gave him a seventy-five dollar a week raise. He'd be getting four hundred dollars a week, the highest paid messenger on Wall Street. Chuck was happy. He had become part of the American Dream of upward mobility where everybody goes up up up till they disappear in a balloon of their own hot air.

15

OUT OF NOWHERE my driver, Said, decided to move back to Egypt. Domestic help came in and out of my life like birds in a backyard tree. I hired a new driver, a Russian Jew named Michael. I was toast for his buttering up, a soft touch for his flattery. Every morning when he picked me up he'd tell me how good I looked. There'd be hot coffee, a fresh roll, and a newspaper sitting on the wooden tray in the back of the Rolls. I felt like I was in chauffeur heaven. He was a real shrewdy. He knew how to play me like a pinball machine by pushing my buttons with a lot of yes sir, no sir crap.

When I got to the gym Chuck was always waiting for me to spar. Now that he worked for me it was part of his job description. We'd always go about ten rounds, trying to kill each other. But we were so used to each other's punches that they didn't hurt much. It was like good sex, we had punched our way into each other's rhythm. Then Michael would drive us over to Wall Street while Chuck and I were in the back seat joking and boasting about our morning fight. Chuck loved being chauffeured around in a Rolls Royce. He was living my life with me.

While I was at work Michael would go uptown to drive Lauren around to shop and lunch with her snotty girl-friends. At first Michael liked her. He thought she was a real doll. She was good-looking. Her blue eyes looked like some gentle sadness was going on beneath their clarity. Michael tried to flatter her like he did me with his clumsy Russian charm. When he put a cup of coffee on her tray in the back seat of the Rolls she said, "What makes you think I drink coffee?"

"I just . . ."

Lauren was very direct. Being a good-looking woman, she was used to turning down people who were trying to hit on her. Lauren didn't really need other people so she didn't go out of her way to appeal to them. She said what was on her mind. In chess, she'd be looking for check-mate. I just enjoyed moving the pieces around. She was a winner. I wasn't.

Michael complained but all he could hear from the back seat was Yak. Yak. Yak. He said she drove him crazy with requests—I'm getting a chill, turn on the heater. I'm too hot, turn on the air-conditioner. I'm too lukewarm, open the windows. Don't step on the brakes so hard. I'm getting nauseous. I'm getting whiplash. Don't speed. This is a Rolls not a Corvette. It doesn't look right to speed. You're driving around in a museum. It's priceless. Stop at Saint Laurent's. I'll be fast. An hour later she was back. Let's stop at Bergdorf's. No, I'm not going to rush. My hus-band will have to wait. You'll get to him when you get to him. You work for me.

Michael would show up for me long-faced and apologetic, "I'm sorry I'm late, boss. Your wife . . ."

I suppose I should have told him not to complain about my wife but I was seduced by his calling me boss. He reminded me of my vice president, Kelly. They were both operators.

I often wondered why my wife was so hard on the help. Was it because she was annoyed that I was such a sucker? That I forgave them anything? That I treated my employees as my best friends? It didn't occur to me that Michael might be exaggerating about how difficult my wife was.

My doormen told me that the wives of all the rich men in the building were harder on them than the men. There's something about having earned your money that makes you more considerate. I think the wives felt guilty about living off their husbands and struck out at the help because they were available and weaker.

I would get angry at Lauren's lack of consideration until I noticed that all her friends were worse than her. She was actually one of the more considerate ladies of the manor. Her friends were brutal. I don't even know if the Upper East Side women realized how they treated subservients. Perhaps their behavior was like a New York accent to a New Yorker. It was transparent. They didn't notice it. It wasn't obvious or strange like a British accent.

•••

We sold our weekend retreat in Westhampton. Lauren and Graham cried, putting a wreath on the door. I felt sad too but I hadn't enjoyed the house much ever since Lauren made me get rid of the motorcycles. We got four hundred and fifty thousand dollars and dumped it and other monies into an elegant pre-war building at 31 E. 72nd Street. It was a steal—one million, one hundred thousand dollars. It was a wreck. I told Lauren I wanted nothing to do with furnishing it and that we would stay in our apartment on 72nd Street and 3rd Avenue until it was ready. I gave her an open wallet and told her to decorate it as she wanted. I didn't want to control bullshit like decorating. I figured Lauren appreciated me for this. What woman wouldn't? After she spent a million dollars on repairs she invited me over to see her work. It looked like something out of *Architectural Digest*. Marble floors, chandeliers and sinks with gold faucets. A rosewood paneled library. Stark carpeting.

"I feel like I'm at the Frick museum," I said.

"Do you like it?" Lauren asked.

"You're a great decorator."

"Thank you," she said. "I did it for you."

Well, maybe not so much for me. She loved to shop and was thrilled with her own handiwork. She lived for the apartment. Still, it was nice of her. She went way out of her way for the both of us. I felt cool about it but I really didn't give much of a damn. In fact, its beauty made me feel uglier inside. The larger my life style the smaller I felt. I was in a palace. Disappearing into the janitor's lounge of the heart. I looked into a bucket and saw my own skeleton.

"I'll see you later," I said and headed out to Gleason's.

It was fight night and I ended up matched against a kid named Morales from Fort Apache Boxing Club in the South Bronx. Fort Apache was a no-no word where I came from. It scared the crap out of the average Upper East Sider. They wouldn't even drive through it in a locked car. Directors made movies about how rough that place was. *Bonfire of the Vanities* took place up there. To fight a boxer from Fort Apache you had to be out of your mind.

Last year Morales won the Junior Olympics. This was his first adult match. He was a stocky Hispanic kid who looked like he had a streak of black blood in him. He was seventeen years old. At that age kids didn't get tired. I wanted to knock the kinky hair off his head. I knew this was going to be a slugfest. I figured I was a father figure and that Morales would probably want to kill me. But I had just beaten Gonzalez and I was feeling confident. The bell rang and Morales came at me like a little bull. He was thrashing around, throwing punches from every angle. And I was firing back. Crash. Boom. Boom. Boom. We were trading punches on the inside. That's where I liked to be. We were in a rhythm like Fred Astaire and Ginger Rogers dancing cheek to cheek. I was in too close to get hit at the end of a long punch. The sweat was flying. Bruises were peeking out of my face. The adrenaline was rushing. Move. Countermove. Punch. Counterpunch. I loved it. I got hit with a hook in the corner of my right eye. I felt the skin pressing into the bone. I knew it was going to be black and blue. That was good. I was going to look like Halloween. I was excited. After the final bell I waited nervously. I needed this decision to prove that Gonzalez wasn't a fluke. The ref held up my hand. I had won. I had beaten the seventeen-year-old champ of the Junior Olympics. I thought the closest I'd ever get to anything to do with the Olympics would have been sitting in front of my television set. What was Morales going to say when he got back to his friends in the South Bronx? I lost to a middle-aged Jew? His trainer, an old Puerto Rican about my age, was slapping him in the corner. He had disgraced him.

I felt bad. I felt great. I didn't feel anything. I had my chopsticks in so many dishes. I was a global dim sum of feelings. After the fight I met Lauren for dinner at Mr. Chow's. I was wearing dark shades. She asked me to take them off. I tried to look away but there was nowhere to turn. She grabbed my chin like she was grabbing a dog's muzzle to stick it into its own shit and she made me look at her. She gasped when she saw my shiner.

"What truck did you get hit by?" she said as I went to the marble bathroom to take a peek. It was purple with streaks of black and yellow. It was a mess. Fuck it. I was proud. I beat the little bastard. Nice kid. I hoped I didn't ruin his career. He had nothing else besides his boxing. I felt bad. When I came back to the table, I half expected Lauren not to be there.

"Grow up. Fighting's for the lower classes," she said. As if she came from the aristocracy.

The maitre d' came over. He was a fan. "Are you still boxing, sir?"

"What do you think?" I said, taking off my glasses and showing him my eye. He was startled.

"Did you get him back, sir?" he asked.

"Don't encourage him," Lauren said. "Where's my squab with lettuce leaves?" Men loved to discuss boxing. Lauren just couldn't understand it. She hated violence.

●●●

It was about a week after the Morales fight and I was back in the gym sparring a tough session against a light heavyweight. I still had a black eye. I heard Hector yelling in the background, "David's gonna get knocked out." It was obvious to everyone but me. I saw another trainer shaking his head with disapproval. I was doing too much. Then I got shouldered in the nose. It swelled up like a turnip. It looked misshapen, like something that had just been pulled out of the earth. It was at that point that Bruce came over to me, "David, you need a rest. You're killing yourself."

"Please, I need the practice," I said. "Do you think if I drop to 139 pounds I'd fight better as a Junior Welterweight?"

Bruce looked at me curiously like I was anorexic and said, "You're already so skinny you look like you have AIDS. Ira thinks you're going to drop dead in the ring."

I listened to him but secretly decided I'd try to get down to 139 pounds anyway. I only had to work a little harder. I could drop six pounds. A few days later after a particularly rough sparring session where I got knocked down, Bruce came over to me and said, "You're suspended."

"You can't do that," I said.

Bruce took me over to a bulletin board hanging from

the gym wall and said, "Look at this." It was a five-page list of fighters who had been suspended by the New York Athletic Commissioner for lacerations, broken bones, and knockouts. Tough names, Spanish names. And ring names like the Butcher, the Assassin, the Hammer. I felt proud. I was part of the list of the toughest guys in the world. Even if I wasn't on the Athletic Commission's list, I was on Gleason's. I was one of the boys. I was a member of the foreign legion of the wounded. I was honored to be in their company. It was something to be suspended for being too tough for my own good. That was better than being given a plaque by the Young Man's Philanthropic League. It was ironic, knowing secretly in my heart of hearts that I was a coward, that I really didn't have it, that I was still afraid. Then again, I thought of my business friends who were honored for things they didn't deserve, of philanderers who got awards for promoting the quality of family life, of alcoholics who were made dinner chairmen for drug abuse benefits and of financial cutthroats who were made honorary Boy Scout leaders. Was I any less deserving than they were? When you really measure a man, we all fall short. At least I paid for my phony recognition with black eyes, broken ribs, and separated shoulders. I felt somehow real.

I thought back to when I was sixteen, when I first started seeing a shrink. At that time, I had been in a few street fights.

"Why do you fight?" my shrink asked me.

"Because I'm afraid not to," I said.

It was the sixties and my shrink was a hippie. He said, "You should love people not fight them."

"Yeah, right," I laughed.

"Listen to the Beatles. Songs like 'Love Me Do,'" he said. "What do you think the girls are listening to?"

It hit me like a revelation. I hadn't been doing too well with girls. The hippies who were always talking about love were stealing all the hot chicks. If I was ever going to get laid I had to give up this violent shit, grow my hair, and get some beads. That very afternoon I went into Greenwich Village and got some bell-bottoms and a shirt imported from India. I bought the novel *Siddhartha* by Herman Hesse. I put a flower behind my ear. I was going to get laid. I buried my hostile feelings in order to fake that I was sensitive just so I could get girls. I wasn't angry anymore. Now, twenty odd years later, I found myself regressing to my adolescent fury, fighting with other young men. I was really tough. I had been honored. I was suspended.

Four years ago I was afraid to enter Gleason's, where the weakest of the fighters looked like Freddy from *Nightmare on Elm Street*. Now I was the mayor of Gleason's. The injured clown. All the champs knew me. Michael Olajide, Jr. congratulated me on winning my battle against Morales. Buddy McGirt said he heard I was improving. Jose Rivera asked me when I was turning pro. Renaldo Snipes said he'd like to come to my next bout. Juan La-Porte said he'd like to spar with me sometime.

After a week I couldn't stand being away from sparring. I went up to Bruce and asked him to remove my suspension.

"I'm worried about you," Bruce said.

"I'll be more careful," I said.

"Give it another week for the swelling on your nose to go down and I'll let you," he said.

"Shit," I said.

"Is that a yes?" he asked.

"Yes, sir," I said. I wanted to fight today. But I didn't want to argue with Bruce. I liked him. I didn't want him to throw me out forever.

It was a long week waiting to return to sparring. Michael, my driver, teased me about my suspension, "I've never seen someone being banned for getting beat up too much, sir."

"I don't think you'd want to fight me," I said.

"I wouldn't want to hurt you, sir," Michael said. He looked in the rear view mirror and suppressed a giggle. I shouldn't have let him tease me like that but I was a regular guy and I let him talk the way he wanted. I didn't use my position as his boss to bully him around.

"You have permission to hurt me," I said. "I'll fight you when Bruce lets me back."

"It's your life, boss," Michael said, real cocky like he thought he could kill me. Michael was about 190 pounds and an ex-Israeli paratrooper who was born in Russia. He thought of himself as a tough guy. Did he think he'd just step in the ring with no experience and whip my ass? Would he challenge Jimmy Connors to a tennis match? Or enter a giant slalom race against Ingemar Stenmark? Why does everyone think he can be a boxer even if he never threw a punch? Something in the male ego doesn't let him admit to being a wuss. It relates back to caveman days when if you weren't tough you didn't eat or get laid.

I liked Michael. But he was stepping on my pride.

When I got back to the gym, I got right into the ring with him. In the first round I moved to the side and hit up under his ribs. He dropped to one knee just like that. His parachute didn't open.

"No more," he said, struggling to his feet. He had lasted less than twenty seconds. It wasn't right for me to hurt a beginner but he had asked for it. He sat on the side while I sparred six rounds with Chuck. The rest of the day he was groaning. While he was driving me back to the city he said, "Nice shot boss. Didn't really hurt me, you know. I'm just a little sore."

The next day while I was at the office Michael went to the hospital during a break.

"Gee, boss, you really hit hard," he admitted as he was taking me to my next appointment. "You broke two ribs."

What a kick. Two ribs! I liked Michael. I was wondering if I should feel bad for him. Or pretend I felt bad? No. He deserved the injuries. He disrespected me. He never should have thought he could stay in there with me. Did he think he could beat Tyson? And date Miss America while he was at it? The ego of men. You have to beat it out of them. I was the ego beater. The boxing psychiatrist.

•••

My next fight at Gleason's arena was against Angel Cordero. He was a wiry Puerto Rican with a skinny ponytail that snaked down his neck like a worm. I watched him warming up behind some of the other chairs. He looked like an open class fighter. He had a long snappy jab, the kind that whipped out there and snapped back to cover his face. And he threw classic combinations, working off his jab. With that style I could see that he was an outside puncher and would probably try to stay away from me. My mission was to get inside and crowd him. When the fight started I was all over him. Working the body. On the inside. Roughing him up. Between rounds a cute round card girl came by. She was a brunette with pudgy cheeks like tapioca pudding. She winked at me. I felt desirable, masculine. After the bell I tried to wade in on Cordero. He was a classy fighter. Olympic style. I was a club thug. With a million dollars and a Rolls Royce. You can't buy fighting styles. You are what you are. I fought like I was from Bed-Stuy. He fought like he was from the Upper East Side. No one got knocked down but I managed to outpoint him on pure aggression. My hand was raised in victory at the end. The round girl applauded. I waved goodbye to her. I'm sure she was disappointed that I didn't invite her to come along with me. I was more impressed by my fighting than my Rolls Royce. When I wasn't knocking myself I, too, was impressed by my image, my razzle dazzle.

Michael took Chuck and me back to the city. I told him to stop at the Iguana Café and I invited them in for some drinks and Mexican food. I was hanging out with my crew. I felt like I was part of a rap group. They were my posse. I liked them more than my millionaire buddies. They were not walking around with golden rods up their asses. They were broke. They were there to see me fight. They witnessed my love of risks. I was high on danger. I didn't like successful people. They became their occupations. I had no wish to chat with an occupation. Michael and Chuck were down with me. But after all they were only the hired help.

Shakespeare liked the rabble. So did Francois Villon. And James Joyce married rabble. Great minds gravitated to small minds. They didn't have time to mess around with over-achievers. No genius would waste his time listening to the boring arrogance of doctors and lawyers. Or, God forbid, dentists. He'd rather listen to the amusing patter of the uneducated.

When I got home my wife demanded, "What took you so long?"

"I stopped for drinks with Chuck and Michael," I said.

"Chip West invited us to dinner," she said. "Now it's too late."

"Thank God."

"You're slumming, David. You have no ego. You should be hanging out with investment bankers and people like Chip."

She was always trying to get me to do what she thought was best for me. I was more bent on self-destruction. I didn't want to tell her that I hated businessmen. They traveled through the city thinking that money was love and love was money. I remembered the business majors in college. The liberal arts fanatics considered them idiots. We didn't even think business was a subject. It was a pseudo-science like sociology. Business majors didn't get any brighter as they got older. They disappeared into skyscrapers like lapses in intelligence.

"Yes, maybe I'll try that," I said.

"Yes, you should."

●●●

My next fight I was matched up against a black guy named Duncan. Last year he had been a quarter-finalist in the Gloves. He looked like a crackhead. Stoned glassy eyes. He was wearing dirty wrinkled shorts and had a stupid expression on his face. Hector whispered in my ear, "Body punches." With his shorts hanging down so low, I could hit him almost anywhere without throwing a low blow. My hook to the body was my best punch. I was a natural rib breaker. I had no leverage up top. But when I dug down into the body, I shifted my whole weight into each punch.

The bell rang. I smashed across the ring and started banging Duncan's body. He was taken by surprise like someone smoking a crack pipe and getting busted by the cops. He didn't expect such an attack. I was slamming into him. Busting him up good. He punched my face in self-defense. But every punch he threw I banged him in the ribs. I didn't even bother to block his punches. I felt I had to take punches to give them. I was keeping the pressure up. He was cracking. He was against the ropes and not answering the body blows. I was feasting on him. Chewing him into little pieces when the referee stepped in and gave him a standing eight count. The ref asked him if he wanted to continue. He shook his head, no. I was euphoric. I had won by TKO. I was a killer. I was beating guys from the Gloves. I had improved like an urban rehab project. I was building edifices to my own fighting. I imagined *Awesome Lawrence* in graffiti on the side of subway trains.

16

IT WAS CHRISTMAS, 1989 and it was time to go on vacation. I hated going anywhere because I preferred to be home where I could train at Gleason's. All the ostentatious folderol of resorts didn't turn me on. I wasn't looking for glamour outside. I was looking to cuddle up with myself. I wanted to see if I could withstand punches, internalize them.

We decided to go to Florida. Lauren and I stayed at the Boca Raton Hilton while my son lodged with my parents in their condo at Deerfield Beach.

Lauren and I argued about nothing. I was hurt. I felt she didn't love me or even like me. I was jealous of possible suitors. What if she cheated on me? I wanted to beat someone up. Not that I would. I never started fights. I had no evidence of her doing anything wrong but my hurt feelings.

I went out for a walk. When I came back she was talking on the phone. She was laughing, having a good time. I felt like the duke in Browning's "My Last Duchess." Was she talking to a friend? Did she have a lover? There had been minor incidents where we had both been dishonest with each other. Was this another one?

I was not a wife beater. I went into the bathroom and started punching myself in the eye. I was taking no prisoners. I pounded away on myself. It was the same shit I used to do as a kid. Once I scraped my face against the bark of a tree and told my mother I wasn't able to go to school because some bullies beat me up. Another time I punched the cement wall on our driveway until I broke my pinky in order to get out of gym class for six weeks. Still another time I cut my face with a razor blade so I could watch it bleed and scare some of my friends at a party. I did a lot of stupid, hurtful things when I was young. But I was no longer young.

I looked in the mirror. My right eye was already purple. I had some punch! I felt proud of the way I hurt myself as I went back into the bedroom, looking forward to Lauren's reaction. But Lauren hardly looked at me. She was too busy chatting away on the phone to some friend. Or was it a friend? I grabbed the phone out of her hand and slammed it down. She looked at me full in the face to ball me out and noticed my eye.

"You're nuts," she said. "What do you want to hurt yourself for?"

"What hurts is your ignoring me," I said. "Who were you talking to?"

"Just a friend."

"That didn't sound like a friend," I said.

"You couldn't even hear who I was talking to," she said. "I'm going to tell your parents you're mentally ill."

"You drove me to it," I said, pointing to my eye.

"I'm not getting suckered into feeling sorry for you," she said and picked up the phone.

I was tempted to grab the phone from her and slap her across the face. But I didn't. I was not the type of guy to hit a woman. Instead, I went back into the bathroom and punched myself in the face again. But I didn't punch hard. Then I felt like I was a chicken for not punching hard enough. So I bashed myself harder to prove that I was no coward. But I still didn't hit myself hard enough to feel that I had real balls. I always fell short. That's why I boxed. I looked in the mirror. My eye was ripe. It was rich. Better than I thought. It looked like I had been in a fight. I liked that. It was stupid. But there was something romantic about being all caught up in your injuries. I stayed in the bathroom. I didn't want to share my nervousness or jealousy with Lauren. She wouldn't understand it.

●●●

A month later *USA Today* filmed a show on yuppie boxers. I was the focus. It was the same old same old. David Lawrence arrived at the gym in his Rolls Royce. David Lawrence sparred with Chuck. David Lawrence went back to his office on Wall Street and discussed business with his staff. The story was done over and over again. And played everywhere. I was an international phenomenon. I was nothing.

My wife and I watched *USA Today* when it was broadcast a week later. I asked her, "What do you think?"

"The media's only interested in you because of your Rolls."

She was right. The difference between me and other fighters was my car. I wanted to hit her, but I didn't believe in being clumsy or ugly. I don't know why she got me so angry. I guess it was because I was so attracted to her. I was not a wife beater. I didn't consider it aesthetically correct.

17

I FOUND A NEW sparring partner from Mexico. I nicknamed him "Mexico." I always called fighters by their na-
tionality. I never bothered about their real names. Mexico
had only been in the country a year and didn't speak much
English. He sold peanuts on the corner for a living. When
I told my father I was sparring with him he said, "Very
classy, you're now friendly with a peanut vendor." I was-
n't a snob. I liked peanuts. He boxed like all Mexicans
boxed, leading with his head and not bothering to protect
himself with his jab. Nothing hurt him. He was a donkey.
A few years down the line he'd turn pro and get knocked
around a lot.

Mexico and I always banged on each other hard. One
morning I was getting the better of him when he landed a
good thud on the side of my head. I looked at him and
there were suddenly three of him. I was surrounded by
him. I didn't know which Mexico to punch at first. I finished the round as best I could and went over to Hector
and said, "I can't see."

Hector disappeared. Then he was back. Then he was triple. My eye was all fucked up. Bruce gave me the name of an ophthalmologist in the city and I called him. Michael drove me over there. I was worried that I was going blind. I was scared shitless but I tried not to show it. A doctor with coke bottle lenses in his glasses examined me. I got a headache looking at him.

"Am I going blind?" I asked.

"It's a visual migraine, set off by the boxing," he said. "You'll be back to normal in a few hours."

I gave his nurse what looked like three credit cards. Later that afternoon the world came back to one image. Now, I only had to deal with the brutality of the real world and the financial pressures of producing enough business to offset the staggering expenses of running a Wall Street office. Not only was I spending like a pig but so was my wife. If that wasn't bad enough, I gave wide-open expense accounts to my employees. They lived in expensive restaurants for breakfast, lunch, and dinner. I never really monitored them. They charged their vacations to me and whenever they needed a bonus all they had to do was ask. As long as the firm was producing business, I kept doling out the incentives. I didn't care about balancing the books. Insurance was the kind of business that you could borrow from the premiums you collected in the trust fund and pay them back tomorrow. What did they call it? Rob from Peter to pay Paul. That was it.

●●●

One morning I was at Gleason's Gym watching a short, stocky, tattooed Italian sparring in the first ring with his trainer, Edwin Viruet. Edwin was impossible to hit. He had fought Duran twice and was never knocked down.

"Who's that Italian?" I asked Hector, thinking I might go a few rounds with him.

"Sammy the Bull," Hector said.

"Gravano?"

"Yep."

"I don't think I'll spar with him," I said. Sammy was John Gotti's main hitman. It was rumored that he had murdered eighteen men. It was not a good idea to hit him.

"Good choice," Hector said.

Michael had left the Rolls outside in the street. We didn't worry about that because no one wanted to steal a Rolls. It was too noticeable and you couldn't sell the parts. Michael was hanging around the gym, bullshitting with Sammy the Bull's driver. It was like a club for drivers. They had their own way of talking.

Gravano was a lot stronger than Edwin but he couldn't lay a glove on him. Edwin threw a couple of light jabs. Gravano flinched. I wondered what he was doing flinching. Here was a man who had murdered a bunch of people and he was afraid of a jab. If I were a killer like Gravano, I would have told Edwin to give me his best shot. If you were gonna give it, you should be able to take it. Bullies made me sick.

●●●

I got all the downtown billionaires into boxing. I called my little group the Billionaire's Boxing Club. I talked David Moross, Mark Dudelson, and Evan Greenberg into taking boxing lessons at Gleason's Gym. Moross was the son of the English billionaire, Mandy Moross. His family had worldwide oil and shipping investments. They had bought an insurance brokerage for their son David to play around with. He thought it was a class operation. It was a bucket shop. David wasn't very brilliant. His brokerage was only worth about thirty million dollars so the family didn't care if David fucked it up. Dudelson was an old friend of mine from high school. His family owned Taurus Films. He was only a millionaire, the poorest of the group next to me. Evan Greenberg's family owned the largest insurance conglomerate in the world, AIG. I used to play tennis with him, his brother Jeff, and his father Hank Greenberg on their private grass tennis court in Brewster. By bringing these guys into the gym I had turned boxing into an upper class sport like polo.

Hector was training them all. He cursed them out and bossed them around. He showed no respect for their fortunes. They loved it. It was nice for them to be treated like regular guys for a change. A kind of vacation for the very rich. It was fun putting billionaires in the ring together. Their combined assets could buy a small country.

Hector put Dudelson and Moross in the ring to spar. They almost scared each other to death. They were so busy backpedaling that they never hit each other. Evan got so nervous watching that he ran into the bathroom to take a dump. He didn't come out until the end of the lesson.

A few days later Moross called me up to his office. I was sitting in this huge conference room with a desk that sat twenty. "My dad wants me to quit boxing," he said.

"Why?" I asked.

"It's not dignified."

"That's ridiculous," I said.

"If I don't quit he's going to sell my company and bring me back to London," he said.

I called Dudelson and bad-mouthed Moross. I said, "Can you believe that pussy. His daddy won't let him box."

I was expecting him to say Moross was a jerk. Instead he said, "I have to stop, too. I'm falling behind in my work."

Then Greenberg told me, "I'm having stomach problems. My doctor wants me to stop boxing." That was the end of my billionaires boxing club.

Cover of *Men's Health*,
photo by Mark Seliger,
1991

18

I WAS IN THE DRESSING ROOM at Gleason's for a tournament. I was worn out and I felt like I had the flu. My last fight was a joke. Bruce had set me up with some sucker and told me to go easy. I was landing punches on him like commuters stepping into subway cars. It was hardly a workout. This time I got a tough match, Ted Robinson. He had just won the Empire State Games. I was feeling really sick and would have dropped out except a couple of my friends were in the audience and I didn't want to disappoint them.

When the bell rang my sick body sprang to life. Robinson was a slick outside fighter and he was slapping me around from a distance. I tried to get inside to exchange body shots with him but he kept stepping away from me. In the second and third rounds he tired out and I was able to catch up with him and land some clean shots. I kept coming forward and forcing the action. I pushed him against the ropes and landed hooks to the body and the head. When the fight was over he could hardly stand up. A round of applause burst through the arena.

I was convinced I was the winner until I heard a bunch of boos go up and saw the ref raise Robinson's hand. This was as phony as a Don King fight. I had won hands down. I was disgusted. Still I tapped gloves with Robinson. The decision wasn't his fault. I guess the judges didn't want to see a promising kid who won the Empire State Games losing to an old man like me. I went up to the dressing room. Robinson's father was there talking to his son. The father was younger than I was. He came over to me and said, "You really won." That was incredible. I couldn't believe he said it.

"No. Your son was the true winner," I said. He wasn't. But the father was so polite I had to say it. His son was exhausted. He threw up in a trashcan. Vito Antuofermo, who used to be middleweight champion, came into the dressing room. His face was so scarred from fighting that he looked like Frankenstein.

"You're great," Vito said. "How old are you?"

"Forty-two," I said.

"I'm thinking of making a comeback myself. I'm only thirty-five."

"You're a young man," I said.

"You're right. I can do it," he said.

When Vito tried to get his boxing license back, he had to go for a brain scan. He failed the MRI. Whole pieces of his brain were missing.

MTA photo of David Lawrence as bum posted in all NYC subways for seven years during the 2000s

He may be without a home, but he's not without help.

MTA/Connections Outreach tries to offer the homeless in the subway something more lasting than money or a meal. They connect isolated, troubled people to medical and psychological care, substance abuse treatment, and shelter. And they follow up on their progress. Connections workers, affiliated with BRC, include trained social workers. They're the only people authorized to do outreach in the subway. If you see someone homeless, call the BRC Homeless Helpline at 212-533-5151 (24x7). Thanks to their caring efforts, the subway doesn't have to be a permanent address.

Article written about David Lawrence and award-winning musician, Sam Wayman (Nina Simone's brother) for his album, *Magic Man*

THE WORLD'S No.1 SOUL MUSIC MAG

BLUES & SOUL

No. 494 October 13-26, 1987   + Black Music & Jazz Review   UK: 90p

BLUES & SOUL 494

SAM & DAVE
(WAYMON)   (LAWRENCE)

Behind the dark glasses of these two friends lies a series of stories which, one day, could easily make a wonderful film. Mark Webster dips his toe in the water and finds out that still waters still run deep

Lauren and David in their
dining room from an
article in *People Magazine*
about their rap music

David with Lauren
(above) and Graham
(below) in Paris

Lauren, Graham, and David
in the late 80s in St.
Thomas

David as a model

Graham's graduation from Collegiate High School
in 1997

Joe:
Drug addict.
Health problems.
Can be violent.
No family. Homeless.

David modeling for a Salvation
Army poster

The bell rings. I am calm. The world is in slow motion.

How I Won the Most Educated Fight in the History of Pugilism

By DAVID H. LAWRENCE

76 • BOXING SCENE

From an article David wrote
about his fight with Doc
Novick in 1990

Lauren, from her album,
Terrorist Lover, 1995

Merrill Lynch was doing an article on me for their in house organ, *Pursuits Magazine*. It was a beautiful, slick magazine. Michael Kaplan was writing it and Mark Seliger, a famous photographer, was taking the pictures. I was going to be a cover boy. Seliger took pictures of me jumping rope for hours on end. Everywhere I looked the shutter was clicking. He was a perfectionist and took a hundred roles of film. On Saturday he wanted to take some pictures of me sparring. I was training for an upcoming police charity fight in honor of some cop who was shot. My nose was sore from a sparring session I had earlier in the week. I probably should have rested it but I wanted to get ready for the cop fight.

I practiced with my usual partner, Chuck. We were going at it pretty strong when Chuck took a step back and threw a perfect straight right, shifting his weight from his ankle on up to his fist. I heard the loudest crack echo through the gym like a bone had been snapped. It was my nose breaking. I wanted to kill Chuck. I started throwing punches from every angle. I smashed his lip and opened up a two-inch gash. My blood was covering us like a swarm of bees. I fought blindly until the bell rang. Like a Pavlovian dog I stopped. I became calm. The adrenaline rush was over. I got out of the ring. Guys were looking at my face and turning away green. Hector took me into his office. He could hardly look at me. "It's broken," he said, like I didn't know that. The reporter, Michael Kaplan, came in to interview me but he couldn't look at me either. Seliger asked, "Can I photo it?"

"Not now," Hector said and kicked him out of his office. My nose was numb from swelling and I didn't feel it much. Chuck was standing around me like a big dummy not knowing what to say.

"I'm sorry," I said to Chuck.

"You're sorry?" he asked, puzzled.

"Sorry I let you break my nose. Now my dad's going to kill you," I said. I laughed. He laughed.

"Do you want to look in the mirror?" Chuck asked.

"Are you crazy?" Hector said. "He'll scare himself to death."

"I don't want to see me. There's nothing there," I said. "I'm Dracula."

I could feel my nose hanging under my right eye like a door off its hinge. It was pushed way the hell to the side.

My driver, Michael, drove me to the Ear, Nose, and Throat Hospital. A nurse put me in a room in the emergency section, next to an eighty-year-old lady with a broken hip. She was moaning and mumbling, "Help, help," but all the nurses and doctors were ignoring her. She yelled to a young doctor in a white coat, "Can't you help me? I'm in pain."

"You have to wait your turn, lady," he said, and walked away.

I wanted to speak up for her but I was afraid if I complained, I'd antagonize the staff and make things worse for her. Worse for me, too. Not very gallantly, I kept quiet and to myself, wondering what was in all the cabinets and happy to be in the hospital. After about twenty minutes my wife came darting in spewing anger, spitting out curses and chewing her gums, "Look at your nose, you idiot."

"Want to pick it?" I said.

"Fuck you," she said.

"Is that a promise?

"You have to stop fighting. You're killing yourself."

"Leave me alone," I said.

"I don't even recognize you anymore. You're leaving yourself alone. And your family," she said and flew out. I guess she couldn't take too much more of me. She hurt inside for me or was disgusted by my masochism.

A doctor came in and looked at me. "It's too swollen to x-ray," he said. "Go home and ice it. Take Percodan and go to a plastic surgeon in a couple of days to get it looked at."

"Can you take a look at the old lady?" I asked, gathering my courage.

"I don't do hips," he said and walked out. Feeling guilty, I left her there. I had done nothing for her. What was she doing at the Ear, Nose, and Throat Hospital anyhow if she had a bad hip?

Michael dropped me off at my building. The doorman, Fred, was working. He was a six-foot-three inch jolly monster with a limp. He walked like a sailboat beating into the wind and dribbled saliva on his lip when he spoke. I always expected him to trip over his clubfoot but he never did. I liked Fred. I held a towel up to my nose so he couldn't see it too well.

"Who won the fight?" he asked me.

"You should see the other guy," I said.

He took me up the elevator and I rang the bell. My wife and son weren't home. I didn't have the key. Fred took me back down to the lobby where I had to wait, covered with blood, holding a towel to my nose. Some horrified elderly neighbors passed. "Does he live here?" the old lady whispered to her husband. "I hope not," he said.

Lauren and Graham came home about an hour later and took me upstairs.

"Where were you?" I asked.

"Just because you were stupid enough to break your nose is no reason for us to miss lunch," Lauren said.

"Daddy, will you be all right?" Graham cried.

"I feel great, son," I said. "It was fun to see the hospital."

I went into my room and lay down on the bed. Lauren came in and said, "Are you crazy? You'll get blood on the pillowcases. They're Pratesi. They each cost five hundred dollars."

"For a pillowcase?" I asked.

"Don't you know anything about decorating?" she asked.

"I'll sleep on the floor," I said. About an hour later Graham woke me up and said, "I want to show you something." He led me down to the end of the hall by the hand and showed me a pile of all my boxing clothes. He jumped up and down on top of them, all red in the face. "Mom and I are throwing them all out," he said. "I don't want you getting hurt anymore."

It was pretty embarrassing getting balled out by a ten year old and knowing that he was right. I was touched. I loved him. If I could get out of the mess in my own head I might have the clear-sightedness to see that he was reaching out to me. But my vision was obscured by internal compulsions. I was already addicted to boxing. My injuries committed me further.

"You better quit, dad," Graham said.

"I promise I'll quit," I lied. I didn't like lying to my son but he was ten years old. I couldn't reason it out with him. If I quit, then I'd be diminishing all the suffering I had already endured. I could only ratify my dedication to boxing by sticking with it. I couldn't tell him that I was afraid that if I quit boxing I'd fall apart. I had a lot of business pressures and my marriage was on edge. Lauren was jealous of my boxing. More like she was disgusted by it. She obviously felt it was lower class. It was. That's what made it appealing to me. It freed me from snobbery. As much money as we were pulling in, we were always spending more. I was always borrowing from my business's trust account to pay bills. I'd wait anxiously for the next large commission check to come in to cover the deficit. I was running my business like a bucket shop. Boxing was the only thing I had that made me feel good about myself. It was ironic. Everyone else admired my business. It was quicksand. They looked down on my boxing. It was the bedrock of my substantiality.

•••

Dr. Tabal was a famous plastic surgeon on East 72nd Street. He didn't deal with many accident cases. I was his first boxing injury. He handled accidents of birth—big noses and ears, ugliness. He fought against the ravages of old age, popping out wrinkles and stretching the skin like a balloon. He specialized in making squeaky mouthed, Upper East Side women prettier. He defied Darwinian natural selection by turning survival of the prettiest on its ear. A lot of ugly women got rich husbands thanks to his work. These women would have been spinsters and worked as low paid secretaries if it wasn't for Dr. Tabal. Now they were ordering their doormen around and riding in limousines.

"I can scrape out the inside of your nose and make it like new but it would lose some of its strength," he said. "You won't be able to box."

"I have to box," I said.

"Your nose would break if it got hit," he said.

"Just push it back into place," I said.

"It won't look as good. It might be a little crooked," Dr. Tabal said.

"It'll give me character," I said. I wasn't looking to be a beauty boy. It gave me a kick to not care about my appearance when everyone was spending so much to look good. I felt sorry for the ugly women around me. They were like one large tear dripping from a damaged eye. It was sad to hate yourself. I loved myself. I wanted to hurt myself as a test. I had to pass through the fire to become purified.

Tabal booked an operating room in five days at Lenox Hill Hospital. I stayed locked up in my room at home until the operation. I was embarrassed to let anyone see my nose. When I looked in the mirror, I looked like Mr. Potato Head with the wrong nose pinned to my face. I hated not being able to work out. I did a few push ups at home and my nose started bleeding.

When the day arrived, they rolled me toward the operating room high on Valium. I pulled up along side of an old woman in a wheelchair. I felt like we were two teenagers lined up at a traffic light in our hot rods. "I'll drag race you for registration," I said to the old woman as I was wheeled past her.

After the operation I wasn't supposed to do any exercise for a few weeks. I had a small bandage across my nose but otherwise I looked all right. I spent a lot of time lunching and drinking with clients. Everyone asked me, "You quitting boxing now?" I always said, "No." Some clients were impressed by my stick-to-itiveness. Most of them thought I was a moron. I didn't care what they thought.

Chuck slinked around the office, scared of his own shadow. The fact that he had broken my nose so badly didn't make him too popular with my dad, who was busying himself these days by reading the *Wall Street Journal* and *Barron's*. My father insisted on staying in the back of the office because of his previous reputation and business failures. Occasionally, he'd check up on supplies or personnel. For that I paid him about five hundred thousand dollars a year. Or something like that. I never really knew. I signed blank checks for him. Who cared? We were making money and he had given me my start in business. He was my dad, family, blood. I loved him.

I didn't know what was the big deal about my broken nose. I would have broken Chuck's nose if I could have. And I wouldn't have felt guilty about it either. Why was my dad pissed? He was a tough guy in WWII. He had taught me to be a man. Had he forgotten how to be one himself?

A week after the operation I was back at Gleason's hitting the bags and working out. I told my family I was only there for exercise and I wasn't ever going to spar again.

I went out and bought one of those headgears with a nose protector. That way I wouldn't get any bruises on my face and no one would know I was sparring again.

The first person I started sparring with was Chuck. I hated wearing a nose protector. It made me feel like a pussy. Still, I had seen top pros use nose guards when their faces were sore. So who was I to think I was so tough? My nose had almost been taken off my head. I was no chicken. I didn't have to prove anything. I was a jerk. I was exhausting. My personality was fatiguing me. I was growing tired of my confusion and the boasting of my inner voices.

After the workout I went back to the office and stared at my memorabilia. My notoriety as a boxer had grown. It was as undeserved as I was unusual. People were fascinated by rich people boxing. Just step in the ring and you were bound to get an article written about you. The walls were filled from floor to ceiling with newspaper and magazine articles about my white-collar boxing. *People Magazine, Sports Illustrated, Esquire, GQ,* they were all there. The office was so filled with trophies and magazine pictures of myself that my employees used to call it "The Shrine." My face hung on the walls like pictures of Lenin in Russia before the end of the Cold War. You'd think I was Muhammad Ali instead of some novelty fighter. But the media loved me. My life was a sound bite. I didn't care about landing accounts. All I wanted were trophies to affirm that I was alive, a champion, a somebody. The fact that I was a someone in business didn't faze me. I was trapped in some adolescent fantasy of being a great athlete.

19

I HAD JUST finished working out for the morning and Bruce came over to me and said, "I'm taking a team of American boxers over to fight in Norway. You want to fight?"

He had to be kidding. It was a dream come true to fight on an international team. I wanted to go. But I was scared. What if the guys were killers? I wasn't suicidal. I asked, "Who will I get to fight?"

"Some Norwegian kid who didn't quite make the Olympic team," he said.

"How far off was he from making the team?" I asked.

"Don't worry about it," Bruce said.

Everybody who set up matches for me always said, "Don't worry about it." I often found out that I had to "worry about it."

"As long as he wasn't in the Olympics I'll fight him," I said. I figured I could handle any of their Norwegian fighters except the best. I was used to fighting good fighters at Gleason's. No Norwegian Eskimo was going to beat me up.

I went downstairs and got into the Rolls. I said to Michael, "Guess what?"

"You're turning pro."

"No. I'm going to Norway to fight."

"Let me come, boss," he said. "We can stop in Russia and buy art. There are some great deals over there now."

"I've seen a lot of that shit floating around New York," I said. "Everyone's selling Russian art."

"I know where the good stuff is. And I can get it really cheap," he said. It sounded like it would be fun. I wondered what my wife would think of my traveling around the world with my chauffeur. She'd probably look down her nose at me. She was such a snob. Or a realist.

I had some T-shirts printed up—*Norweigian Boxing Tour,* and I gave them out around the gym to other fighters who were also going on the trip. The T-shirt company had misspelled Norwegian but none of the guys in the gym knew it. I was so excited to be in an international event that I wore my black *Norweigian Boxing Tour* T-shirt under my white dress shirts just to feel close to it. You could see the letters through the fabric. I felt almost like I was in the Olympics. Two weeks before the trip I was in Bruce's office when he got a call from the international committee. He called me in and put the call on his speakerphone. "What the hell are you doing? Lawrence is too old to fight," a gruff voice barked at Bruce.

"He's fighting very well," Bruce said.

"You want to be banned from international events?" the voice threatened.

"Can he go as a coach?" Bruce asked.

"He can coach all he wants. I just don't want him fighting." The phone line went dead. Bruce looked at me and said, "Well, you can still go."

"I'm no coach," I said. I looked down at my *Norweigian Boxing Tour* T-shirt and felt that at least I had that. My wife would be happy that I wasn't going. Michael would be pissed but that was his problem. He worked for me rather than vice versa, although sometimes we both forgot.

•••

I used to ask a lot of questions about my opponents. But Hector told me that a true fighter didn't care who he fought. I was in the dressing room at Gleason's arena. I got paired up with some black guy, Claude Nesbit, who I knew nothing about. I didn't ask any questions. This was my first fight since my broken nose. I figured I'd move my head a lot. I wasn't sure how strong my nose was and I didn't want to risk breaking it again.

Nesbit was a technical fighter. He had no power but a lot of skill. I got in and swarmed on him with my Jake LaMotta style. He did his best to move away but I stayed on him. It was a pretty even fight. I had the strength and he had the moves. I didn't bother slipping his punches. I liked when they bounced off my face. I had this crazy theory where I used my opponent's punches as part of my own combination. My jab would be 1, then his jab to my face would be 2 and then I would complete the flurry with a right, 3, and a hook, 4. It was ingenious. At least I got a kick out of it. I was clearly the aggressor and won the decision. I was developing quite a collection of trophies.

One morning I was shocked to read in the *Post* that a scandal had broken out in the boxing world. Bruce was accused of skimming from the Amateur Boxing Association. He lost his job as president of the association and he was no longer able to hold amateur tournaments at Gleason's. Bruce was worried that they might send him to jail.

"What's it all about?" I asked.

"It's over a lousy four hundred dollars I didn't get receipts for when I took the amateurs over to Sweden last year."

"I hate that petty receipt shit," I said. I kept receipts for nothing. I charged everything to my business. I'd be dead meat in an audit, but who cared?

"Like I was supposed to keep receipts each time I bought a kid breakfast."

"If they don't trust you, you shouldn't work for them," I said.

The handwriting was on the wall for my amateur fighting career. Without Bruce as President of the ABA, they'd never let me fight. I was way past the twenty-seven year old age limit.

20

THE ARTICLE Michael Kaplan was writing for *Pursuits* finally came out around the time I broke my nose in the fall of 1989. My picture was on the cover. That was my first cover. I felt like a top model. Maybe I was pretty good-looking. I never thought about it much. That picture was taken just before I messed up my nose when I was a lot better looking than I was afterwards.

As much as I enjoyed the *Pursuits* article, I was blown away when Seliger came back and asked me if he could photograph me for *Men's Health*. It was a national magazine with huge circulation. It appeared in most of the newsstands throughout the United States. I gladly acceded. We spent another fifteen hours in Gleason's Gym taking pictures of me jumping rope. I didn't know why he took so many pictures—thousands. What was he trying to get? A hit-or-miss photo of my soul jumping rope? Imagine my thrill when a few months later I appeared on the cover. That was big. Even I was impressed.

There was a tough fighter down at the gym named Donnie Poole. He was built like a fire pump. He was the

Canadian national welterweight champ. When I came in one morning he approached me and said, "Doc Novick thinks he can take you."

I remembered the first time I saw the Doc about five years ago. He was hitting the bag at Gleason's. His body was tight as a drum. His abdominals were like a mogul field. At that time I wouldn't have fought him for all the tea in China. His nose turned around on itself like a snail. It was sick. Sickening. I wondered how a person could willingly misshape himself so. Yet, he must have been proud of his nose. It was a trophy, a trumpet of his toughness. Otherwise, why not fix it? His face was gone. Who would fight him? He had nothing to lose. I didn't want anything to do with the Doc. But there was no way I was backing down. He was a good test for me. Beating the Doc was a rite of passage. Like winning a tennis club championship.

"The Doc bets five hundred dollars he can beat you," Poole said.

Hector overheard and said, "David can beat the Doc."

"You want to bet?" Poole asked.

"David bets five hundred dollars too," Hector said. "You kill the Doc, David."

Thus spoke Hector. If I backed out now I'd lose face. The date was set for two weeks later. I went up to Bruce and suggested, "Why don't we start a new league, White-Collar Boxing."

"Why?"

"You can't hold amateur fights since the ABA kicked you out," I said. "This will give you a chance to get audiences and charge admissions. Give out trophies again."

"Let's do it," Bruce said. Making a few more dollars from shows would help him. And that was the beginning of White-Collar Boxing at Gleason's Gym. The first fight to inaugurate the new program was between Doc and me. We made it a 5-rounder for the New York State White-Collar Welterweight Championship. It was a club fight, unsanctioned by either the Amateur Boxing Federation or the New York Athletic Commission. I felt like the nineteenth century fighter, Bill Heenan, who wore disguises and sneaked around the London countryside to fight.

The fight promised to be the most educated battle in the history of pugilism. The Doc had law and veterinary degrees. I had a Ph.D. in literature and was the President of a Wall Street insurance brokerage firm.

Later that week I was down at the gym sparring with Donnie Poole, who had set up the fight. He was taking it really easy on me. He probably didn't want to give me any good practice for the Doc.

"If the Doc wins he's giving me the $500 he collects from you," Poole said between rounds.

"I'll give $500 to Hector," I said. Hector overheard me in the corner. Now he had a stake in the fight. He wouldn't let me lose. Even if he had to come out of the corner and hit Doc himself.

I wasn't sure I was ready for the Doc. He was an ex-pro who was into self-destruction. He didn't care about getting hit. I told my wife I was going to a business meeting. She didn't suspect my adulterous liaison dangereuse with a pair of boxing gloves. If my face was battered, should I say negotiations were rough? Or quip that we clashed heads for a while, then saw eye to eye? I had to come home unblemished.

I was eager. I was nervous. I was scared shitless. Yet I

was anonymously making history. Two fighters with their educational titles on the line. A freak show.

The night of the fight I checked out the arena before anyone arrived. The cavernous space was dark except for a lone spotlight on the ring. I thought of Rocky Balboa going into the gym late at night to have a private grudge match with Apollo Creed. Just to do it. To see who was the better man. I went into Bruce's office. Doc Novick arrived. We exchanged pleasantries. *How have you been? Long time no see.* He handed me a piece of paper to sign.

"What's this?" I asked.

"A waiver. In case you get hurt," he said. The nerve. What made him think he was going to hurt me? I signed the stupid piece of paper. I didn't want to lose my concentration by arguing before the fight. It pissed me off that he was losing the poetry of the moment in legal concerns. He was not concentrating on the fight. I wouldn't have sued if he killed me. This was about honor. This fight was above the law. It was illegal in the first place. Waivers were candy ass. I was surprised at the Doc. We were here to die and he was worried about the law. There were greater laws than what he studied in school. The laws of nature. Thousands of years of civilization and we were still animals. Why else were we fighting? The Doc was becoming too civilized. That was a weakness, an Achilles heel. Perhaps he was vulnerable.

Look at that nose. Doc had lost all perspective. He was in love with the ugliness of his own nose. His goal was nasal annihilation.

Bruce placed two huge trophies in the ring. They were beautiful. "This is the beginning of a series of white-collar tournaments, which hopefully will grow into an international event," he announced to an audience of about twenty people. "This fight will be for the vacant, welterweight crown."

Hector hadn't showed up yet so my friend Chino worked my corner. I was pissed that Hector hadn't showed up for such an important fight. I depended on him. The bell rang. I was surprisingly calm. The world was in slow motion. Every punch I threw landed. I was in the zone. His face was swelling up like a pink water balloon. I double jabbed him. I sneaked in a straight right and knocked him back fifteen feet into the ropes. The ref, José Rivera, former contender for the middleweight crown, gave the Doc a standing eight-count. I didn't try to finish him off because I was worried about conserving energy for the full five rounds.

When I got back to my corner Hector had arrived. He looked like he had had a few beers. I never knew him to drink before. His balance was a little off and he didn't climb up to the apron of the ring. He shouted at me from the floor. He shouldn't have been late. I needed him. He was my backbone. He was my courage. Chino told me to uppercut and hook. Hector said, "You doing good. We go pro after this."

In round two, the Doc became a human punching bag. His head snapped back, then forward every time I hit him. He had no defense. His nose was onion purple. I think he liked it. I liked getting hit because it gave me a chance to prove that I could take it. He liked it because he was a real masochist. He was sick. Round three exhausted both of us. Donnie Poole kept yelling, "You got him, Doc." Which fight was he watching? I was killing the Doc. Between rounds,

Hector told me to go easy and save it for the fifth. I danced. I was Baryshnikov playing Gregor in The Metamorphosis. I was a cockroach. Fast and indestructible. I didn't get hurt.

In Round Five I was smoking. I was Gene Kelly, tap-dancing on Doc's face. He knew he had to stop me or he'd lose the decision. He threw bombs. But I caught them and threw them back like grenades. He liked being blown up. He never quit. He fought till the last bell.

I was exhausted when Bruce raised my hand and announced to the mostly vacant arena, "The new welter-weight champ and king of white-collar boxing, Awesome Lawrence." The victory was mine. It was sweet. The 20 or so people there applauded. The decision was unanimous. I couldn't believe how easily I mastered the same fellow who scared the shit out of me a few years before.

Doc came in to the dressing room to congratulate me. We hugged. Pals to the end. He split without saying anything to me about our bet. Poole came in and said, "Doc's trying to stiff you out of the $500. Come down with me and tell him to pay."

"I don't want to fight over the money," I answered.

Poole went over to Hector, "Help me get the five hundred dollars from Doc. David's supposed to give it to you." They went off. I already gave Hector $200 to pay the referee for officiating. I was supposed to be winning money, not losing it. After all, I did win the fight.

Poole came back. "The motherfucker won't pay. He's a disgrace. I thought he could fight. He's only good for sparring. David, lend me the $500 so I can pay Hector."

"I'll pay Hector," I said. I wasn't going to let him fuck me over like I was a sucker. Why should I give Poole five hundred dollars to give Hector when Hector was right there? I could give it to him myself. But what was I to give him? The Doc hadn't paid me.

"The Doc made me look like a jerk. And he's not taking us to dinner. He was supposed to treat all of us. He's the worst sport I ever knew. I'll break his fuckin' neck. He's embarrassed cause he thought you were nothing, but you're a better man than he is. He's a faggot," Poole said.

Hector returned.

"Don't worry, Hector. I'll pay you for helping me even if the Doc doesn't pay," I said. He was a poor man. The money meant nothing to me. And he hadn't tried to cheat me like the others.

"Forget it. You won. That's all that counts," Hector said. He was a friend.

•••

The next morning the Doc called me in the office, "I'm taking you to dinner like I promised. But the $500 I knew nothing about. Poole made that bet on his own."

"I had promised the money to Hector, Doc. It doesn't matter to me personally, but he could use it," I said. I figured if I could get the Doc to pay up it would be better than my forking out the money to Hector.

"But the bet wasn't mine. Poole set up the whole thing. Even the fight," he said. "He was so sure that I'd win that he figured he'd get five hundred dollars from you easy. He never expected you to beat me. Neither did I. He said you challenged me."

"I didn't challenge you. Poole said you wanted to fight me," I said.

"Then Poole tricked us."

"Forget about it, Doc," I said.

•••

A few days later I got an urgent call from Poole, "That cheap son of a bitch. I'll break his fuckin' neck. I thought he was a friend but he's just a faggot. He's just not paying because he's so embarrassed he lost."

"Forget about it, Poole. I'm sure there was just a miscommunication. Let's all try to stay friends." I was the good guy. I couldn't believe these creeps going through gyrations for a lousy five hundred dollars.

"He shouldn't have done that to me," Poole said.

"It's me who got stuck for the money."

But the money wasn't the issue. All that mattered was that I was now Gleason's New York State White-Collar Welterweight Champion.

•••

It was the third month in a row that I had received my vice president Kelly's corporate bill from American Express for over forty thousand dollars in expenses at the Waldorf Astoria. It was like he owned stock in the place. I was in my father's office and I called Kelly down to speak to us. I had warned him before, but he lied to me that he was going to change. He came into the office with a hangdog look. He knew he was going to get punished. But I couldn't fire him because he was too profitable. Just last month he had written an account where he had buried a two hundred thousand dollar fee for my firm. That paid his monthly Amex bill eight times over. He also knew too many inside secrets about our operation. Such as the games he played. It was ironic. He'd break the rules and then use his indiscretions as a form of covert blackmail against his dismissal. He was a smart prick. Skinny and small, a diminished form of Frank Sinatra. An energetic punk. His favorite song was "My Way." And yet, no matter how dangerous he was for my operation, I liked him. Maybe it was because of the way he flattered me. He always referred to me in front of the staff and clients as "The Boss." He and Michael used the same term. Kelly drove the business; Michael drove my car.

"It's a waste of my breath to ball you out," I said. "Give me your Corporate American Express card."

He took his time taking it out of his wallet. He had it in its own leather folder. He loved that card. He handed it to me with tears in his eyes. I took out a pair of scissors and cut it up. He winced like I was cutting off his finger.

"What am I going to do for money?" he moaned.

That was a problem. He lived off his American Express Card. I gave him about sixty thousand dollars a year in salary. He took that home to his wife. The rest he used for himself while his family lived in a little, lower white class community in Bohemia, Long Island. He charged over five hundred thousand a year to me on his Amex card, his restaurant charge accounts, his car and limo expenses and a couple of VISA cards he'd have me reimburse him for.

I had an inspiration. I could make up for taking his Amex Card by giving him the service fees we were getting from Schwartz. Schwartz was an unlicensed broker who used to charge his clients consulting fees instead of commissions. The Insurance Department had no control over these fees. Who knows if they were legal? They were larger than the premiums. For example, he'd buy insurance for a client from us for fifty thousand dollars and sell it to his client for three hundred thousand dollars. He'd call the two hundred and fifty thousand dollar mark-up a service fee. He did this to hundreds of clients. And kicked us back about five percent. We learned from him. We later quoted premiums to him for his personal clients and jacked them up just like he did.

"Take the Schwartz fees," I said. They're thirty thousand a month. About the same as your Amex bills at the Waldorf."

"You're too generous," Kelly said. "I have to give you back some of it."

I liked the idea. Bribing me with my own money. It was ironic. I bit into the apple.

"I have a banker friend at National Westminster Bank," he said. "He can cash the checks."

The Feds were putting money launderers away for eight to twenty years. They were down on that kind of shit. Without realizing it I had just become the key man in a money-laundering ring. If I had any idea of the implications, I wouldn't have done it. I was no chiseler, no weasel. I was cool and careless. I had no intention of committing a white-collar crime. If I was going to do a crime, I would have done the big kahuna of all crimes. I would have killed. There was something romantic about death. We were all headed there anyhow. I saw life as a giant slide we were all going over into death's abyss. When I closed my eyes I sometimes saw skulls. They were calling to me. But I could never understand what they were saying.

David fighting Rodriguez at Trump Palace in
Atlantic City

21

I WENT SKIING in Aspen with Michael Douglas. My son Graham and his son Cameron were schoolmates at Birch Wathen. My wife had become friendly with him and his wife Diandra. Lauren, like most Upper East Side women, wanted to hang out with celebrities. I didn't mind. I liked stars. They shined on me. But at the same time I resented Michael's fame. Why not me? Right? What for? The world's most distracted insurance executive.

When we were on the liftline all the girls were staring at him, flirting with him. What about me? Was I chopped liver? I used to be a ski racer. I was ranked in both slalom and giant slalom in the USSA. But when we came down the slopes, Michael stem-turning next to me like a ruptured turkey with a knee brace, all the girls would applaud him. I could carve turns with independent leg action better than most of the instructors and I was merely the guy who blocked their view of Michael.

It was an uneventful trip and Michael was too busy with an estate he was building out there to spend much time with us. Most of the time I babysat on the slopes for Cameron and Graham. I was like the hired help. I didn't mind. I liked kids. I had trained my son to ski since he was three years old. I used to put him on short skis and hold him between my legs as we skied down double black diamond expert slopes in St. Moritz, Courchevel and Vail. Cameron wasn't too good. Michael didn't spend much time with him. Not that he knew enough about skiing to teach him. In the Hollywood community he was known as a good skier and a good father. He was neither. There's something about being on the big screen that magnifies your accomplishments. It's like stars are always hiding behind their make-up. They are hidden by the airbrushes of their own invention.

When I got back I bragged like Douglas was my best buddy. I didn't tell people that he mostly ignored me. Not that he was a bad guy. He was nice. I just qualified as other-things-to-do, which weren't done.

Kelly was now rolling in cash. Since I cut up his credit card, he'd been cashing the checks I gave him from Schwartz with his Westminster friend. He called me into his office and took out an envelope with thirty-five grand in it and gave me seventeen thousand. That was a beautiful looking pile of dirty bills. It rained from a black cloud in heaven. It was a fringe bonus. Money I could do whatever I wanted with and there would be no trace. My wife wouldn't have a clue about what I was earning or spending.

That summer Kelly went to Atlanta on a business trip with my other vice president, Mark Cramer. I didn't like Cramer. He was ugly and neat. He wore corny, Brooks Brothers clothes. He had hair plugs. In fact, he had charged them to me. I kept him around because he was profitable. Like Kelly. He had one account that I placed the insurance on for three hundred thousand dollars and he charged his client eight hundred thousand dollars. I made a five hundred thousand dollar profit on that account alone.

When Cramer and Kelly came back from Atlanta, Kelly said, "Cramer's in with us on the cash."

"Why?"

"It's the only way to control him," Kelly said.

"I don't trust the bastard," I said.

"If you don't let him into the deal, he'll fuck you," Kelly said.

"I don't know," I said.

•••

A couple of days later a short, ugly nerd with thick glasses and chino pants with coffee stains on them showed up at the office. Kelly introduced him, "This is Toni Dantinas."

I didn't shake his hand. It looked clammy or like he had just picked his nose.

Toni handed Kelly a big fat brown manila envelope. I was uncomfortable about this guy. Something stank. Toni looked gay. I knew Kelly wasn't. He was a man's man. But there was something going on there. I couldn't quite put my finger on it.

I left Toni alone with Kelly for a while. The air was stale in Kelly's office. I couldn't take too much of these creeps together. I heard girlish giggling as I closed the door behind me. About a half hour later Toni left and Kelly called Cramer and me down to his office. He opened up the envelope and there was thirty thousand dollars in cash. There was something funny about so much money. We all cracked up and had a grand old time. It was only a lousy ten grand to me. I earned that much on the books every couple of days. But it was the fact that it was cash that was such a thrill. Even if it was my money. I was stealing from myself and dividing it with these two thieves. When I thought of the simple honesty of fighters risking their lives in the rings, I couldn't compute how I could be part of this flaky shit.

I asked Kelly, "Who's this creep Toni Dantinas?"

"He's our banker from Delaware," he said.

"I thought you had a friend up here at Nat Westminster who was cashing the checks for us," I said to Kelly.

"Don't worry so much," he said. I didn't want to seem like a worrier so I dropped the subject. It was probably best that I didn't know anything about what the guy was doing. Then I wasn't a party to it. I had seen that in crime movies. The less you knew the better. I felt clever.

22

I FELT GOOD at Gleason's, away from the corrupt atmosphere of my office. But in August the arena shut down.
Gleason's couldn't afford to hang onto it. All the fights
were moved to Gleason's Gym up the block from the
closed arena. Tonight Bruce was having the first open call
for white-collar fights at the gym. It was a follow-up to the
fight I had with Doc Novick six months before.

All the fighters went into the office and weighed in. I
was paired off with a Gleason's fighter, Gus Blight. He'd
never seen a white collar in his life. He was a black street
kid. The same kind of fighter I'd get in the amateurs. But
I wasn't worried about him. I had plenty of experience. I'd
rather fight him than the businessmen who were hanging
around there. I didn't want some easy crap.

Bruce announced me as the white-collar welterweight
king. I liked that. He made me want to beat the shit out of
Blight. But he was too fast and slick. I couldn't catch up
with him. He ran from me the whole time. I won by an uneventful decision. It was boring. I didn't get that thrill like
when I was on the edge between hurting someone and

seeing myself hurt. But the hidden, cowardly part of me that was tucked inside my brain like a pod of raw nerves celebrated its escape from danger.

I didn't fight again until November. This time I defended my welterweight title against my sparring partner Chuck. Although we always tried to kill each other, even in sparring, there was something comforting about fighting an opponent I knew so well. I sometimes kept my hands down so he could hit me in the face. This charged me up. And I came after him harder. As usual, I hurt him in the body. His punches bounced off my head. I controlled the tempo of the fight and I won.

"The judges gave you the fight because you rich," he said.

"I was the aggressor," I said.

"Like shit."

"Here's your twenty dollars for sparring," I said, and handed him a twenty.

"You can't pay me off," he said and gave me the twenty back.

"The judges made the decision," I said.

"This wasn't sparring," he said. "It was a fight. I should get more."

I gave him fifty dollars. He looked happy and pocketed the money. He was stupid when it came to his principles. Everyone was. It was like politics. There was no sense in arguing with a wall.

•••

My buddy Ken Friedman flew into town. He was a Hollywood screenwriter and my oldest friend. He was with his
ex-girlfriend Angela. She had Betty Boop hair and angry
eyes. She chain-smoked Gauloises. After a Japanese lunch
where we all had a lot of saki Angela said, "You've led a
fascinating life. I'd like to do a short movie about it."

My hobby had always been writing. Actually, it was
more than a hobby. I had a Ph.D. in literature and had published hundreds of poems. I had also published literary
criticism. Not to mention four unpublished novels and five
plays. I was busy at my lack of success. I gave Angela some
autobiographical writings. She took them home to see if
there were any ideas there for her film. A few days later
she called me. She wanted to speak to me about her movie
idea. We went to lunch and she told me, "I'd like to do a
sixteen millimeter, black and white, short film based on
your writing. It's brilliant."

"How much will it cost?" I asked.

"Twenty-five thousand dollars," she said.

"OK," I said. I never haggled over price. I knew nothing about movie costs.

"When can I get the money?" she asked.

"Tomorrow," I said. What was the rush? I was a fool. I
trusted everyone. I was so rich that I didn't realize twenty-
five thousand dollars was a fortune to her and she was
going to find it hard to resist wasting it. While I was rich
compared to Angela I was poor compared to all my billionaire friends. Rich people didn't give away money.
Money stuck to them like warts.

Gary Braverman, the self-promoting hustler who went to jail for robbing Paul Simon twice in one night, invited me to fight in the Celebrity Fights at the Taj Mahal in Atlantic City. He was a large man who liked to wear pajama tops. He talked a bunch of famous fighters and ne'er-do-well actors into participating under the guise that it was for a charity. Somehow Gary decided that I was also a celebrity. He called me the Wall Street Boxing Champion.

Lauren hadn't attended one of my fights since the Wall Street Charities four years ago. Not that she knew about all of them.

"Are there going to be celebrities there?" Lauren asked when I told her about the fight in Atlantic City.

"Yes," I said.

"I'll come," she said.

•••

The Celebrity Fights were held in December in Atlantic City. Angela and her husband, Jean Marie, came along to film me for the movie we were doing. I strolled the lobby of the Taj Mahal with my own film crew following me everywhere. I liked the attention. I was a star. I often fantasized about being stretched out in a coffin and having a room filled with people crying over me. But I knew that the only people who would show up would be my parents and my son, Graham. What about Lauren? She might show up just to wear a new black dress from Chanel and tell the rabbi that I didn't leave her enough life insurance. She didn't like me. Or she loved me and was bitterly disappointed. Why? I loved her when she wasn't picking on me. I wasn't a nostril. Why couldn't she leave me alone and let me breathe the rarified air of my own fantasies? I was difficult.

There was a long hall with a line of dressing rooms at the Taj Mahal. On one door it said, "Larry Holmes" and "David Lawrence." What a high! I was sharing a dressing room with Larry Holmes, the former heavyweight champion of the world. He was a friendly, teddy bear of a guy. He was a little punchy. He told me stories about how he used to go up to training camp with the Rams football team and beat them up in the ring one after the other. "Huge guys," he said. "They couldn't fight at all."

Donald Trump stopped by to say hello to Holmes. He was a chubby, arrogant man with hair that lay over his head like a gull's wing. He reminded me of the rock group A Flock of Sea-gulls. The real estate market had crashed and he was in debt billions of dollars in 1990. But it didn't take any of the wind out of his sails. He gave me one of those nods as if to say I didn't exist. He was the supreme egotist. Worse than me. I'd seen him speak at an insurance engagement. Mindless. He had some sort of idiot savante talent for building. His self-assurance contrasted with my self-doubt.

Larry was singing "Sweet Georgia." Having a good old time. Angela and Jean Marie showed up and captured it on film.

At fight time, Macho Comacho entered the ring wearing a Dracula cape. He was my opponent. He was a famous fighter, a wildman. He was known to have the fastest hands in the business. He looked stoned out of his mind.

Like he'd been partying for the last three days. Hector said, "Let them fight without head gear."

Did Hector want to see me killed? Was he crazy? "No way," Michael Buffer, the announcer, said.

"It's just an exhibition," Hector said. "It's not a fight."

He was right. But what if crazy man Comacho decided to turn it into a fight? Then I'd really want that headgear.

"Let's get ready to rumble!" Michael announced. Comacho and I went right after each other, exchanging punches rapid fire, in flurries. We were going side to side and spinning each other around. Doing a lot of professional moves—bobbing and weaving, attacking at angles. I wasn't the slightest bit scared because I figured he was too good to sucker punch me. Near the end of the first round I tapped him and he fell to the canvas. I was sure he did that on purpose to make me look good. Or he was so stoned he tripped. I certainly didn't hit him hard enough to knock him down. Nice fantasy, though.

The second and third rounds were more of the same. I was feeling his rhythm. He was smaller than me. I felt I could take him in a slug out. He had no weight in his punches. But I held back. Out of respect. I would never sucker punch a champ. And the fight wound down to an uneventful, professional conclusion. There was a lot of applause. Comacho's manager came over and congratulated me for a beautiful fight. Hector was praising me. Even my wife thought I was the best fighter there. Of course it was just an exhibition. We weren't really trying to kill each other. And I knew he wasn't going to hit me hard. But I managed to stay with him. And that's a lot to say when you're talking about one of the fastest fighters in the world. I felt like I was world class.

We gambled, drank and hung out that night and the next morning we went to the awards ceremony to pick up our medals. *Here. Here. You did great, son. I didn't know you could fight like that,* was the kind of shit I heard from everyone. I thanked Comacho for boxing with me. He was a gentleman despite his bad boy image. The celebrity fighters trash-talked each other when they picked up their awards. *You fight like a woman. You don't deserve shit. I beat your sorry ass. You're a faggot.* No class. It was always the worst fighters who resorted to name-calling. When they had a chance to fight with their fists in the ring instead of their mouths they came up empty. I headed to the gambling tables with my wife and blew a few bucks on roulette. It was no thrill to me. Once she tried to bet after the croupier said, "No more bets."

"I know Donald Trump," she said. She did. She pushed her chips forward.

"So do I, ma'am," he said and gave her chips back to her.

Gambling didn't turn me on. In business I didn't gamble. I stole. I liked to take my chances with life and death. Real men's stuff. No sublimation crap.

•••

A boxing team from Dallas came up to fight the Gleason's White-Collar fighters. They were clean-cut men with gray-haired flat tops in their forties and fifties. They looked like they could row crew at a college reunion. They even wore blue blazers like they were on the American Olympic team. They took one look at us and none of them wanted to fight. There was something about living in New York that made us look degenerate and rough. They didn't want to dirty themselves by getting into clinches with us. They looked like athletes; we looked like muggers. So I fought another guy from my gym, Jimmy Monteverde. He worked for UPS and was trying to be a screenwriter in his spare time. He talked on and on about his movies. He showed me a script about two brothers who were fighters. Poor Jimmy! He was a nice guy but he didn't have much of a chance of ever having one of his scripts made. I felt sorry for him, so I didn't hit him too hard. Somehow I broke his nose. But I didn't mean it. We were friends. I was undefeated in the white-collar league.

Even though part of me was afraid of everybody on the planet, the other part of me was cocksure that I could kick everybody's ass, that I could turn pro. I figured I could become famous. It was the logical next step after so many fights, so I applied to the commissioner, Randy Gordon. "You're forty-three years old. Are you crazy?" he said. "Why do you want to get hurt?"

"I'm not going to get hurt," I said.

"Go out of town and win a fight. Then I'll let you fight in New York," he said. A lot of newspapers picked up the story of this old nut who wanted to fight pro. I liked the chatter about me. Attention splattered over me like paint from broken balloons. I was colorful.

I had two more fights over the next couple of months. I boxed this young strong black guy, John Bridges, and beat him by unanimous decision. They wrote me up in some local press. I was becoming so good that I felt an urgency to go pro. The Greek warriors fought so they could be remembered in the poems of Homer. There was nothing wrong with being written about in the local press even if it was not quite *the Iliad*. I also beat Lawrence Chenko, a short, mafia-looking guy who worked out in the morning with a muscle-bound friend. He looked like he came from the streets and knew his way around. Just looking tough doesn't make you tough. Still, I was a little unsure of Chenko's strengths. So I decided to take the fight to him and destroy his confidence. Within thirty seconds his eye was swollen and black and blue. Hector was yelling at me, "Take it easy on him." It occurred to me that I didn't have to kill the guy. He was no match for me. I backed off and played with him. I won another shutout. And another trophy.

•••

I used to take my son Graham to Alex & Walter's trendy gymnastics studio in the East Fifties. People like hotelier Ian Schrager and jeweler Nicola Bulgari worked out there. Alex, a sixty-something-year-old gym instructor, was giving lessons to the rich who wanted to learn to bend, stretch and do minor moves on the parallel bars and the rings. I took my son there and we shared lessons.

One day as we were leaving, Alex introduced us to Tom Foley, the Speaker of the House, and his wife, Heather, who would fly up to New York from DC to take lessons three times a week. I was impressed. I knew some billionaires but not the number three man in the US government. Alex introduced me as the "white-collar champion" boxer. We all agreed to go to lunch sometime.

Sometime came the following week. We all went to Cipriani's on 59th and Fifth, where I had a house account. It was very friendly. I felt like we were family. I was a little surprised when Heather ate a salad that she took out of her knapsack. I guess when you're running the US Government you don't have to worry about manners. Not that she wasn't nice and polite. But p-l-e-a-s-e. She was wearing jeans.

Tom promised to come to one of my bouts. I don't remember if I forgot to invite him or he turned me down. It doesn't matter. He became a stamp in my collection of famous faces.

•••

I decided to follow Randy Gordon's advice to take a pro fight out of state and then come back and go pro in New York. I was friendly with a top ten middleweight contender, Michael Olajide, Jr.

"Do you know anybody who can get me a fight in another state?" I asked Michael.

"I got a friend Ziggy," Michael said. "He's setting me up with one down south."

I went to Ziggy's flower shop on the West Side. Ziggy

was sitting in the back of the store. He had one good arm and one withered with a little hand hanging from its end. Ziggy was a real small time mafia type. He was chain-smoking in the middle of all those flowers. I was worried that he'd give a tulip lung cancer. When I asked Ziggy if he could get me a fight he said, "Sure. I'll get you a fight. But not at 43. You need a fake birth certificate."

"Where do I get one?" I asked.

"Don't worry. I'll take care of it," he said.

"Thanks a lot for doing this for me," I said.

"I could use a little help too," he said. "I'm managing this Israeli heavyweight—Tim Puller. I want to sell you a third of his contract for $10,000."

"You got it, partner," I said, shaking his hand without even questioning the ten grand. I didn't stop to think that it was a bribe or that I was doing something corrupt. Corrupt didn't mean anything to me. I wanted that damned pro fight. I was going to make history as the oldest first time pro. I didn't give a fuck about ten grand.

"I'll call you within the week and give you the lowdown," he said.

"I hope this fight isn't going to be too tough," I said. "It's my pro debut."

"Don't worry about a thing. I'll get you a tomato can," he said. He called me in five days and told me he didn't want to talk on the phone. I went back down to the flower shop.

"The fight will be in Denver on May 31st," he said.

"Who am I fighting?" I asked, nervous.

"Some bum who never fought before. He can't hit at all. Just like I told you, a real tomato can," Ziggy said.

I gave him a check for ten grand. He gave me a birth certificate saying I was thirty-three years old and a contract for one third of Tim Puller's management.

●●●

Bill Levi, a clerk in the accounting department, called me into his office and told me we were running short on money again. He told me that Cramer was giving the service fees he was charging over to Kelly instead of the corporation.

"Screw that," I said and went down to Kelly's office. He looked nervous when I asked him, "What are you doing with Cramer's fees?"

"You know," he said.

"No, I don't," I said.

"Toni's been cashing them. You got your share," he said. I knew I got some bundles of cash but I never thought it was enough to put a dent in the office's cash flow. I never cared about money and I never counted it. I suppose that was because I always had so much of it.

"This shit's got to stop," I said. "You're bankrupting us."

In the last few months Kelly's work was sliding downhill. He had been on the bottle big time. He never got to the office until four in the afternoon. All red-eyed and hung over. He was testy, always snapping at everybody. He used to be my key man. Now he was a used-up, drunken slob. I took out a five hundred thousand dollar key man insurance policy on him just in case he died. I used to get a kick out of him. Now I wished he were dead. I couldn't trust him anymore.

23

IT WAS A balmy April day in 1990 when Cramer got a telephone call that would change all our lives. He came into my office and told me that he just got a call from an FBI agent asking why we were cashing checks in Delaware. "I told him we're opening an office in Delaware," he said.

"Are you crazy? We're not opening any offices down there. You don't lie to the FBI," I said.

My life had become simplified. It was punch or be punched. My business problems were too rarefied for me. I couldn't relate to them anymore. I didn't know what this was all about. I just knew that I was in deep shit and it was beyond my control. Something was going on in Delaware behind my back and the FBI was looking into it. I had no experience with the FBI.

After Cramer got the call from the FBI about bank accounts in Delaware, I called my corporate lawyer who recommended I get in touch with Ben Brafman.

In the nineties Brafman was notorious for handling hitmen Mafioso cases. It never occurred to me that he might not be so hot at white-collar cases. I'd never been in trouble with the law before. All I knew was that he was famous. I was thinking that maybe the media would pick up on Ben Brafman handling my case. I liked press. I was always being covered as a businessman boxer. I couldn't understand people who hated the media. Like Sean Penn who actually punched the paparazzi. I wanted to kiss them. Maybe I'd get really famous like Ivan Boesky or Milkin, other businessmen who had gone to jail, landsmen. Then I could write my life story and make a bundle. I'd be rich again.

We went over to Ben Brafman's office in the Rolls and Ben told us that he had already spoken to the prosecutor in Delaware and gotten a feel for the case. He assigned Gus Newman to Cramer and Barry Kaplan to Kelly. Newman was like the dean of criminal attorneys. He was a senior, respected guy. Kaplan shared an office with Brafman. Our little team of expensive lawyers was assembled.

Brafman presided over the meeting. He was a Michael Douglas look-alike, only five inches shorter. He spoke authoritatively and well, with stage presence.

The three lawyers were a formidable defense team. And an expensive one. They looked worried that we might not be able to pay their fat fees.

"My retainer is twenty-five thousand dollars," Newman said, puffing on his pipe, getting the money issue on the table right away to make sure we weren't wasting their time.

"Mine too," chirped in Kaplan.

"I'm thirty-five thousand dollars," Brafman said proudly. "I'm the quarterback."

They sounded like hookers negotiating their tips. I was tempted to ask how much they wanted for a blowjob.

"You're hired. Send the bills to me," I said. They leaped to their feet and shook our hands like we were getting bar-mitzvahed. We had passed the test of manhood. We were paying customers. I held my dick. I didn't want to get circumcised.

"Delaware. A strange state," Brafman said.

"What were the checks doing there?" Newman asked.

"We were thinking of opening a branch in Delaware," Cramer said, reiterating the bullshit he told the FBI.

It didn't make sense to me to lie to our own lawyers.

"He's full of shit," I said. Cramer looked pissed off.

"Nick was cashing the checks there," Kelly chimed in.

This caught me off guard. Kelly had told me Nick was his boyhood friend who worked at Nat Westminster in New York.

"I thought he was cashing them at Nat Westminster in New York," I said.

Kelly squiggled in his chair, "No. Nick lost his job at Nat West."

"What?"

"I didn't want to bother you with details, boss," Kelly said. "That's why he was cashing them through a friend in Delaware."

I should have fired him on the spot for lying. Was I afraid to fire him? I had never fired anyone before. No, we were both involved in a federal investigation. If I cut him loose, he'd turn federal witness against me. I had to keep him and Cramer on staff. All that kept them from snitching about the shit that went on in my operation was their paychecks.

"I wouldn't have let him cash checks in freakin' Delaware," I said. "You should have checked with me."

"Never lie to the FBI," Newman said to Cramer, puffing on his pipe.

"About what?" Cramer said.

"About anything. They can get you on perjury. That's five years," Newman said like he was addressing first year law students. Puff puff.

"I'm innocent," Cramer said, looking like he was about to burst into tears.

"You lied to the FBI," Brafman said.

"I didn't know," Cramer said.

"We didn't do anything," Kelly said.

Cramer and Kelly burst out with a chorus of denials. I imagined their spines bending like hoola hoops as they rolled out of the office into some hopeless digression.

"I spoke to the prosecutor in Delaware," Brafman said.

"Prosecutor?" I asked.

How'd things get this far? There was a prosecutor after me for something I had done in Delaware and I had never been to Delaware. I felt like I was in a Kafkaesque nightmare. I was the Hunger Artist. Everything I did was from hunger. I was trapped by my own negligence. This was beginning to look like it was no joke. Was Delaware a state or just a city?

"The prosecutor's no match for me. I could run circles around him. When I was assistant prosecutor in Brooklyn I won awards. But this young hotshot thinks he's gonna get you guys in jail. He's preparing a case against you for evading taxes," Brafman said.

"We didn't evade taxes," Kelly said.

176

"Did you report your cash income to the government?"

"No."

"Then you're a tax evader," Brafman said. "They also got you for structuring and money laundering."

"What's structuring?" I asked.

"When you withdraw cash from a bank in amounts under ten thousand dollars so that it does not have to be reported to the federal government," Brafman said.

"I wasn't involved in this," I said.

"Did Kelly and Cramer report to you?"

"Yes."

"Then you're the ring leader, the key man."

"Great," I said. I was the key man in a scheme I knew nothing about. "Can't we just pay the taxes now?"

"Too late. You've defrauded the government. They're not after the money. They don't even care how much they spend on prosecuting you. They just want to make an example out of you."

"And money laundering?" I asked.

"That's the catch-phrase. They use it for any diverted funds. They can throw you away for twenty years on that alone, easy. "

"Anything else?" The Feds were acting like I was a serial killer. What had I done? Let Kelly cash a few checks. By the time the Feds finished calculating my thoughtless offenses I could be doing life. Did they ever execute anyone for white-collar crime?

"Kelly, did you really put a two hundred and fifty thousand dollar bribe in writing?" Brafman asked. It seems Brafman had a direct line to the prosecutor. He knew more about what we had done than I did.

"The cost of doing business," Kelly said. "Everyone does it."

"Not everyone puts it in writing," Brafman said.

Our largest account was American Risk. We wrote it for a Connecticut broker, Bill Dunst.

AIG had canceled the American Risk liability policy and Kelly had offered the underwriter a bribe of two hundred and fifty thousand dollars to reinstate it. The idiot had put it in writing.

I can't really blame him for trying. The account was a seven million dollar premium and we had piggybacked six million dollars in service fees on it.

"The prosecutor's got some witness who claims you guys owe her seven hundred and fifty thousand dollars," Brafman continued. That was my fault. I had offered to pay some clerk off to give us inside information on Bill Dunst's internal pricing on American Risk. At least I didn't put it in writing.

The prosecutor really knew what he was doing. He was probably playing with Brafman, letting him know only a piece of what he knew. Why was Brafman so confident? Was he blowing smoke up our asses or his own?

I felt like I was part of the Gang That Couldn't Shoot Straight.

"That clerk was my friend," Kelly moaned.

"She's not your friend now," Brafman said. He liked the way that sounded. He cleared his throat and said it again, "She's not your friend now." She was ratting us out the way she had ratted Dunst out to us.

"It's all your fault, Kelly," Cramer said, scratching on his hair plugs.

"You gave me nine hundred thousand dollars worth of checks to cash," Kelly said. Cramer had been taking service fees onto his personal insurance accounts and giving them to Kelly to cash for him in Delaware.

I was shocked by the amount. I thought Cramer only gave Kelly a few checks to cash. Nine hundred thousand dollars of checks from Cramer? Where was my piece? I was given a few piles of hundreds here and there. Kelly and Cramer must have split up the balance between themselves. I was not getting my share of my own money. I had never even known how much that was. I was an afterthought. They tipped me with my own money. I had been suckered into allowing them to cash the checks in the first place. I should have never allowed it to get to this extent. I was more a victim than a criminal. I was a fool. I thought I was a genius but I had inadvertently become involved with the dumbest crime anyone every committed.

"Those checks were service fees. We can't get in trouble for that. Charging service fees that are more than ten per cent of the premium is a misdemeanor. Not a felony," Cramer said.

"How do you know so much?" Kelly asked.

"When I break the law I make it my business to know what I'm breaking," Cramer said, proudly.

"Maybe I should hire you as my lawyer," Kelly said, sarcastically.

"Maybe you should," Cramer said.

"Hey, we're the lawyers here," Brafman interrupted, protecting his fee.

"That's right. You just hired us," Kaplan chimed in.

I ignored them. I was still thinking about what Kelly

had said about Cramer giving him nine hundred thousand dollars. "Did you fucks really get nine hundred thousand dollars?" I asked.

"No! No! I exaggerated," Kelly said.

No way he was going to admit he robbed me along with everyone else. Not even to himself. He thought of himself as a nice guy. Unlike Cramer, who really enjoyed being a prick, who exulted in it.

"I'm not going to jail," Cramer cried.

He waddled up from his chair and grabbed Kelly by the throat. Kelly grabbed Cramer back. It was a joke to see them trying to act tough. They were like two chubby girls mouthing off at each other on the subway. I separated them. Even though I didn't know they were cashing checks in Delaware, it was still my fault. I should have kept track of the checks coming into the firm and not let them cash them anywhere. Yeah, hindsight is always twenty-twenty.

"Your fight is with the Feds, not each other," Brafman warned.

"We have to gather the wagons round," Newman said.

"To keep the Indians out," Kaplan added.

I imagined myself in the Wild West surrounded by attacking Apaches with only Kelly and Cramer to defend my back. I'd be better off shooting myself in the head than depending on these two to keep me from getting scalped.

"How many years can we get?" I asked Brafman.

"Twenty years for money laundering alone," Newman interjected, taking a long slow drag of his pipe and blowing out slow smoke rings. He added, "The Feds think money launderers are drug dealers."

"I'm an alcoholic. Not a drug dealer," Kelly cried.

Kelly was right. We weren't criminals; we were dunces. Wasn't there anything in the law to respond to such circumstances? Wasn't there a penalty for idiocy? Couldn't they make me sit in the corner wearing a dunce cap?

"The money laundering probably won't stick," Brafman said. "But they'll use it to get you to admit to tax evasion."

"I'm not going to jail," Cramer cried again.

"You'd look good in khaki, Cramer," I quipped. I wasn't going to admit how much this upset me. I was afraid of being a crybaby. When I was sixteen I broke my hand against a concrete wall to show how tough I was. I smiled through the pain because I didn't want to admit how much it hurt. There's intimacy to suffering. I didn't want to share it with creeps.

"Go home. Don't speak to anyone. I'll get in touch with the prosecutor again and see if some deal can be worked out," Brafman said.

"Just keep us in business as long as you can," I said.

"Make sure you don't speak to the Feds. If they call, refer them to us," Brafman said.

I kept my panic to myself. No way I wanted the business falling down on top of us right then. If I was going to end up in jail I needed time to get together some money for my son's education and my wife's rent. I wanted to make sure my parents were taken care of. I wanted to plan a new career for when I got out. I pretended that bad luck was good. It took me off my pedestal and let me play tennis with the ants on the curb. I hit good topspin. I won crumbs.

"If we go under, I'll kill myself," Kelly said.

There was nothing else for him. He had no talents. His one skill was leaching onto me and using my business relationships for his own profit. Without me, he'd never be more than a clerk. And he knew it.

"I'm not going under," Cramer said.

There were tears in his eyes. He was determined to survive this debacle. But I didn't realize that he might try to sink us to save his own ass.

We all shook hands and left Brafman's office. We went back downtown in the Rolls. I tried to lighten the mood, "If I bunk with Bubba in jail, he's not getting any." Kelly shifted in his seat and smiled. Cramer almost cried. No one was laughing. We were lost in our own worlds. Tragedy is always personal. Two people getting eaten by the same shark are two thousand miles away from each other in their own minds.

I didn't look at it like Kelly and Cramer. I saw it as an adventure, exciting. I was going to be a big con. But another part of me was scared. And the other parts? They were just commenting on each other trying to drive me crazy. I was fragmented, fractured and narcissistically attracted to all the broken pieces within my puzzle.

We thought we were marked men after our meeting with Brafman. Now that the FBI was on our trail we felt like the whole business world would be watching us. We felt like Jews in Nazi Germany wearing yellow stars on our raincoats. We were Jews. Not Kelly. I was in the Warsaw ghetto. How was I going to eat? We thought we'd be out of business by the morning.

But disaster doesn't always rush in like a volcano. It doesn't burst into color like Vesuvius. It sometimes sneaks up on you in a gray sweater. Its agents study dossiers in smoky back rooms. Tragedy follows you around like a dog sniffing at your cuffs. Your fate simmers rather than burns. The FBI was doing a private little dance with us. It was a slow marathon. We were almost innocent. We were on a carousel. They don't shoot horses, do they?

Word hadn't hit the street yet. At first, no one noticed we were under investigation. It was business as usual. We began to relax. We continued to write accounts as if nothing had happened. We landed some big insureds. We bought a new office computer. We began to doubt that we were even under investigation. Maybe we had just had a bad dream. Maybe we'd wake up rich and successful again. We'd take bonuses. We'd buy an office yacht.

●●●

We went back to Wall Street and Kelly followed me into my office. He was stammering and jammering. He finally dribbled out, "You're going to find something out you're not going to like."

"Like I like what I found out today," I said.

"This is worse," he said. "I'm gay."

"You're not," I said. He was always bragging about his prowess with women and his big dick. I hated to think of him squirreling up a man's ass. But I didn't really care about it now. "Look, my whole business may be going down the tubes because of your friends in Delaware. I don't give a shit if you're gay," I said.

"All those guys who were opening accounts for Toni in Delaware were gay too."

"Great. Now I'm the head of a gay money laundering ring," I said. This was a homophobic's nightmare. I should have known there was something wrong with him when he was bragging about the size of his dick. He was probably drunk so often just to forget what he was. Lauren always said I was a bad judge of character. She was right.

"It's worse," he said.

"You're a woman?" I asked, sarcastically.

"No. My boyfriend Joseph is. Or wants to be. He's costing me a fortune. I have to pay for all his hormone shots. He's planning to have an operation. To become a chick. I don't like chicks. I love him as a man," Kelly said.

This was getting too weird. I thought of *Dog Day Afternoon*. In the movie Al Pacino robbed the bank so he could pay for his boyfriend's sex change. Only Kelly didn't really want Joseph to become a woman. He confided in me, "I want him to keep his dick. But I love him too much to fight him." He also told me that part of the reason his bills were so large at the Waldorf is that he had talked a cashier into overcharging him and kicking back some of the money for the hormones.

"Where'd you meet this creep?"

"Toni, you know, the guy who cashes our checks at Nat Westminster. Well, he and I own this male escort service," Kelly said.

"This just keeps getting better and better," I said.

"You want the truth?"

"Go on."

"Joseph doubled as a male escort for our firm, 'Discreet Gays.'"

Great. Kelly was a gay entrepreneur, pimping his own boyfriend.

"But, you see, I fell in love with Joseph. I can't stand

him sleeping with anyone else. So I pay him ten thousand dollars a week to keep him from hooking with other guys. That way he's all mine. Makes sense, right?"

"What's to keep him from cheating anyhow?"

"Because I also stock his Village apartment with antiques. If he got caught, I'd take them all away," he said.

I should have strangled Kelly for involving me in such a decadent spool of corruption. But I took pride in not caring. If I didn't feel anything nothing could get to me. With so many people out of control around me I had to shut down. I was in a parking lot surrounded by other collisions. I didn't want to start up my engine, howl, grind gears, stall. I pulled the blinders down over the windshield and mentally went to sleep. I needed time to figure out where I was parked.

Lauren getting out of the Rolls in the early 90s

•••

Life goes on even when the FBI's up your ass. I went to Jones Beach with Michael Olajide, Jr. to shoot a scene for my boxing movie. I figured I might as well get famous before I lost my business and they locked me away. I had to do something with my life that would set me apart from the typical loser. I had to find a new direction. I'd be a movie star.

We shot some lovely, moody scenes of Olajide and me crawling around on the rocks with the seagulls flying over the shore.

Angela said, as we were packing up, "We could make this film really beautiful if we switched to thirty-five millimeter film. Instead of a short we could make it a feature length movie."

That sounded good. A feature length film of me. What could be better? The narcissist in me rolled over itself like a whitecap.

"How much more will it cost?" I asked.

"Seventy-five grand, give or take," she said.

"It's yours," I said. "And I'll tell you something else. I have a pro fight in May in Denver."

"Wow. That will really make the movie," Angela said. "We'll bring Jean Marie and a sound man."

I didn't ask how much more that would cost.

•••

I wasn't exactly making money in the fight game. I flew seven people out to Denver with me to see my pro debut.

186

Mark Cramer, Bruce Silverglade, Hector, Angela, Jean Marie, and a soundman who wore earphones all the time. I already paid ten thousand dollars to get on the fight card. The trip itself, including three days lodging, cost another twenty grand. I felt no sympathy for those crybaby fighters who complained they got their brains beat in for four hundred dollars. I was paying about thirty grand, all in all, to get punched in the head. I could have gotten laid for a lousy hundred dollars. My priorities were all fucked up. I bumbled along making mistakes believing every move I made was a thousand percent correct.

When we landed we took a cab to the Regency Hotel in the foothills of Denver. I'd been in Colorado a dozen times skiing. It usually took me about twenty-four hours to adjust to the altitude. This time I was dizzy as hell. It was probably a combination of altitude and nerves. That night I went to the weigh-in. I wished I had gotten out there a few days earlier to get used to the thinner atmosphere. My opponent, Steve Valdez, was a pudgy, short Mexican. I was going to kick his ass. I said a silent prayer of thanks to Ziggy for picking me a sap for an opponent. Valdez looked like he ate too much rice and beans. I wanted to say, "Go home on your donkey, asshole."

I weighed in at one hundred and forty-five pounds. Valdez weighed in at one hundred and fifty-three pounds. Hector told him he better go jump rope for a few hours and get down to the welterweight limit – one hundred and forty-seven pounds. Hector figured losing weight would dehydrate and weaken him.

The next night I met Tim Puller in the dressing room. He was a gentle giant. He had only been fighting a few years. I had more experience than him. I now owned one third of his management. He'd been training in Vegas with a well-known trainer, Panama Lewis. Panama was famous for stripping the padding from Billy Collins' gloves that ended up blinding his opponent. Then the blinded fighter killed himself. Panama Lewis was banned from working fighters' corners. But there was no rule against his training them. Tim Puller never even had an amateur fight. What was he doing fighting pro with no experience? Most real fighters started at seven years old. I couldn't believe I had bought a piece of this inexperienced guy. When the official came into the dressing room, he checked my wraps and put an X on them with a magic marker. They were done up so tightly that they felt like concrete. Hector squeezed them into the gloves. They felt like bricks inside little mittens. I could kill someone. Holy fuck, this was a different ball game from the amateurs. I didn't even have headgear to deflect the punches.

I walked up to the ring with Hector.

"In the red corner we have Awesome Lawrence, the Wall Street boxer, making his professional debut," the announcer said into the microphone. "And in the blue corner we have Steve Valdez from Denver with a 3 and 0 record."

Ziggy fucked me. He had told me that my opponent had never fought pro before. I didn't want an experienced opponent with a winning record. This fuck could kill me but I couldn't leave the ring now. I was in cowboy country.

"Don't worry about the record," Hector said. "They made it up."

I didn't believe him but I wasn't going to argue with my only friend there. "Play with him. Don't try to take him out early," Hector said.

When the bell rang, I charged straight at Valdez. I was still dizzy at this altitude and I wanted to get the fight over with before I collapsed on my own. I went to his body first and landed some good shots. I was winning for the first minute. I was ready to celebrate. Then Valdez pivoted on his back foot and landed an overhand right on the side of my head. I went down like a drunk who missed a tricky step from the dining room down to the living room. What a punch! He threw it like a major league pitcher. A loose, relaxed arm. Bam! I had to give him credit for it. Strike one! The fans went wild. I heard someone yell my name. I thought he was rooting for me until I realized he had yelled, "Go back to Wall Street, Awesome." I struggled back to my feet. My head felt a little numb and there was a buzzing in my ears, but I was somehow happy. I had survived a professional knockdown and I was going to come back and knock him out now. I started swinging again. I heard my punches thwacking against him. I was landing some good shots with no effect. I should have expected that. Mexicans take the best punches in the world. They love it. I was just getting him mad like a fly buzzing around a pitbull. Then he wound up and let another knuckle ball go at me and blasted me right in the temple. The next thing I remembered was waking up and looking from the canvas sheepishly into Hector's eyes and smiling. I had been somewhere far away and was amused by it. Hector didn't look too happy. "Shit," he said.

I was embarrassed. But I was still alive. I was glad it was over. I had déjà vu to my amateur fight where Medina knocked me out. But this time I landed all right and didn't separate my shoulder. I felt good. It was better than getting beaten to a pulp against the ropes. Getting knocked out was so much cleaner. I was proud that I had fought my first pro fight. It didn't matter that I lost. I had lost my first amateur fight, too. What was the difference? I wasn't discouraged. I knew that I could improve.

Back in the dressing room I said to Hector, "This guy was supposed to be a real tomato can."

"He was," Hector said.

"He hit hard," I said.

"You shouldn't have slugged with him. Mexicans have hard heads."

"I was so dizzy I wanted to end it fast," I said.

"Well, you did end it fast," Hector said. "You ended your pro career."

"Sure, sure," I said. But I was thinking to myself that nothing was finished until it was finished. I looked at my gloves and thought, *Man these fuckin' gloves are small.*

Old reliable Hector tried to cheer me up, "You rich, David. You no need to fight."

"Reason not the need, the poorest beggar is in the least thing superfluous." He didn't know I was ripping off Shakespeare.

After changing I went back upstairs to the auditorium and bought a wine spritzer. Three cowboys standing at the bar asked me, laughing, "Why is a clown like you fighting?"

"Mine is not to reason why. Mine is just to do or die," I said, joking around.

"Keep it up and you will die," the most rugged one wearing a ten-gallon cowboy hat said. They all cracked up. I did too. "A man who can laugh at himself's all right, partner," the short cowboy said and slapped me on the spine. "You a Jew?" the fat one asked.

"I'm a New York Jew," I said.

"You guys have a good sense of humor," he said, and slapped me on the back too. I escaped from this jolly crew of idiots and sat down to watch Tim Puller fight. He was fighting some guy who looked like he was trucked in out of a fat farm. He was short and way overweight. Tim knocked the guy out of the ring in the first round. Unlike me he won his pro debut. Lucky bastard.

Cramer saw me in the audience and came over. "Are you all right?" he asked.

"Fine," I said. I'd died and gone to heaven. I was the real thing, a professional fighter.

"I threw up when I saw you get knocked out," Cramer said. As if he really cared. He probably got sick thinking about it happening to himself.

"I like getting knocked out. It's a great feeling. You ought to try it," I said.

He thought I was kidding and smiled.

Angela and Jean Marie came over. "Don't worry. We got it all on film. It will be beautiful," Angela said. She held up a microphone and asked me, "How does it feel to get knocked out?"

I played for an imaginary audience, "It's like taking a trip to a deserted foreign village. You walk around hearing the echo of your own boots on the cobblestone. You look at the clock tower and there are no hands. A purple cow comes up to you and moos. You are happy."

"Wow," she said.

On the plane home I told Hector, "I'm glad Ziggy got me an easy opponent."

"David, you embarrass me," he said.

"At least I try," I said.

"I'll give you that," he said. "You got heart."

"Thank you," I said. That was a biggie. To be told by a Panamanian that you had heart was like being told by a Black that you had a big dick or by a WASP that you had a nice yacht.

David's rap CD, *Lyfestylz* by The Lost Trybe of Hip-Hop

24

BILL FASHINOU of the British BBC came over to visit Gleason's. He was a famous footballer who was hosting a new television show in England, *Good Sport.* He was in the States to report on businessmen who box. They'd heard about me in London. I was the perfect eccentric; I was England's kind of gentleman. And I was chauffeured around in the queen of English vehicles—the Rolls Royce.

Fashinou wanted to get some footage of me in an actual fight so I showed up at White-Collar Night even though I was already a pro. He brought his film crew, as did Angela and Jean Marie. As an extra treat, the film crew from CBS's *48 Hours* was there. I think I was getting as much film coverage as Tyson. They put me against some guy from upstate at Floyd Patterson's gym, Lawrence Ambosino. He was heavier than me, about one hundred and seventy pounds. And around fifty years old. I was figuring he was an old pro who wanted to make a comeback and was trying to make a rep off beating me. Hector didn't know anything about Ambosino. He told me to belt him a few times in the gut to get some respect out of him.

The bell rang and I raced across the ring and started slugging him. I was hitting him with body shots that you could hear across the street. Thud! Thwack! Thud! He fell to his knees. Between rounds his cornerman came around and told me if I hit him hard again he was going to stop the fight. Shit! Not that! I had three camera crews filming this. I promised Ambosino's cornerman I'd go easy.

The next two rounds I danced with him. I stayed on my bicycle, moving, tapping him, carrying him. I wanted to get the whole fight on film. I was at the point in my boxing where I was good enough to take it easy on guys. I didn't have to beat them up because I didn't have to be afraid that I'd get hurt. I won by a shutout. I hung around after the fight talking with some fans. I was all caught up in self-admiration.

•••

A month later in August it was another glorious night for White-Collar Boxing at Gleason's Gym. I was a little disappointed that no news stations were there. At least I had my personal film crew—Angela and Jean Marie. I even made up a poster advertising the fights with my picture on it. I called myself Gleason's White-Collar King. Tonight they matched me against a tough black middleweight, Irwin Phipps. He was a stocky mother. This guy was about as white-collar as a guard in an insane asylum.

He hit like a bull. I tried to play with him like a matador. I tried to lead him where I wanted, punch him and then get out of there. But as much as I tried to finesse him I'd lose my cool and end up in wild exchanges. It reminded me of the Morales fight where I got a black eye that lasted for two weeks. I liked this fight. There was a rhythm to the punishment. I had fight fever. As old as I was, I was in great shape and I wore him out. The same way I used to wear down opponents in tennis. No way I was going to lose. It was a battle of the wills. I kept coming and coming. I exhausted him. I felt like I could go on forever and never take a step backwards. I was on my way to heaven. I was going to come out cloudside. And the decision was? Could there be any doubt? Another shutout for Awesome Lawrence.

Everything was just a matter of hanging in there. The champions in every sport were the ones who were willing to take the most beatings, who never quit. It was the same thing with an artist. He had to take the most criticism. I was learning how to be disliked. I was learning how to win.

David in the ring at the Mirage Hotel the day before his fight with Caveman Lee

25

GARY BRAVERMAN was hanging around Gleason's gym. "You want to fight on the Tyson card?" he asked me.

"Are you kidding?" I said and laughed. Who wouldn't want to fight on the Tyson card?

"I'll get back to you in a couple of days and let you know," he said.

He had let me fight in the Celebrity Fights for free. That wasn't like him. Somehow he hadn't hustled any money from me yet. Maybe this was his opportunity. I saw him at Gleason's later that week. "I can't do it. It's all booked," he said. "But I can get you on a Chavez card out at the Mirage Hotel in Las Vegas." Don King managed Chavez and Gary's dad, Al Braverman, was King's matchmaker.

"Wow," I said. Chavez was a world champ and the Mirage was a major venue.

"It'll cost ten grand," he said. Well, he was a hustler and it was time for him to take a piece of me. It was a fair price. Same thing I paid Ziggy in Denver for the bogus Tim Puller management contract but this was a much bigger deal. Maybe they'd even put my fight on television. I signed a contract getting one dollar for the fight instead of the usual four hundred for a four rounder. What the hell? I had pissed away ten thousand dollars for a week at the Breakers Hotel in Palm Beach and had nothing to show for it but a suntan. Fighting at the Mirage on a championship card was priceless. Ten thousand dollars' worth of pricelessness. Any up-and-coming fighter would have died to fight there.

"We'll get you the opponent," Gary said. "Some lump of shit that you can kick around." Ziggy had told me the same thing about the Mexican, Valdez, who knocked me cold in Denver. But I wasn't nervous.

"You got a deal," I said to Gary and we shook hands.

Later Michael Olajide, Jr. showed up at the gym. Hector invited him to go to Vegas with us. "David will pay for your plane ticket," he said. It would look good to have a world contender in my corner. This was ticket season. It was raining plane tickets. I bought tickets for Olajide Jr., Angela, Jean Marie, their soundman, Cramer, Bruce, my brother Pete, Chuck, and Hector. I didn't even bother to get a group flight rate.

Lauren knew I was going to fight. She didn't know I was treating the world. I don't know how much she would have cared. We weren't paying that much attention to each other at the time. Although we lived together, what we did didn't register that much with each other. We kind of lived alone in the same home. I was dedicated to boxing. She was involved with shopping. We visited each other at restaurants.

Stan Gold told me he was going to be out there with his fighter Dennis Milton, who was fighting Julian Jackson. That was one plane ticket I didn't have to buy. Mobster Lenny Minuto managed Milton. Stan was the adviser. He was the fight consultant. It was a great job because he didn't have the aggravation and expense of being a manager. He did nothing except set up the fight.

I paid for everyone's hotel room, except mine and Hector's. We got free rooms at the Mirage. In addition to all these expenses, I was sure to get charged back by Cramer and my brother for any money they lost gambling. They'd just put it on their expense sheets. There was so much money in the world. I spread it around. It meant nothing to me. I didn't even understand it. The FBI was in my face but my eyes were closed. I was driven forward by inner obsessions. I didn't look at the road's shoulders.

●●●

Two days before the fight I flew out to Vegas with Olajide Jr. and Hector. My film crew was going to meet us out there. We checked in at the Mirage. This was some nice shit. I had been here last winter with my client, Bob Dubofsky, and we played on Steve Wynn's private golf course. It was so exclusive that he only allowed four guests on it a day. Bob loved that. It was a businessman's wet dream but it was nothing compared to fighting on a championship card. I was here to put another notch in history. I was going to be the oldest fighter ever to fight at the Mirage. Not that they'd know that. I still had Ziggy's birth certificate saying that I was thirty-four.

Hector and I went over to train at Johnny Tocco's Gym. Another one of Hector's fighters, Chinito Sanchez, met us over there. He was the Dominican champ and he was fighting on the same card with me. He was in the corner of the gym skipping rope like mad to make 140 pounds. Eddie Mustafa was also there training Mike McCallum. Michael Dokes was slowly riding an exercise bike. He was a whale of a heavyweight fighter. He had recently been busted for coke. But there was talk about getting him a title shot. He said, "Hey, Wall Street. Can you give me a loan?"

"I'll give you my purse," I said. "I'm getting a dollar."

"I thought you Wall Street guys were smarter than that," he said, laughing. "I never fight for less than fifty grand."

I was so proud that he was talking to me. I was one of the boys, part of the fight crowd. I shadowboxed alongside him in the ring. Then I hit the heavy bag, speed bag, and jump rope. No sparring. I was fighting tomorrow. I had to stay fresh. I didn't want to leave it in the gym. Whatever it was. After training I bought three t-shirts that said "Johnny Tocco's Gym" on the front and on the back, "You gotta have balls if you wanna conquer the world."

There was another press conference that night at the Mirage. Chavez's opponent, Lonnie Smith, who I knew from Gleason's, acted like an asshole. He boasted and threatened. He started a ruckus. Chavez tried to take it all with good humor. But he was getting pissed.

I figured Lonnie was just hyping the fight, but it was poorly done. I hated rudeness. And what about the asshole who was putting on the show—Don King? King was like a crass, human version of the trashy volcano in front of the Mirage. He reminded me of Trump. Donald was one of the few billionaires with the lousy taste to have running Italian fountains in his apartment.

I wasn't a WASP but I was beginning to respect their subtlety and reserve more and more. I understood why they disparaged the nouveau riche. Not that I wasn't nouveau riche also. It's just that I had pretensions of being blue blood. I felt kind of aristocratic. At least my education was proper. I had the advanced degrees and erudition. My doctoral dissertation on the Metanovel was kind of like wing tipped shoes. My nose turned up a bit. I was stately.

I almost tripped over Mike Tyson who was sitting in the audience at the press conference surrounded by women. They were vying for his attention. He was an ugly man. Girls liked me too. Was I an ugly man? No. I was cute. That was my ticket. I was a charmer. Anything but threatening. Somehow Mike recognized me. He was a lot friendlier than Don King.

"You're the Wall Street guy, right?" Tyson said, smiling.

"That's me," I said.

"Knock him dead," he said. He thought I was a Wall Street big shot. But I was nothing. I only had one Rolls and it was leased. I was much to do about nothing. Tyson used to give away Rolls Royces to the cops when he got traffic tickets. I was under investigation by the FBI. A small detail I kept putting out of my mind. I hadn't heard from them lately. If they had anything to communicate, they spoke to Brafman. It was all very lawyerly and nice. They were in no rush. Apparently, nothing much was moving forward. Brafman only bothered to communicate with me when he wanted a free lunch or was sending me another bill. The FBI had a limitless budget. They had all the time in the world to nail you and they liked to leave you hanging out there so that you could make other mistakes.

••••

It was the morning before the fight and Angela and Jean Marie showed up with their soundman. He had a new pair of earphones on. He usually wore black. These were purple. I felt good to have my film crew with me. Even if I was paying them to follow me around. I figured they must be filming someone important. I was like a vanity press. They followed me around for my morning jog. I stopped in front of the fake volcano at the Mirage and shadowboxed. No one really looked at me. They couldn't wait to get into the casino to lose. The Mirage was the image of everything that was wrong with America. It was Don King's American Dream. It was thousands of lost people chasing polka chips in a pre-fab city planted in the middle of the desert. There were sand dunes in the pockets of our hearts.

The film crew followed me to Johnny Tocco's. Hector was pissed off. "Are you making a movie or are you fighting?" he said.

"I'm not doing anything wrong," I said.

"You want to get knocked out again?" he asked.

"I won't pay attention to the camera," I said.

"This no joke, David. You could get killed," he said. "This not Hollywood bullshit."

"Let's work," I said and hit the heavy bag. I liked joking around with the film crew. It kept me loose. But I ignored them because I was afraid Hector would hit me. He thought nothing of whacking me when he was pissed.

I went to the weigh-in. There was press everywhere. It was an egotist's wet dream. I stripped down to my shorts and got on this scale in front of a couple hundred people. I was lathered in diamonds. A diamond boxing necklace, a boxing bracelet and a boxing ring. I loved boxing jewelry. It went with the blue tattoo on my left arm of "Awesome A" with two boxing gloves. I had that etched in there about two years before. I was a walking billboard for boxing. They could put me in front of one of those West 47th Street jewelry stores as a sign.

I saw my opponent, Caveman Lee. He looked impressively large for a welterweight. I got a foreboding that I'd be knocked out again. No, you got to think positive. Right. I didn't want to think about it until tomorrow.

"I haven't seen a Jewish fighter in twenty years," the doctor said at the physical.

I never really thought of myself as Jewish but I now felt part of the Hebraic tradition. I was wandering around the desert looking for fights with Egyptians. The doctor looked at my birth certificate from Ziggy and said, "You look older than thirty-four."

"My eyebrows are prematurely gray," I said.

"And your chest?" he asked.

"That too."

"I'm Jewish too," he said. He let me pass the physical.

•••

At three o'clock in the afternoon the next day they moved me into a trailer behind the stadium. It was hot as a concentration camp oven. No air-conditioning. A guard said it was a hundred and fifteen degrees in the ring. Chinito was there with Hector who gave him a shot of vitamin B. When a cop later found the needle in a wastebasket, he brought his troops in to search for drugs. They found nothing. I was getting real nervous waiting for the fight. I couldn't wait for it to start. I knew that I'd relax after I threw the first punch. I tried to calm myself down by telling myself that this was easy. At least I wasn't a boxer in Auschwitz where the guards used to have you beat each other to death for their amusement. If you lost they shot you. At least that's what I had heard. Willem Dafoe made a movie about this. He used to train at Gleason's. He wasn't very good but everyone praised him because he was a movie star.

At four o'clock Olajide Jr., Bruce, and Stan came back to the trailor. Stan was with some English reporter for *Star Magazine* in London. I started clowning around with him, "We never should have won the revolution. I want to be English."

"You're a smart American," the reporter said.

Hector smacked me, "No joking before a fight." I wasn't joking. I thought Americans were stupid. The English wouldn't build something as ugly as Las Vegas. They had style. Hector taped my hands. An official put an x on them with magic marker like they did in Denver. I liked the way that felt.

A few minutes later, an usher came to the trailer to get me. It turned out that I was the first fight of the night. I guess they wanted to get rid of my fight before the audience started showing up. I put my gloves on Hector's shoulders and followed him out. Olajide Jr., Bruce, and Stan followed behind me. They were my entourage. This was a ritual. I felt my face should have been painted red like a sacrifice. I was prepared to die. We marched through the parking lot, around the back of the stadium and down a long walkway into the empty arena. There were eighteen thousand empty seats. I could hear the echo of claps that didn't happen. Security guards and workers were milling about in the emptiness of the desert afternoon. As I got near the ring I saw my brother and Cramer sitting in the press section. There were a few heads sprinkled around like soccer balls.

My opponent, William "Caveman" Lee, was shadowboxing on the other side of the ring in a blue terrycloth robe with the hood over his head. He must have been sweating to death. He looked even bigger in the boiling heat. He looked like King Kong rotating his arms in that robe. I felt like I was going to be eaten. That he'd bite me off down to the ankles and my boxing shoes would fall on my brother's head twenty rows up. The heat rolled across the canvas like the ocean. The salt of my own sweat was burning my arms. I was going to die. I didn't give a shit. My business, the FBI, and my unhappy marriage were killing me back in New York.

"Stay away, David," Hector said. "Don't let him hit you." He looked nervous.

When the bell rang, I started dancing around the ring like Chicken Little. Caveman came right after me and started throwing bombs. The wind from his punches was almost enough to knock me over. I was in fear for my life. Why'd I take this stupid fight? This guy was tougher than Valdez in Denver. I threw a few punches and ran. I wanted to give him something to think about. I could punch too. I stuck and moved. I was in and out. I danced around him in a circle. This was exhausting in the heat. He was standing in the center like some glassy-eyed ape, wondering why I was bounding around him in circles. I confused him. I was getting dizzy myself. Then he came after me with chopping wild swings. Thud. Thud. The ring shook. A few punches hit me in the face. I ran like a coyote. He couldn't catch me. The bell rang and I went back to my corner exhausted. For ten grand Braverman could have found me an easier opponent. He was fucking me. He didn't care who he set me up with as long as he got his fee. I was a punching bag that paid middlemen to get beaten up. Back in the corner Hector put an endswell on my eye. The top of my right eyebrow was all scraped. It was swollen and a trickle of blood was dripping down into my eye.

"Kill him now, David," Hector said. "He tired in the sun. Go to the body."

With Hector's encouraging words in my head I charged out after Caveman. He charged right back at me. We met at the center of the ring and started swinging. He pushed me back towards my corner. I belted him with a few slugger body shots and he hobbled. He was off-balance and took a giant swing at me, falling to the canvas. I hadn't even hit him. Was he throwing the fight? Damn, I wasn't looking for a fix. I felt like helping him off the canvas. I looked down and I whispered, "Get up." I saw that there was water on the canvas. He must have slipped on it. He wasn't taking a dive. He was swimming on the canvas like a fish, trying to get up. He then rose from the sea like King Kong with flippers. The amphibious bastard. I began to wish he hadn't gotten up. Damn, why hadn't I fixed the fight? He was going to kill me. We started banging into each other. The punches were going back and forth like a presidential candidate shaking hands. Then we fell into a clinch. The ref separated us. Caveman was getting bored with me. He wanted to take me out. He raced forward but forgot to raise his hands. He was charging with his head sitting on his neck like a golf ball on a tee. I stepped towards him and unleashed a huge straight right. I felt like I was knocking his head three hundred and fifty yards onto a par 4 green. He was out cold on the canvas like a golf ball in the rough. The ref counted him out. Hector almost tripped over him as he ran into the ring and held up my hand. His corner picked him up and put him on a stool in the middle of the ring. King Kong was defeated. They were going to send him back to Africa and take down the circus tent. This was some lovely shit. Hector was holding my hand up, shouting, "The champ."

I had to admire myself. I was like a character out of *Ripley's Believe It Or Not.* I was so stubborn I could accomplish anything. I now had a professional win. Olajide and Bruce were slapping me on the back. My brother and Cramer were cheering near the press box. The security guards were dazed. Angela and Jean Marie were standing there applauding. Where was their movie camera? I later found out that Showtime wouldn't let them in with it. I had flown a film crew two thousand miles to have them watch my fight without filming it. The soundman was with them. He had his purple headphones on. I felt like my bank account had sprung a leak.

Later I was the hero of the security guards who kept patting me on the back and saying, "Good fight." The audience for the real fights started trickling into the stands. Chinito was the fourth fight. I saw Hector working his corner. I felt proud that he had just worked mine. Chinito knocked his opponent down in the third round but ended up winning an eight round decision. That gave Hector two wins for the night.

Julian Jackson knocked out Dennis Milton in the first round. No surprise. Jackson was one of the hardest hitters in the game. Milton was a nice guy but had no punch. Stan, the consultant, must have made a pretty penny from Minuto on this loss. There was always someone making money off someone else's disaster. Usually, his best friend.

The main event didn't start until almost eleven o'clock. It had been seven hours since my fight. I had been there all day. Big brave Lonnie Smith turned out to be full of prefight hype and ran from Chavez like a chicken. From the first bell he was doing everything to survive. He had no balls at all. "Hi, Wall Street," someone said next to me. I looked over. It was Comacho. I was flattered that he remembered me. He started yelling to the audience, "It's Macho time."

Lonnie lost by decision. I couldn't figure out why he would have talked so tough at the press conference just to come here and run for his life. Men weren't like that back in the days of Rocky Marciano and Jake LaMotta. They had some pride.

After the fight I went to Caesar's Palace with Stan and his wife, Lou. I looked like fuckin' Liberace with my diamond bracelet, necklace, and ring. Security guards and bus boys flocked to me. I was king of the blue-collar class. These workers were all my audience. I had shown them something they'd never seen before. This wasn't some little club fight. I had won a professional fight on a championship card in Las Vegas. Some people wanted to go to baseball fantasy camp. But how many guys got to play in the major leagues? Or to fight at the Mirage? If I had died in this arena it would have been worth it.

26

IT WAS FIGHT night at Gleason's and Bruce put me with Irwin Phipps for a rematch. I was now a pro. Phipps was still an amateur. They let us fight because the rules on White-Collar Night were eclectic. Bruce followed his own internal logic in matching people up. He had a good feel for what made sense. Phipps was a rough, black amateur. This was a smoker. No sanctioning body. It was kind of a waste to fight someone as tough as Phipps and not have it count as a professional fight. But it was good to get the practice.

The ref announced that I was just back from my knockout victory in Las Vegas. That sounded like some tough shit. Now I had to go hard. The bell rang and Phipps and I started out the same way we did in our first battle. Banging each other with overhand rights and not even bothering with defense. At the end of the first round I landed a smashing uppercut and his headgear went flying into the air. Too bad his head didn't go with it. Not to be nasty. But, hey, I was here to win.

In the second round the same thing happened. His corner gave him new headgear and we continued boom bam de bing. It was an even match all the way. I didn't know if I deserved the decision but I got it. I guess the flying headgear had a dramatic effect on the judges. I must have caught a few good punches in the eye because I was seeing spots. Phipps told me, "I'm planning to go pro next month like you."

"Cool," I said. I felt great. This guy was heavier than me, planning to go pro, and I still beat him twice in a row. Maybe I wasn't as shitty as I thought. Not that I ever thought I was shitty. In relation to a normal person who wasn't a boxer, I was freakin' Roberto Duran. But in relation to Roberto Duran, I was shitty.

●●●

Gleason's decided to have pro fights again. The arena was long gone but Bruce figured he could make some money having them right in the gym. Bruce found an opponent for me but when I got there he was a no-show.

"You want to put on an exhibition against Pedro Saiz, the New York State Champ?" Bruce asked.

"I want a real fight," I said. I didn't. But I wanted to sound tough. "Well, if you got nothing else, I'll spar with Pedro." I was delighted. Pedro was a friend of mine. He was New York State Junior Welterweight Champion. He wouldn't hurt me. I'd get some exercise and not get injured. This was the first pro exhibition ever in New York State. It seemed that I was breaking all kinds of records. The boxing commission was there and approved it.

Pedro and I fought an uneventful three rounds. There were a lot of exchanges but neither of us really tried to hurt each other. My camera crew captured it all. The same idiots who weren't allowed to film in Vegas. I showered, changed, and watched the other fights. Jean Marie filmed some of them. They were much more exciting than mine. They were good, bloody, honest battles. I was jealous.

●●●

Bruce made it up to me for not having a real fight at Gleason's. He got me a fight at the White Plains Civic Center. I was on the undercard of Lou Savarese. He was an up-and-coming white heavyweight. White heavyweights were worth their weight in gold. Lou wasn't a bad fighter. He had won the Golden Gloves. Ken Weiss, who was paying him ten thousand dollars a month, managed him. That was a lot of bread for a guy who fought for a couple of thousand dollars a fight. Ken felt he could build him up for a shot against Tyson where he might make ten million dollars like Gerry Cooney did against Larry Holmes. Ken and I became friends through Bruce. Ken was a wild man who liked to carry a gun, drink a lot, and go to nudie bars.

Doug DeWitt was also fighting on the card. I knew him from Gleason's. He was the guy without the nose. He had it broken so many times that he had a surgeon take out the bone and it sat against his face like a herring.

"Who am I fighting?" I asked Bruce down at the gym.

"Some tomato can," Bruce said. "My friend Jimbo from Woochester, Massachusetts got him for me."

"Where'd he find him?" I asked.

"On some municipal basketball courts. Never been in the gym," Bruce said. I didn't know whether to believe him or not. Everyone always lied in boxing.

●●●

I was in the dressing room in White Plains. Sergiev Artemov, the Russian lightweight, was fighting a six rounder later that night. This was a few years before he became the lightweight champion and got brain damage, almost dying in a title defense. He was clowning around with me. I already knew him. He got a kick out of my fighting pro. I loved it when I was accepted by the real pros. Hector's assistant, Yiyo, wrapped my hands. Hector was out of town. Yiyo didn't speak a word of English. He brought another trainer with him, Angel. Angel spoke English. They were both going to work my corner.

Bruce introduced me to Jimbo, who had set up the fight and was working my opponent Tony Diaz's corner.

"Don't worry," Jimbo said.

"About what?" I asked.

"Your opponent," he said. "The guy can't punch." Was Jimbo telling me that to get my guard down or did he want me to win so he could set up other fights for me? Did he want to be my promoter? Did he think he could ride me to a title shot? I was no champion. I was a Jewish, forty-four-year old, upper middle class fighter. That's the best you could say for me.

•••

I was in the ring looking over at Tony. Jimbo was behind him with a bucket and a sponge. Tony was a friendly looking, short, pudgy guy. He looked like a teddy bear, Winnie the Poo. I felt like waving hello to him. But I had to keep my fight face on. I stared at him like I wanted to kill him. When the bell rang, the teddy bear came racing across the ring at me. He was swinging wildly like he wanted to murder me. What did I ever do to get him so pissed? I got worried that I'd get knocked out again like in Denver. I held back. I didn't want to walk into any punches. I figured I'd wear him out a little so he couldn't hurt me if I did get clipped. He looked out of shape and like he didn't have too much wind. He was telegraphing his punches and I was able to slip some. When he charged at me I tied him up. Then I unleashed some bombs. But the little tree stump just stood there like he hadn't been hit. I must have gotten hit in the head because my mind clicked into slow motion. The canvas looked like a field of snow. I felt like I had slipped through a time warp and I was lost somewhere on the North Pole. I was wandering around with a cloud around my head. Then the bell brought me back to reality. Things started speeding up. The world came back into hard motion and I went back to my corner. My cutman was Al Gavin. He was one of the best in the world. He put some magic lotion around my eyes. My face felt swollen. I was sure it was going to be a mess. I had caught a few good punches.

Round two buzzed and I walked back out to fight. I felt like I had taken his best punches. He was sloppy and wild.

I could take him. He started chasing me around the ring. I was countering as I stepped back. He didn't move his head much. It was a ripe target. I was hitting him in the body to get his hands to drop. He was slowing down from a nervous hop to an unsure slide. I slipped a few round-houses and then came up the middle with an uppercut. His head flew back into his neck. I unleashed a left hook and his head knocked to the side. Then a straight right and his head almost came off his shoulders. He was on his ass. Out cold like an ice cream cone that had been dropped on the sidewalk. His seconds brought out the stool and seated him on it in the center of the ring. He was sitting there exhausted, dazed, like a trophy of my conquest while Angel and Yiyo were hugging me. I wanted to scream out my own name, *Awesome*, but I liked to be modest in victory. I did it again! I was the champ!

As I was walking out of the ring, the commissioner, Randy Gordon, got up to shake my hand.

"I didn't know you could fight like that, son," he said. He was younger than me.

"I did my best, sir," I said. I cut through the crowd like a Viking war ship on the way back to the dressing room. Angela and Jean Marie followed me with their camera.

"Don't worry," Jean Marie said. "We got the whole fight on film this time."

Jimbo came in and said, "We're going to the top. I'll line up your next ten fights."

I didn't think that it was a good idea for Jimbo to be talking to me about promoting my fights. I hardly knew him. Bobby Halpern came into the dressing room to congratulate me. He was that famous crazy fighter who did seventeen years for rape. His girlfriend's hit man shot him but he didn't die. He was still fighting in his late forties. He was punchy. One of the lunatic legends in the fight game. It couldn't get much better than this. I felt like a banana peel in a garbage can even though everyone thought I was a big success. It was ironic that I was being celebrated as a man who used his poetic brain as a punching bag. Only in America, Don King said. He was a slob but he was right.

David's first rap CD, *The Renegade Jew*

27

IT WAS SNOWING out and Gary Braverman, who had done the Celebrity Fights and set up my Las Vegas fight, was hustling another event. I met him in Bruce's office at Gleason's. This time he was promoting the Rapper's Federation World Championships. In order to fight you had to be a rapper.

"You can fight in this, David," he said.

"I'm not a rapper, Gary."

"I thought you said you were an English major."

"I have a Ph.D. in English Literature. I'm a poet," I said. When I was in college I published some poems in places like *Poet Lore*. I also wrote the lyrics for Nina Simone's brother's album, *Magic Man*. It made the charts in London in the mid-eighties.

"I'm putting you in these fights," he said, proudly. "You just have to write some rap songs." Maybe he planned to fleece me on this whole event. I figured I'd worry about it when he tried something. The chance to box in another tournament was worth it. And if it meant

I could launch a career as a rapper, all the better.

"I'm going to set you up with Grandmaster Melle Mel to write some rap songs." Braverman said.

"Who's he?" I asked.

"Only one of the founders of rap," Braverman said. "He's an old school hero."

•••

Melle Mel was a stocky, muscle-bound black guy who was also going to fight. He was a friendly, funny guy and not at all conceited about being famous. We went down to Funky Slice Studios in Brooklyn. We rented a studio there at sixty dollars an hour and he laid down some beats that I rapped along to. I really liked being at the studio. I felt like a rock star and we spent about thirty hours a week recording there. In no time at all I was going through thousands of dollars. But I felt it was worth it. I was looking for a new career. I thought I was adding a new linguistic sophistication to rap. I combined street language and literature. I was writing rap lyrics by the bushel. The fights were set for May 1992. I wanted to have a bunch of great songs by then so that I could say that I was a real rapper. I didn't want to keep it real. That was street talk for imitating a fake, pseudo-tough life style. I wanted to be real.

•••

Before the Rap Fights came around I had the chance at another professional fight at Trump Palace in Atlantic City. Michael drove Hector and me down the night before the fight. We entered the hotel lobby where Stan Gold was talking to Bob Arum. Arum was a legendary promoter in the fight business. He was a short, ugly, Harvard educated lawyer. He was everything that bigots hated about Jews. He was an embarrassment to me and my people. He had a reputation as a sleezebag. He was a white Don King. I said hello to Stan and started shadowboxing in front of Arum. I was joking around and I said, "Come on, Arum. Let's box." I could see that no one liked my joking around with him like that. Arum, Stan, and Hector all looked away from me like they didn't want to see what an asshole I was. This really pissed me off. I was used to dealing with billionaires so why should they expect me to respect this little shit? What was the big deal about my shadowboxing with Arum? Fuck him and the horse he rode in on. I was supposed to be impressed by some lispy midget who made money off watching athletes beat each other to death? He thought he was too big for me to joke with? He was giving me dirty looks. I kept my mouth shut. I didn't want to dirty myself by arguing with him. I didn't want to ruin my fight career.

•••

I weighed in at one hundred and forty-six pounds. That was perfect. I met Tim Witherspoon who was promoted by Dennis Rappaport. I liked both of them. Tim had been fucked over by King and was suing him. Tonight he was the main event again. He had once held the heavyweight title but King squeezed him out of boxing and he couldn't get a fight for years. Everyone was suing King. But fat King was like a pig basted in butter and too slippery to grab onto.

Hector and I met Jimbo in the cafeteria.

"Don't worry about a thing," Jimbo said. "I got a real easy one for you this time. Rodriguez, the guy never fought before."

It turned out *USA Tuesday Night Fights* was down there to cover the event. That meant I could be fighting on national TV. Wow, what a rush. It was a pleasure to know me. I felt like I was being introduced to my new partner. The announcers, Sean O'Grady and Al Albert, tracked me down. "Amazing that a businessman like you is fighting," Sean said.

"Why are you doing it?" Albert asked.

"Can I sell you guys some insurance?" I said, joking.

"I hope you don't need any in the ring there," Sean said. I hoped so too. I hoped Jimbo didn't set me up with some killer.

It was fight time and Angela and Jean Marie were filming. Fifty of my friends were in the audience. I had rented a bus to have them driven to Atlantic City and gave them all free tickets. I wish I knew a guy who was as much fun as I was. I'd attend all his events. As I went up to the ring, a song I wrote with Melle Mel came over the loudspeaker, "Hard-On Attitude." Even though I had given it to the soundman to play, I didn't actually think he'd do it. I felt cool as hell as I pounced into the ring and started shadowboxing to my own music, "Hey dude, hey dude, you got a hard on attitude."

Rodriguez came into the ring. They announced his record as two and one. I was one and one. Jimbo had

never said that Rodriguez had two wins before. Rodriguez looked big for a welterweight. He definitely
looked like he was more than one hundred and fifty
pounds. Jimbo was probably planning to get me beaten
up.

The first round I went right after him. He was
backpedaling. I had him on the defensive for about twenty
seconds. Then he started coming after me and landed a
sharp punch above my eye. It was a real zinger. I was told
after that I staggered but I was unaware of it at the time.
He stepped back when I was about to counter. I came after
him but his defense was too good and I couldn't catch him.
He just kept moving. I didn't understand why he didn't stay
and trade with me after landing that shot. Was he scared
of me? Maybe he was a counterpuncher.

Between rounds Hector attended to a cut over my left
eye. It was only dribbling a little blood. Hector slapped me
across the face. It hurt. I was more afraid of Hector than
Rodriguez. "I stopping the fight unless you fight harder,"
he said. The bell rang and I stepped out to fight. I attacked
Rodriguez like a mad man. I got him against the ropes and
hammered his ribs. My body punches have always been
my best shots. They came effortlessly. I knocked Rodriguez onto his butt. The referee pushed me back. Rodriguez wobbled to his feet. I stormed back all over him
like a squid. He was sinking against the ropes when I
landed a clean shot to his head and he fell over backwards.
He couldn't get to his feet and the ref ended the fight. Applause went up throughout the arena and I was in fighter's
heaven. Jimbo brought a stool into the ring and sat Rodriguez on it, who was holding his side. He had had

enough. His ribs were broken. My friends had seen me in all my glory. I had executed this guy.

Everyone congratulated me after the fight. I went to the casino and did some gambling. I had a drink with Rodriguez and Jimbo.

"You broke my ribs," Rodriguez said.

"I'm sorry," I said.

"I don't care," he said.

Sean O'Grady and Al Albert congratulated me. So did my friends who had taken the bus there. I didn't have my wife with me. I was in love with myself at the moment. I didn't want to share my affection with a woman. If there were time and a place to jerk off I would have done it, so I could admire my own prick.

A bunch of newspapers covered the fight praising my second round knockout of Rodriguez. The only one who criticized me was Michael Katz of the *Daily News*. He wrote that he thought Rodriguez took a dive. I was furious. I later heard Katz wasn't even at ringside. The promoter, Arum, probably put Katz up to dissing me. Arum hated the fact that I was close to his age yet I was good-looking and had the balls to fight. Katz was a fat, dirty looking man with a beard and a neck brace. The Katzs and the Arums of the world didn't mind if the niggers were tough. They didn't even consider niggers the same species. But when one of their own class and color was tough, it was a threat to them. It made them look like fairies. Their wives probably asked them why they couldn't be like me. I was a hell of a lot sexier than they were. You think I'm conceited? No, I'm just defensive. I'm angry. Fuck Michael Katz! The Atlantic City papers said I was the toughest fight of the night. So did the *Philadelphia Daily News.*

But Katz hurt me. After all the beatings I'd taken and the times I'd been in the hospital it was insulting to be mocked by some overweight scribbler in a neck brace. I wanted to kill him. He was bringing out the worst in me. I had a hard-on attitude.

•••

Lauren caught our driver, Michael, billing his laundry and groceries to us on our charge accounts.

"Fire him. He's a thief," Lauren said. Michael had put five sirloin steaks on the Gristede's bill. He was charging the cleaning of his girlfriend's blouses to us.

"These are perks. Forget it," I said. She showed me the bills. I wouldn't look at them. She never liked Michael. But I didn't particularly care if he was stealing a few bucks here and there. Everyone had to live.

"You're an asshole," she yelled. Later that day she fired Michael herself. I didn't rehire him. It just wasn't worth it to fight over a chauffeur. Even if she was wrong. I was never right in the long run. She was a twelve round fighter. I was a preliminary pro—good for four rounds but not for a championship marital spat. I learned you couldn't beat a woman in a fight. It meant too much to them. They were in it for the long haul.

I drove the Rolls myself down to Harrah's Marina in Atlantic City for my next fight. I was now a 2 and 1 fighter. Hector and Bruce came with me. I was on another Dennis Rappaport card; Witherspoon was the main event again. When I pulled into the hotel in my Rolls the valet said, "I saw you fight at Trump Palace. You were great." I tipped him twenty dollars. I checked in and hit the gambling tables. But I was bored. Chips didn't mean anything to me. I went to bed early.

Next day at the weigh-in I saw my opponent, Daniel Flores. He was 142 pounds from Connecticut. He had a chubby, friendly face. Jimbo was there with him, picking out all my opponents as I fought my way up the ranks. Three film crews—*Sean O'Grady's USA Tuesday Night Fights*, *The George Michael Sports Machine*, and Angela and Jean Marie—followed me around. You'd think I was a candidate for President I was getting so much media coverage. Harrah's was giving me VIP treatment. They gave me a special welcome gift—a boxing uniform with *Awesome Lawrence* stitched on it.

I was excited about my fight while I was waiting in the dressing room. I was anxious to prove that I could win a fight and that my last bout wasn't fixed. J.T., the friend I fought my first fight against after my separated shoulder, visited me. I had no idea he even knew that I was fighting. It seemed like ages ago when I patty-caked around the ring with him. I had come a million miles since then. Reporters were following me around everywhere. Everett Martin was in the dressing room with me. He was a tough light heavyweight. He was with his trainer Victor Valle. Valle used to be Gerry Cooney's trainer. I knew them from Gleason's. Witherspoon had his own private dressing room. I wasn't allowed in there.

●●●

When the bell rang I started jabbing with Flores. He was shorter than me and I was able to land some. His nose started bleeding. I felt good about that. He was having trouble getting me into range. But he was a good fighter. I could see that Flores was experienced. He kept his hands up nice and maintained good balance. His footwork was real professional. Not some wild amateur shit. But my jab was better than usual and a thin line of blood was dripping from his nose. He stepped in and caught me with a few punches but they didn't hurt. He was more like an overblown lightweight than a true welterweight. You'd be amazed the difference a few pounds makes in your punches. I couldn't feel his. And my confidence grew so I kept landing stiffer and stiffer combinations, dominating most of the fight.

"Kill him, Doc," someone in the audience yelled. I guessed one of the newspapers mentioned I had a Ph.D. I must have been the only doctor who was a professional fighter. Doctor of Literature, that is. Well, so I wasn't a real doctor. Still, it took me six years to get my post-graduate degree. I was a poet. An angry poet. When the fight ended, the decision was unanimous. I won. The crowd went wild. I looked over at Flores. His face was all swollen. I felt bad for him. I think he was better than I was. I was just stronger, more dedicated.

I was at the bar bullshitting with my brother and other people from the office.

"Flores didn't hurt me a bit," I said.

"You're getting good," my brother, Pete, said. I thought back to how my brother had started with me. I was proud of how far I had come. Dennis Rappaport said, "Those were great knockdowns in the fourth round."

"What knockdowns?" I asked.

"The two times you knocked Flores down with body shots," Rappaport said.

"Oh those. Yeah thanks," I said. I didn't remember a thing about knocking Flores down. It was like that part of the fight was completely blank to me. I was totally exhausted. Maybe I had lost some brain cells. Who cared? I was born with enough brain cells to light a whole village in the mountains. I could afford to lose some of them.

When I got home from Atlantic City, Lauren had hired a new driver, Ram. He was a polite, well-dressed man in his thirties from India. It was nice to have a driver again. It was a lot more convenient than driving myself, calling Communnicar, or hailing a cab.

28

I MET BRAVERMAN at Gleason's Gym to discuss the Rap
Fights. He was short on money. I gave him twenty grand.
He didn't even have to pressure me. I was worried that the
FBI would eventually close down my business. I could tell
from my lawyer Brafman's bills that he had had numerous conversations with the Prosecutor; they were probably
trying to work out a plea bargain. I needed another career
to go into when I bombed out of insurance. Maybe I'd become a famous novelty rap act. You could say I was throwing my money down the sewer. But there was the chance
that I'd become a star and dance on top of the sewer cover.
It was a long shot. But the world was closing in on me and
there were no other escape routes.

A few weeks later, Braverman called me to another
meeting at Gleason's Gym. I was really pleased about the
promotions for the Rap Fights. He sponsored a police es-
corted drive through all the boroughs. He put on radio ads.
I was looking forward to fighting.

"Things are going bad," he said.

"What now?" I asked.

"I went through your twenty grand just doing the promotional tour and renting the armory for the fights. Not to mention the cost of fliers and radio ads," he said. "I'm tapped out. I can't afford to hire security or buy insurance. I may have to tank the whole idea of the Rap Fights. What a shame to get this far."

Shit. I thought of having blown my twenty grand on nothing. I really wanted these dumb fights.

"David, can you invest another twenty?" Braverman asked.

The swindler had come to the right place. I could see he was a con man but I couldn't help going along with it. I wasn't a sucker. A sucker doesn't realize he is being sucked in. I was a jerk. I knew what was happening and I went along with it anyhow on some magical whim, some dream of being a rap star. It was like when I was ten years old and I used to throw pennies down the sewer saying that it was hungry while the kids on the block watched me. I would steal those pennies from my mother's penny jar. I was a child Robin Hood. I wanted to dance on the sewer cover.

"I'll give you twenty grand tomorrow," I said.

I didn't have much choice. If I didn't throw in the money I'd lose the first twenty grand. This was my only chance to save my investment. Braverman said, "Don't worry. You can station your own Pinkerton guard in the ticket booth to watch over your money for you." The sewer belched. The next day Braverman was all psyched about the fights. "Don't worry. It's gonna come off great. You're gonna make all your money back, plus. And none of that Puff Daddy, CCNY basketball rap riot shit is coming off at my fights. I got top security," Braverman said.

Rap events had a bad rep. A few months earlier Puff Daddy had arranged a basketball game for rappers at CCNY. He oversold the event. A stampede ensued where nine kids were trampled to death.

"I'm looking forward to fighting," I said.

"You know how many of those suckers are too chicken to show up at the Rap Fights?" Braverman said. "All the big names, like LL Kool J and Ice Cube ducked the bouts, pretending their managers won't let them fight. At the last minute, Dres from Black Sheep and Tim Dog dropped out. Followed by Raheem."

"Rappers are artists not fighters. Their fronting is ridiculous," I said.

"Chicken shit motherfuckers. You got more balls than all of them put together, Awesome," Braverman said.

I liked when I was called my nickname, Awesome. I guess that compliment was worth forty thousand dollars.

"Oh, by the way, I got a call a week ago from Boxing Commissioner Randy Gordon. He said if you fight in this thing he's gonna suspend your pro license," Braverman said, casually, like it was nothing. Gary could have warned me about this earlier. The prick. I was spending a fortune just to lose my pro license. I should have dropped out of the fights and kept my license. But the lure of becoming a famous rapper was too much for me.

●●●

An hour before the Rap Fights I was looking around the Armory in Harlem for signs of life. It was a huge place that sat thousands. There were only a couple hundred people spread around like mountain goats. Puff Daddy had sold

228

thousands of tickets to a lame basketball game. Here we had real fights, something the rap community should love, and the place was deserted. We had a car parade and radio ads to promote this damn thing.

What had Braverman done wrong? I had hired a Pinkerton guard for five hundred dollars but Braverman wouldn't let him into the ticket office to count receipts. "It's against armory rules," he said.

Fat chance! Not that it mattered. Hardly any tickets were being sold. I changed in the dressing room and followed my opponent, Kurtis Blow, down to the ring. He was a famous rapper and was known as a tough guy. He had beaten up John Diehl at the Celebrity Fights. He turned to me and said, "You better not beat me in Harlem. This is my backyard."

I didn't like to talk trash so I just smiled. He had to be kidding. No way I was going to lose to a musician. A rapper. Let's see how he boasted when I punched his head off. I heard the song I wrote with Melle Mel blasting over the loudspeaker, *I'm the Wall Street Rapper, very dapper / Very slick, and eccentric.* I felt pumped. Hector was working my corner. I was in the ring, looking at the crowd. There were about two hundred people there. I was going to lose every penny I had invested. The cash register groaned. The sewer roared. Crazy Sam, the mad host of *Video Music Box,* was there. I met him at an earlier press conference and we hit it off. He was a three hundred pound black dude with dreds and was yelling, *Awesome! Awesome!*

Round one: I came in thinking this was a joke. Blow was a decent fighter but I had fought pro. I was cocky. I thought I'd kill him. We traded punches. He was about twenty pounds heavier and hit harder than I expected. He was fast, too. But I had fought in Las Vegas, Atlantic City, Denver. I was on another level. About half way through the round he surprised me with a tremendous uppercut that he threw from his ankles and lifted me three feet into the air and dumped me on my ass. I found myself lying on the canvas, staring at Kurtis jumping up and down like he was Muhammad Ali. It didn't hurt. But it shocked me. Kurtis thought he'd already won. I laughed to myself, embarrassed, that he knocked me down. No fuckin' rap punk was taking me out. I got off the canvas and went after him like a wounded lion. I hit his body so hard that you could hear his *ughs* resonate through his rib cage. I was breaking him up inside like brittle glass.

Round two: I went straight for his body again. I was right there bobbing and weaving, landing hooks from both sides. He managed to hang onto me and survive the round. If I were his weight I would have put him down. He would have died of shame in front of his Harlem people. Fuck him for knocking me down.

Round three: He was out of gas, running on empty. I kept digging punches into his ribs. I heard a cracking sound like tinder on fire whenever I connected. He was whimpering like a woman. I didn't know what was keeping him on his feet. They rang the bell early to save his ass.

The crowd was roaring for me. Crazy Sam was yelling, "Did you see that white boy fight?"

I went back to my corner. "You won," Hector shouted.

"The Doc beat the shit out of Blow," a big black guy in the audience yelled.

Then Michael Marley grabbed the mike and announced, "The new Super Middleweight Champ, Kurtis Blow."

Boo! Boo! Kill the ref. The audience pelted the ring with ticket stubs and programs.

"You crazy," Hector yelled. "Lawrence won." Then he said to me, "Maybe Marley thought there would be a riot if a white man beat Blow in Harlem."

"What do you mean? All the blacks were rooting for me," I said.

The Source and a bunch of rap magazines and video shows ran over to Kurtis Blow to interview him. He was a big celebrity. They were all kissing up to him. When Kurtis got away from the crowd he came over to me and said, "I think you broke my ribs."

"I hit hard to the body," I said.

"You're telling me," he said, rubbing his side. He ended up in the hospital later that night. I had broken three of his ribs. I wish I had broken his head. He was a nice guy. But I don't like losing.

There were a lot of celebrities in the audience at the armory—KRS-1, King Sun, Erik B. & Rakim, Choice, Son of Bazerk, Red Alert, Kevin Kelley, Buddy McGirt, and Iran Barkley. It was a real black crowd. I was part of their culture. I loved boxing, rapping, and their broad smiles. The blacks had a sense of humor about the world from being so beaten up by it. They retreated into laughter. Chuck D from Public Enemy got up in the ring and performed, "Shut 'em Down."

I went up to Gary Braverman and said, "What's going on here? You know I won that fight."

"I'll check it out with the judges," he said. He went up to their bench and read through their scorecards. He came back and said, "There's a mistake." Marley added up the rounds wrong. It was a draw.

I wondered if Marley really did make a mistake in the scorecards. "I'll take a draw," I said. "Are you going to announce it to the audience?"

"No," he said. "It's too late. But you'll both get championship belts."

I loved belts and trophies. I did win. I really did. Whatever the decision or revision.

•••

I went up to Gary Braverman's office to talk about the fight. I had already read the *Philadelphia Inquirer* and *Crain's* which both said mine was the fight of the night. The *Inquirer* said mine was the most brutal. I liked being brutal.

"Am I getting any of my investment back?" I asked Gary.

"Are you kidding?" he said. "I lost my shirt. I still owe the security guards. I can't afford to edit the video I'm making of it. I want to sell it to Pay-per-view for a fortune. It was a great show. Can you give me another ten thousand dollars to edit?"

Even I, sucker of the western world, couldn't believe he was asking me for more money. The sewer was affronted. It was full. It hadn't digested the first forty thousand dollars yet.

"I'm tapped out, Gary," I said. "I'm sorry."

"Well, in that case I might as well tell you that Randy Gordon called to tell me that he suspended your professional boxing license for fighting an amateur in the Rapper's Federation."

Can't say he hadn't warned me before.

···

Randy Gordon was only the commissioner of New York. He hadn't told New Jersey that he had suspended my license. I saw another opportunity to fight pro and I took it. I tried to sneak onto a fight card in Atlantic City. I went into serious training. Which I always did, anyhow. But this time I really wanted to kick some ass to show that I deserved to be pro. I was in Gleason's training for this event, hoping I'd get away with it. Hector put me in the ring against some amateur middleweight whose record was 50 and 3. He was a southpaw with an Olympic, stand-up style. That boring jab, jab, cross routine. The kind of fighter I didn't like to fight because I could never get my rhythm against stop and start fighters. I was best when I was on the inside, pounding the body like Joe Frazier. It was hard to get in on this guy. He kept me at the end of his punches. The dangerous spot where knockouts occurred. He had a pretty strong hook, which I managed to block by keeping my left up against my head. Things were getting pretty rough. I don't know how long we were sparring when something happened that I don't remember. Some time elapsed and I found myself in Bruce's office asking, "Did you see me here earlier tonight?" I didn't know how I got there or what I had done just before. I must have taken a concussion to the head and not even known it. Bruce looked at me strangely and got scared. He asked me, "Did you spar?"

"No," I said.

He called Hector in and asked him if I had just sparred. Hector said, "David sparred five rounds."

"Are you sure?" I asked. I didn't remember one of them.

Bruce followed me into the locker room to watch over me while I changed into my street clothes. I didn't remember the combination to my lock. He had to cut the lock for me. I had trouble getting dressed. I didn't know whether my t-shirt went on inside my dress shirt or outside it. Bruce helped me. We went back to his office. Kelly and Cramer showed up out of nowhere.

"What are you guys doing here?" I asked.

"You told us to meet you here for drinks," Cramer said.

"Don't you remember?" Kelly said.

"Sure, that's right," I said. I didn't remember. I wasn't the kind of guy who admitted to being scared. I was scared. I was worried that I was losing my mind and would become a vegetable. I didn't want to be some sorry looking retard, sitting in a wheelchair drooling. Or maybe I did. It might be fun. Less pressure. I could wrap my drool up in a spoon and throw it over my shoulder. I forced myself to not give a fuck because I didn't want to give a fuck. If you gave a fuck, you could get hurt. Bruce slipped me the number of the boxing commission's neurologist as I went out.

●●●

"The investigation's heating up in Delaware," Cramer said. We were in the Lighthouse getting drinks.

"Where's Delaware?" I said. I'm not sure that I ever knew. But I was still confused from getting hit. I couldn't believe I was getting busted for something I didn't do in some little jerkwater state. What an embarrassing way to go down. It was like being sucker punched. I ordered two

Bloody Marys. I wanted to get wasted so I didn't notice that I wasn't thinking clearly. I'd rather feel drunk than brain damaged. After my second drink things started coming back to me. I remembered sparring. But I didn't remember how many rounds I did nor did I remember getting hit so hard that I lost my memory.

•••

A few days later I felt better when the neurologist gave me an MRI and told me, "It's a slight concussion. It happens to boxers all the time." Why was I panicking? It was nothing. Certainly I could handle a slight concussion. But I had to give my head some rest. So I cancelled my upcoming fight. I still couldn't remember the five rounds of my sparring session. It was kind of fun to have chunks of your memory taken away from you. It was only scary if you were scared and I chose not to be scared. It was fun like Halloween. I could face the disappearing jack o' lantern, the howl of witched craziness and the specter of death and still find joy in the world. Disaster was inspiring. It caught you in the balls and made you stand up straight. I figured I wouldn't spar for a while. I'd just hit the punching bags.

•••

Now that the boxing commission had banned me temporarily I was using more of my free time to get into rap music. I felt rap was like boxing. It was from the street. It was all part of the same circle of joyous despair. Rap was going to be my new career. It was a lot easier than getting my face punched in. It wasn't as sincere but it had more potential for profit. I wasn't going to be rich forever. The FBI weren't going to wait too long to indict me or close me down. They already had enough on me and Cramer and Kelly. What were they waiting for? I had to start sorting things out for myself.

I was a great lyricist. I could even rap on beat some of the time. And when I went off beat I could use the equipment in the studio to put me back on. Lauren hated rap as much as she hated boxing. That encouraged me to rap. This was before Lauren decided that she wanted to do some rap songs. I'll never understand why she too became a rapper. I didn't understand that I was forty-five years old and white. I thought I was the coolest motherfucker on the planet, despite the fact that the word "motherfucker" made me wince. Not that I was competing with others. Other people hardly existed for me. I was competing with myself.

I was wearing baggy, purple Girbaud jeans and a Guess hoody when I went down to S.I.R. rehearsal studios to practice my song "The Wall Street Rapper" with three dancers and a choreographer. Billy, the president of Rude Boy Records, was there. He was a chunky black man in his thirties. I had signed a deal with him to put my record out on his label. I gave him fifty grand for promotions. I didn't know what I was doing. I was the only rapper who ever bribed a label to sign with them. The sewer gurgled some more. I was feeding its hunger with lost causes in addition to past occupations. It was a dank weight on the beauty of my pugilism. I was desperate to be a star. I thought being on a black label would give me legitimacy in the rap world.

29

WHILE I WAS banned from fighting in New York, I managed to get another fight out of state. I planned to cut down on my boxing, but not yet. Jimbo set the fight up for me in Boston. I didn't want to tell my wife that I was still fighting so I told her that I was going on a business trip. I flew Bruce and Yiyo up to Boston with me for a fight at the Westin Hotel. The fights were part of some charity event for delinquent children. Rich people loved to see poor folk beat the fuck out of each other. They had no idea that I wasn't from the slums. I checked into the Westin Hotel at noon. I killed the day lying around and went down to the weigh-in at six o'clock that night. It was in the basement of the hotel. The fighters who filled the room were mostly white trash from South Boston. Young men in their early twenties from Italian and Irish backgrounds. Everything was *fuck this* and *fuck that*. I felt out of place. I was more comfortable with the blacks in New York.

Mine was the first fight of the night. They led me through a bustling kitchen filled with pots and pans and chefs and assistant chefs. I came out of a door into the main dining room like I was some kind of dish being served up. There was a ring set up in the center of a large banquet hall with tables around it and men in tuxedos and anorexic rich women in long ugly evening dresses. When I entered the dining room my opponent was standing near one of the tables with Jimbo. He had muscles on muscles and a mean face with a squashed-in nose. Jimbo came over to me and said, "Don't worry about this guy, Novarro. His muscles are all air."

"Are you sure?" I asked. They looked like they were made of stone.

"Don't worry about a thing. Rodriguez knocked him out last month. Attack him before he comes after you," Jimbo said.

Yiyo gestured to me in Spanish sign language that I shouldn't take the fight. Bruce said, "Your opponent looks like he weighs 160 pounds."

Even though I was only 145 pounds, I didn't come all the way up to Boston just to duck out of a fight. I was a seasoned pro. I won the last four fights in a row. I could take him.

The bell rang and I jumped on Novarro. I was going to kill him. I was not taking a chance on any of his big muscles getting active and belting me. I hit him on the forehead with a straight right that would have felled a tree. The bastard looked at me, smiled and rabbit-punched me on the top of the head. I went down. It was more like a push than a thud. I felt like I was at a construction site where he was pile-driving me through the canvas. I got back up onto my feet. The referee made sure I was all right and turned me loose again. I attacked Novarro like a madman. I was in his face. No way he was going to beat me. I gave him a few slugs and then he rabbit-punched me again and my feet almost went through the canvas. The ref checked me out. He asked me, "Do you want to continue?" Like a fool I said, "Yes." I started bouncing around the canvas again, swinging at Novarro's face. I didn't bother with defense. I was going to take that piece of shit out of there, flush him down the loser's toilet. Then Novarro wobbled me with another rabbit punch. Next thing I knew the ref was stopping the fight. "What are you doing, ref?" I asked. "I didn't go down."

"You're out on your feet," the ref said. "It's a technical knockout. Three knock downs in the same round."

"But I only went down twice," I said.

"I'll be the judge of that," he said.

●●●

Jimbo came over to me in the locker room. "I'm sorry. Novarro must have improved a lot in the last few months. There's less air in his muscles."

"Don't worry. I deserved to lose," I said. I should have been able to take Novarro. I had given Jimbo eight hundred dollars to put me on the card and get me an opponent without too much experience.

"Take five hundred dollars back," he said. "This guy outweighed you and was too tough."

"Forget it," I said. "It's not your fault I stink."

I didn't stick around to watch the other fights. I was too embarrassed to be seen by anyone. The last thing I needed was some society chickens making fun of me. I could do that myself.

The week I got back from Boston I started managing a young fighter, Miguel Ortiz. He was a good banger. Reminded me a little of the Morales kid I fought a couple of years before. I think I was the only manager who ever sparred with his fighter. Miguel was good work for me and we practiced together a few times a week at Gleason's. On the weekends I took him with me to the upscale Vertical Club to train and swim in the pool. He loved the luxury. He was a sweet kid but he was a hard luck case. Television was doing a story on him. His father died and his mother was doing a ten-year bid in jail for drugs. Miguel was twenty and bringing up his teenage brother by himself. Hector wanted me to help him so I gave him some money and subway tokens every week.

Bruce helped me get Miguel his first pro fight up in Buffalo. Miguel took a bus up there while I flew up with Hector and Stan Gold. Stan had another fighter on the card. Kevin Rooney was the promoter of the show and he was a friend of Stan's. Mike Tyson had just canned Rooney for saying something against his bitch-wife Robin Givens.

Buffalo was pure winter. Snow everywhere and temperatures below freezing. The fights were held at some small-time high school in the middle of nowhere. For a pro card it was funkier than the amateurs even. Miguel fought beautifully. He knocked out this muscular kid in the first round. We all cheered like we had a champion in the making. Stan's fighter knocked out his opponent in the second round. The opponent was a bum, but Stan was building his fighter. He was the kind of opponent I should have had in Boston or in Denver.

"Why don't you promote some shows with me," Kevin said.

"No thanks, Kevin. I've had some bad luck in promotion." I was thinking of the Rap Fights where I lost forty thousand dollars. But I felt cool that Kevin asked me. He was a real big shot in the boxing game and I liked being associated with him. "Why don't we go for drinks?" he suggested.

"I'd love to but I'm exhausted," I said. I had heard that it was dangerous to drink with Kevin. He was a lush and got into fights. I wasn't a street fighter. I didn't want to get my ass kicked. I went back to the hotel and went to sleep early. I was happy about my fighter winning.

"You can keep the four hundred dollar purse," I said to Miguel. I didn't want the manager's twenty-five percent. I wasn't about to take a hundred dollars from a downtrodden kid.

● ● ●

In order to stay in shape I upped my jogging. I had Ram come to my apartment at 72nd Street to pick me up. Then I'd give him my briefcase and my suit and tell him to drive to Gleason's Gym in Brooklyn and I'd meet him there. I'd run the eight miles from Manhattan across the Brooklyn Bridge to Gleason's. Ram would be waiting for me in front of the gym and carry my suit upstairs for me. I'd then work out two hours, sparring and hitting the bags. I have to admit that I got a big kick out of having my chauffeur drive my suit to work. It cracked me up. I must have been the only businessman that had a driver for his clothes. Of course, I didn't do this too often. As much as I loved to work out, there was only so much exercise I could take.

30

WHILE MY BUSINESS life and boxing career were going on, in February of 1993 Brafman and the other two lawyers went down to Delaware to see if they could get us the best possible deal for laundering cash. The legal team called us up to Brafman's office. "We really did well," Brafman said. "Lawrence, you get a year in jail. Cramer and Kelly get two and a half years each. They're only nailing you for cashing checks and not reporting them as income."

I was glad I was going to jail. I was tired of business. I needed a break. I thought that it would be an experience, that it would make me cooler than the average dork. I would find myself more interesting. I would become nothing like my dippy white-collar peers. I would become one of the fabulous.

If my wife knew I felt this way she would have killed me. Sometimes I'm a real floater. I live in the clouds. She wanted me to come down to earth.

I was jealous that Cramer and Kelly got more time than me. That made them look tougher. Badder. I almost wished I got a longer sentence.

"How come Lawrence gets less time than we do?" Cramer complained.

"Because you and Kelly cashed the money in Delaware," Brafman said.

"I don't like it," Cramer said.

"Are they going to leave the business intact?" Kelly asked.

"Yes," Brafman said.

"Then I'm in," Kelly said. "David, make sure your dad sends my wife a check every month."

The noble husband. The gay blade. The good family man. Right!

Cramer broke down crying. The fat boy couldn't take it. "I'm innocent," he claimed. He didn't want to go to jail.

I wasn't going to be a wuss. Just as long as they allowed my business to stay alive, so I had a few bucks to come out to. I was no girl. And I was not going to jail as one. I would be tough. I had fought in Vegas and Atlantic City. I could fight some punks in jail.

In a private meeting Brafman told me, "Watch out for Cramer. He's going to turn on you. He could be wired."

●●●

Hector and Miguel Ortiz went up to Albany without me. I was too busy with my legal problems. Ortiz lost. He was now 1-1. His professional record was worse than mine. Not only that, he tore a piece of his retina and was going to need an operation. He was probably finished with boxing for good. He had been boxing since he was ten years old and his career was ruined in one fight. Not that he ever

243

had a career. If you aren't the best fighter in your weight division you starve in boxing. There is no middle class. An average baseball player makes a million dollars a year. An average boxer makes about five thousand. And he gets brain damage. That's why the sport is so beautiful. It's not about money. It's about principle. It's about glory and honor, like what the Greek and Roman warriors were after. Fuck the faggots who never boxed and say it's about slum kids wanting to get rich. It's about slum kids wanting to make a name. To achieve dignity. To become themselves. I felt bad for Ortiz. But there was nothing I could do for him now. I was up to my ears in alligators. His boxing insurance would pay for his operation. I had worse problems than him. In my heart I wished him the best. That was not something I usually wished people.

●●●

Bruce managed to get me another fight in Lebanon, New Hampshire, against one of Jimbo's fighters. Jimbo said to me on the phone, "I got you a sure win this time. It will only cost you another eight hundred dollars to get on the card."

I didn't tell Hector I was going. He felt I was getting myself into too much trouble by going against the commission's ban on me and that it was time I hung the gloves up. He told me I'd be better off concentrating on my rap music. I didn't know why I was going. Old habits died hard with me. When I committed to something, I stayed around. I didn't leave my sports. I didn't leave my vocations. I didn't leave my family. I embraced my weakening memory. I was reliable and not . . . .

Bruce and I drove up to Worcester, Massachusetts and met Jimbo. Along the route Bruce told me we had to keep this fight very hush hush. "If Randy Gordon finds out, I'm dead," he said, "particularly after Lauren called Randy and told him if you fought anymore she was going to sue the commission."

"She did that?" I asked.

"Yup," he said.

"If you want to go back I'll understand," I said.

"No. I don't know why. I think it's going to be fun. Besides, I'd like to stick it to Randy anyhow," Bruce said. "You know you're already banned because of the rap fights."

"That's only in New York," I said. "We're fighting in New Hampshire. Randy has nothing to do with it. It's out of his jurisdiction."

"Randy doesn't care where you fight. He thinks he's the commissioner of the world."

We met Jimbo at a diner in Worcester. He had a lightweight Puerto Rican with him. He looked like nothing. I could kill this kid. We all had some coffee and then headed out from Massachusetts to New Hampshire. A couple of hours later we stopped at another diner for lunch. Jimbo said, "Don't worry about a thing." I broke all the rules and had a glass of wine. I just felt like loosening up a little. We arrived at the high school in Lebanon where the fights were being held. It was a pro/amateur card. This was not the high time of Las Vegas. Five amateur fights and two pro. I'd never entered anything that hokey before. I had fallen in the boxing world. I was falling in the business world. I was Humpty Dumpty. Did I even want to put myself together again?

At the weigh-in I was 147 in my underwear. My opponent was 142 in his hiking boots and his ski parka with rocks in the pockets. He probably actually only weighed about 135 pounds. Jimbo came over to me and said, "Your opponent was knocked out last night in Pennsylvania."

"By who?" I asked.

"Some kid who won the Gloves twice," he said.

"Don't you get suspended for three months when you get knocked out?" I asked.

"Don't worry, he fought under another name," Jimbo said.

This was bad news. If I knocked this chump out and the press found out that he was knocked out the night before, I'd look like a complete phony.

"I don't think I should fight," I said to Bruce.

A well-known boxing journalist, Jack Obermeyer, came into the locker room. "Hey, David. I didn't know you were on the card tonight," he said. I couldn't believe that I was famous enough for Jack Obermeyer to recognize me. I loved it.

Now I knew I shouldn't fight. If Jack wrote about this fight Bruce would get in trouble with the New York commission for setting the fight up for me and I'd get in trouble for fighting a guy who was knocked out last night. Why'd they get me this guy? I didn't care much about rules but even I didn't think this was right.

"I just drove up from Pennsylvania," Jack said. "I was at the fights down there."

I was dead. He'd recognize my opponent and know that he was fighting when he should have been suspended. How many laws did I want to break? How many times was I setting myself up to be caught? Bruce and I slipped out to the men's room.

"Go back to the locker room and get my stuff," I told Bruce. "Tell the refs I came down with a migraine. I'll run out to the car." I jetted out the door in my boxing shorts and ran through a snowstorm in the parking lot. It was a spectacular scene with the snow falling down on my bare legs. I was freezing. But I was laughing at the ridiculousness of the situation as I sneaked through the snow. Bruce met me at the Rolls, carrying my clothes from the locker room. After I changed in the back seat, I started the car. We slowly left the parking lot and drove back to New York City. It took us six hours. I hated to miss the opportunity to fight but I didn't want to ruin Bruce's reputation and mine in one night. It was getting harder and harder to fight. It was like boxing was a woman; we were breaking up and I was caught in nostalgia, sadness, and old sweaters.

●●●

I got a call from Jeff Greenberg. He was the son of Hank Greenberg, the CEO of A.I.G., who had been reported in *Newsweek* as the toughest businessman in New York. Tough? How? What? The only toughness I respected was in the ring. I could knock Hank out in ten seconds. Not that I would. He was always nice to me.

Jeff had heard rumors about Kelly having problems in Delaware and told me to fire him or he'd have to close my account. When I told Kelly I had to fire him he said, "I didn't do anything."

"You got us into our Delaware problems," I said.

"Send my salary home," he said. "I'll work from there."

"I'll pay you three thousand dollars a week plus your car and insurance," I said. "But I don't want you doing any work."

"Okay, but I don't want my wife to know what I'm earning," he said. "I'll come into the city and pick up my three thousand dollars every Friday."

"You can do whatever you want with your money," I said. "Now pack up your things before Greenberg sees you around here."

David's second CD which charted in the clubs in the midwest ahead of artists like Fat Joe, Ol' Dirty Bastard, and Cypress Hill

31

BRAFMAN HAD MADE a deal with the prosecutor in Delaware that he would not close down my office in New York, since all the checks had been cashed in Delaware. Nevertheless, in the beginning of June, thirty FBI agents descended on my office at 120 Wall Street and confiscated every file in the place. This was some sort of Israeli commando shit. Some had their guns showing. Like they'd shoot a tax evader? Like I cared? The raid was exciting.

I was a big time, muck-a-muck gangsta. My father and I sneaked downstairs and took the Rolls up to Ben Brafman's office.

"Don't worry, I'll handle this," Brafman said. He called the prosecutor, Falgowski, in Delaware, whom he spoke to for five minutes and then hung up and said, "Falgowski didn't orchestrate the raid. It was the New York Feds."

"So?" I asked.

"Falgowski kept his word," Brafman said.

"We're dead. It will be all over the street within minutes," I said.

"A little more bad news. Cramer has become a federal witness against you. He's been wearing a wire for the last few months and he's getting a 5K Letter to keep him out of jail when he rats you out," Brafman said.

I smiled. What else was there to do? Things had gotten so bad it would have been redundant to get upset. The afternoon had become depressive and humid, the whole atmosphere had gone heavy on me.

When we walked out the door and into the elevator Dad said, "You and your lawyer are ruining us. Hire someone new."

"It's too late," I said. Besides, I liked Ben. Perhaps I was ready for jail. Even though I didn't believe in God I kind of believed that a spirit was watching over me. Let's call him the Absent God. See, the Absent God kept me exhausted so that going to jail seemed better to me than running around trying to save my ass in the free world. It's kind of what I felt about dying. The Absent God gives you a nice disease so that you suffer and are happy to die to get away from the pain. It's all planned in a world without plans. It's accepting contradictions that gives you peace. It's an alternative to stultifying and antiquated Bibles.

•••

I was moving more and more into the blue-collar world of boxers and rappers. My old lifestyle was disappearing. I was going to be sentenced to jail and I'd be gone. I had to finish my *Boxer Rebellion* movie before I went to the joint. I felt I could carve out a future with all my new careers— boxing, rapping, and acting. Fuck insurance.

There was no money coming into my business and I

had to cut back on expenses. I fired my Indian driver, Rom. I had no choice. I was broke. I wasn't even working. I felt terrible. I really liked him. I gave him a month's severance. I went to Carriage House and gave them back their Rolls. They told me I still owed forty thousand dollars on the lease. I told them I was about to go bust and go to jail and I'd give them ten thousand dollars to take the car back. They did.

●●●

Without a chauffeur it was too much of a pain in the ass to go over to Gleason's. I hadn't been on a subway in twenty-five years and was afraid to start going on one again now. I could get lost. I could lose my delusions of grandeur and think I was one of the commuting people. Gleason's would just have to go on hold. One day, maybe, I'd be back.

I started going to Kingsway Gym at 40th Street. I paid Chuck's dues and he came there to spar with me. "Please don't break my nose again," I said. "I have enough problems." I felt like a traitor to Hector and Bruce training at Kingsway but I didn't have much of a choice.

Michael Olajide, Sr. owned the gym. "I'm good friends with your son," I said.

"Oh," he said. He didn't like his son.

My new ritual was to jog from 72nd Street to Kingsway Gym, work out and take a cab home. A couple of times a week I'd run into Geraldo Rivera at the gym. He'd show up in the morning with a trainer and work out. He never sparred. Although I had seen him on television sparring. He was pretty good. He didn't say hello to me. He didn't know me. I wanted to be on his show.

251

32

I WENT TO Delaware to sign my plea bargain. I got twelve to eighteen months subject to the probation officer's report. Kelly got twenty-four to thirty-two months.

Before I went to jail I had to meet with my probation officer. So he could get a sense of me. He was a young black guy who seemed fairly cool. He was very interested in my rapping and boxing. He said, "I have a cousin who raps." We were both part of black culture. I was sure he'd go easy on me. Maybe we could get together and go to a rap concert some day.

A week later Brafman called me to his office. He got a report from the probation officer. "Your probation officer raised your sentence based on your role in the offense. He called you, 'a kingpin.' He boosted you from twenty-four to thirty-two months; Kelly's parole officer raised him from thirty-two to forty-two months."

"Ben. I'm not ratting. But this thing was Kelly's crime. I didn't even know what he was doing in Delaware," I said. "Look. I don't really give a shit about the increase in my sentence but I was no kingpin. I had no major role in the offense. It's principle. I definitely did not mastermind this crime. This was a crime done by Kelly against me, taking my checks and laundering them. Not to mention the other checks he and Cramer colluded with each other to steal from me."

Brafman looked bored. He knew that the truth had nothing to do with the legal process. That I was fighting windmills. I didn't stand a chance.

"We'll ask for a hearing at the sentencing," Brafman said. "We should be able to argue against your role as kingpin. But Kelly has no case. He's guilty as sin."

"I don't give a shit about Kelly. He was the kingpin. He deserves what he gets," I said. That little fuck had ruined my life. I had been so stupidly trusting. "I can't respect a punishment that's wrong. The government is more corrupt than I am," I said. Rah, rah for my politics and sense of the injustices done against me. I was still a crook.

Or was I really a crook? Most of my money was made from straight-up insurance placements. I took roughly ten percent commissions on my placements. The accounts where I charged extra fees, I made the brokers get fee agreements from their clients. It might not have been ethical to get such huge fees but it was legal. My only mistake was letting Kelly get me involved with the check cashing. If I weren't boxing all the time, I might have paid more attention to that.

●●●

It was Saturday and I decided to take a cab over to Brooklyn to train at Gleason's. I hadn't been there in a while.
Bruce gave me some good news: "I got you on a fight card
in Madrid."

I loved it. One last fight before I went off to jail. I
wanted to feel tough when they locked me up. On a high.
Ready to beat the shit out of anyone who started in with
me. If any predator came near me I'd kill him without
thinking twice about it. I was pumped. I was Awesome. But
I knew Lauren wouldn't want me to fight in Spain. She'd
never let me go to Madrid. She'd call the promotors and
have me taken off the card. I tried to throw her off the
track and told her, "They got me a fight in Berlin."

"Fuck you you do," she said.

I figured there was nothing she could do to stop me.
She didn't even know where the real fight was. She'd
never find the promotors.

The next Saturday I went back to Gleason's. Bruce
gave me some bad news, "Your wife called Randy Gordon
at the boxing commission about the fights. Randy found
the promotor and told him if he doesn't take you off the
card they won't let him bring any more fighters into New
York."

That was it for me. I didn't know how she tracked the
promotor down after I told her the fights were in Berlin
but she was like a hunting dog. She'd get a whiff of one of
my mistakes and she'd attack. My fight career was over.
Some people would say my wife was looking out for my
health. But right now I had more problems with my men-

tal stability than with my health. I needed some event to feel good about myself. She had no right to interfere. She had some sort of symbiotic attachment to me where she felt she had the right to control me. She was trying to do good but she hurt me a lot more than a left hook ever could. It's not bruises that hurt a man. It's a sense of failure and not being recognized. How could she understand this? All she wanted to do was dine politely at Le Cirque and attend charity balls in Couture dresses. She wanted me as I was, not how I had become.

•••

I kept pressing on with my rap career. I was spending a fortune trying to get it underway. I went to the Village to shoot a video for another song I wrote, "Hymietown." This was my fourth video and I had no record sales. But I figured I might as well spend the money before the government took it from me anyhow. For an ex-businessman I was acting like an idiot. My wife was furious at me that I was spending my time on my rap and not saving my business. She felt I didn't care about her and our son. She didn't understand that the business was dead. That this crazy rap project was my one chance of salvaging our finances. That even if I was obsessive, I wanted to keep juggling. I wanted to keep all the balls in the air. I was attached to my life. I didn't want it to fall on the circus floor.

I went to lawyers and asked them how I could hide money offshore. No one would give me a clear answer. Either they didn't know or they didn't want to be accomplices.

33

BACK IN DELAWARE the leaves were turning. It was 1993. It was a good year to get sentenced. Why not? I had turned my back against my failures and was looking optimistically into the future. I was going to make the most out of jail. I thought of all the money I had thrown away on excess. I thought of medieval dramas where money was considered filth or dreck. I forgot the names of the plays. I wanted to get rid of dirty, unethical paper. I was a moral crook. I was the clean-up man. A saint.

Prosecutor Falgowski was in his glory. He got off on misinterpreting me. He was an ambitious fuck with slicked-back hair. The bastard had five children on a prosecutor's salary. You figure he had to be stealing to support them. I wished I knew how to get to him. I would have paid him off. One day he would probably end up behind bars. But for now he was the voice of morality. The government's proxy.

Brafman made a speech about what a genius I was and how I should get the low end of the sentence—twenty-four months. I was impressed. I loved being called a genius. But Falgowski jumped in and said, "He's a kingpin. He's rich. He drives a Rolls Royce. Give him the maximum, thirty-six months."

The logic of that eluded me. It would be bad advertising for Rolls Royce to suggest that owning one meant you got a longer jail sentence.

"Twenty-four months," Judge Latchum said and banged his gavel on his desk.

Kelly got the low end of his sentence too, thirty-two months.

Well, that was that. At the train station I said to Brafman, "I don't care about the twenty-four months but I'm not going to be considered a kingpin in something I knew nothing about. I'm no head of a gay money-laundering ring. You have to appeal."

"Appeals have less than a ten percent chance," he said.

"I don't care. What's right is right."

"It's going to be expensive—$20,000."

"Just do it," I said.

I was throwing more money away. It was like I wanted to get rid of it all before the government got me for back taxes. I'd rather piss it away than have it yanked from me. Maybe I would have been better off giving it to them and getting them off my back. No way. They fucked me. I was going to fuck them back. I'd kill the bastards. But I knew I couldn't do that. It was crazy. You couldn't win against the government. They had a royal flush and I was staring at deuces, fours, and fives.

My movie was finally ready for its premiere. Angela showed *Boxer Rebellion* at Du Arts Studio. I invited about fifty friends. Lauren refused to go. She hated Angela and thought she was robbing from me. She was. It didn't matter to me. She still bore a grudge against her because of a food fight they had at a Japanese restaurant in L.A. We had gone there to do some work on the sound track to the film. My wife had come along to try to get closer to me before I left for jail. Angela threw a piece of tempura at my wife. My wife threw tuna roll. Angela walked out. I should have thrown her out. She felt Angela was taking advantage of me and encouraging me to put all my money into my film. Lauren had called her a thief.

The movie had cost me about three-hundred-and-fifty-thousand dollars and now ran about an hour and ten minutes long. It was a feature. Featuring me, financed by me—my greatest fan.

"I'm going to jail in a few weeks. Can't you quit fighting with me and come to the opening of my movie?" I said.

"You're the one fighting," Lauren said. "I want nothing to do with your movie."

Michael Kaplan showed up at the screening and gave me a copy of the *Men's Journal* article he wrote about me. It would be out in the November issue while I was in jail. It opened with a quote of mine, "I just want to kill a man." I loved it. That was the goal of boxing. Its apotheosis was murder. The white-collar boxers who took it up for exercise were jerking themselves off. Idiot softies didn't understand that or looked down on that. It was like hating a fisherman for wanting to catch a fish. The natural conclusion of fishing was a delicious tuna steak. The optimal result of fighting was to see your opponent lying dead on the canvas. There was truth in a box full of bones. The finish line is skeletal.

Jake LaMotta was in the audience with a bunch of my boxing and rapping cronies. I identified with him. He liked to get beaten up too. I sat with my son, brother, and parents. I was worried that my movie would be some corny crap and I would be embarrassed. But from the moment it started with its grainy black and white thirty-five millimeter film I knew that it was going to be good. The idiot Jean Marie had somehow done a beautiful musical score to it. It was the first serious picture about boxing that went outside the clichés.

The movie was painfully serious. It was a ballet of violence like a John Woo film. Only the crusty anger was real. At the end everyone applauded me and told me how much they loved it. Then Angela gave me the good news, "We got into the Sundance Film Festival." What a break! I felt like I might have a future in film when I got out of jail. If so, then it was worth being sentenced. I was sick of insurance anyway. Time I did something I loved.

When I got home I told my wife that I got into Sundance.

"Who did you pay off?" she asked.

I got a letter from the Federal Prison System notifying me that I had been assigned to Schuylkill Federal Prison Camp in Pennsylvania. So was Kelly.

Everywhere you looked there were posters of my album. I spent eighteen thousand dollars to hang them in New York, Beverly Hills, Chicago, Dallas, and Philadelphia. My promotions were in place. And the *Renegade Jew* album was ready. The only problem was I couldn't find it in the stores. I spoke to Billy at Rude Boy. He called his distributor who kept coming up with excuses for why it wasn't in the stores. He said, "None of the stores want to take it because it has 'Jew' in the title." I found that difficult to believe when there was a group out called Niggas with Attitude. I figured I'd make the album famous so that the stores were forced to carry it. I spent twenty-one thousand dollars to give away a CD of *Renegade Jew* attached to the cover of *Spin* magazine throughout Long Island. I was panicking. I was committing financial suicide.

•••

Jean, my young black producer Billy and I decided to throw a party for my going to jail. We called it the "Renegade Jew Lock Down Party." It was held at Club Indigo on the West Side. I hired Crazy Sam to film it. Celebrating going off to jail like it was a vacation or a great treat amused me. I hated crybabies. You got to roll with the punches.

My wife showed up for the party. Afterwards, we went with Billy next store to the Paramount Hotel for drinks. It was one of those trendy, Ian Schrager hotels for the dickheads from my prior life. I made out about sixty thousand dollars worth of checks to *Vibe, The Source,* etc. for advertising. I gave seven thousand dollars to Jack Goose, a friend of Billy's, who was supposed to get my video of "Renegade Jew" on the *Box.* Lauren watched in horror. When Billy went to the bathroom she said, "You should give that money to me. You're throwing it down the sewer."

"And what would giving it to you do for me?" I asked. "Besides, I have thousands of dollars in the bank for you. You own your art and jewelry. You own the apartment. I'll pay Graham's tuition and your maintenance for the next two years up front."

Didn't she understand that rap was my one real shot at a career? This and the documentary movie about my boxing. I had to promote them. That's all I had. I was desperate, I was trapped. Maybe I was panicking? I didn't feel it. I was calm. I would work it all out my way. I was feeling too old and beat up to make money fighting.

34

I HAD NEVER been to jail before. I didn't come from that kind of family. My relatives felt ashamed when they got a speeding ticket. We were Jewish. Guilty. Afraid that if misdemeanors would pave the path to hell then felonies would get us there at the speed of light. Not that tax evasion was much of a felony. Legally it was, but ethically it was no big deal to me. It's not like I had killed or raped anyone. I wasn't going to let jail get me down. If I had a choice of making jail a downer or an upper, I was going to make it an upper. Rather than to define myself by it I would use it as an experience to round myself out.

I self-surrendered to Schuylkill Federal Prison Camp in Pennsylvania on November 4, 1993. My parents drove me. My mother tried to keep me from worrying so we all sang camp songs, "A Hundred Bottles of Beer on the Wall" and "The Bear Went Over the Mountain." It was fun. I was looking forward to jail. I knew I wasn't supposed to. I was supposed to be afraid. I know the things I'd been involved in were contradictions but I was all about contradictions.

I blossomed in the clash of my personalities. I didn't think of myself as a tough guy but I could fight.

After the induction to the prison camp, including a rather embarrassing strip-search, a CO named Grady showed me to my dorm. I was on the third floor, the Ghetto. They threw new white prisoners in there to shock them. I didn't care. Outside of white business people, most of my friends were black rappers and Hispanic boxers. I entered a long narrow room with thirty small cubicles in which were jammed double bunk beds. Grady stopped at a cubicle that was inhabited by a Mexican.

"Julio. This is Lawrence," he said and left us alone.

"First time?" Julio asked me.

"How could you tell?"

Julio smiled and pointed to a picture of his Harley Davidson motorcycle on the wall and said, "I love that bike."

"Beautiful," I said. I didn't mean it. I had no respect for Harleys. The Japanese bikes were built for speed. I actually preferred dirt bikes. You had to be an athlete to fly off the bumps and skid around the turns. It was a little like ski racing. I missed my motocross bike and my home in West Hampton.

My mind was racing. I made an effort to calm down. Why was I always making judgments? I'd hate a person because of the kind of bike he rode, then I'd love that same person because he lifted weights with me or was funny. I had to beat my extremes down into a paste and blend them. I'd use my moods as icing on a cake. My cellmate, Julio, seemed like a nice guy. I didn't have to diss him. I could like him. I did.

A stocky black guy with a shaved head from the next cubicle came over to me with a copy of the *Source*. It was the king of hip-hop magazines. He opened it to an ad with my picture on it.

"That you, man?"

"That's right."

"Holy shit. The Renegade Jew's in the house."

I was the instant hit of the Ghetto. The black prisoners give props to the rappers. Criminals love celebrities. My wife criticized the money I spent on ads. Now it was paying off. I had foresight. I was a star in jail. I had lost my reputation in business society but I had gained it back in the joint. Not only was I a rapper, I was a boxer. Boxers were kings in jail.

A Puerto Rican came over to me and said, "Didn't I see you fight Rodriguez on television?"

"Tuesday Night Fights. Sean O'Grady announced," I said.

"You were the best, man. Knocked him out, right?"

"Second round."

He slapped me a high five.

"What was your ring name again?"

"Awesome."

"That's right. You're the fighter with the Rolls."

"Lost the Rolls," I said.

"It's probably under your wife's name," he laughed, figuring I was a clever business bastard rather than a schmuck. He high-fived me again.

Back in the business world I was a lowlife but in jail I was the man. A lot of the guys had seen me box on television. And all the brothers had seen the *Renegade Jew* ads in the *Source* and *Vibe*. Word was going around the joint, the Renegade Jew was in the house.

Men's Journal was out and was being circulated around the prison. I was glad that they had quoted me saying I wanted to kill someone. It gave me props. I belonged in a place like this, where I got status for being a good fighter. I was happier in prison than I was on the outside. The pressure was off me and I was respected. Respect in prison was the equivalent of riches in the outside world.

There wasn't much room to change in my cube so I stepped out into the aisle to get into my sweat pants. I saw a tall, muscle-bound black with one glass eye staring at me. What was he looking at! When I stepped back into my cube Julio said, "Never change in the aisle. The fags think you want it."

"Want what?" I said.

"It. Up your ass."

"Screw him. I'd shank his good eye," I said.

I meant it. I'd die before anyone touched me. I wasn't afraid to die. And I wasn't afraid to kill. When I was sixteen I tried to kill my best friend by beating his head in with a rock. I don't remember why. I think he had called me chicken. My jacket was covered in blood. I would have killed him if the police hadn't pulled me off him. Should I feel bad about that? I don't know. I was sixteen. It's not that I was really trying to kill him. I just wanted to scare him. What choice did I have? He was dangerous. He claimed he knew French foot fighting. He would have killed me. That's why I had to crack his skull and break three of his fingers.

I was getting worked up about nothing. The one-eyed black punk hadn't started in with me. This joint was only a minimum-security prison camp. You had to be non-violent to get in here. At least you had to have no violence on your record. It wasn't like across the street at the medium facility where the sentences averaged twenty-five years. I was glad I wasn't there. I could handle it but my credentials weren't good enough. To get respect there I would have had to import a few kilos or kill someone. I wasn't about killing. I was a lousy tax evader. All I had going for me was my boxing and rapping. It was enough in Schuylkill Federal Prison Camp. Not in the Medium Correctional Institute.

I made friends with two mobsters from South Boston—Pauli Moore and the Coach. They both had boxing backgrounds. Boxers stuck together. Coach had twenty pro fights a couple of decades ago. He held the record for the fastest knockout at the Boston Garden. Pauli Moore was a killing machine. He was a strong light heavyweight amateur boxer in Boston. One of Marvin Hagler's regular sparring partners. He was also an expert in karate and Kung Fu. He and Coach worked for the Whitey Bulger mob. It was about as notorious as John Gotti's crew in New York. Pauli loan-sharked and bounced at some of the clubs. He was doing ten years for cocaine conspiracy. I had a feeling he did hits for Whitey. But that was just a feeling. Pauli and I ran miles every day on the track. There was a heavy bag and speed bag outdoors in a pagoda near the track. We took turns hitting it. He was a strong lefty. The heavy bag made loud thuds when he hit it with his straight left. He had real knockout power. Sometimes the Coach stood around and advised us. He had a bad back so he didn't exercise much.

Then there were all the punks who walked around talking about their street fights. They were full of shit. They probably had a couple of fights in their lives. I had fought over a thousand fights in the gym. These were the kind of creeps who would bang someone over the back of the head with a baseball bat and brag about how brave they were.

Pauli and I taught a bunch of the other inmates to hit the bags. We formed a little group. The punks never came up to the bags. They were afraid to show they didn't know shit. They'd rather boast about fights they never had.

•••

The administration moved me from the Ghetto to Dorm 2. They figured I'd be thankful to leave the Black and Hispanic dorm. I wasn't.

They put me with a Connecticut banker, Marcel. He was a classy guy who used to drive a Ferrari. He stole some money from Portugal or somewhere.

After a few months he was transferred and they moved in a guy named Spike. He was small time. His occupation was check-kiting. After a few months he told me that he was gay and was in love with another prisoner. I didn't want to be rooming with a gay. I thought the other cons might think I was gay by association. I didn't want to be chasing off fags who mistook me for one of their kind. Hanging with gays on the outside is quizzical. On the inside, it is dangerous. As it was, Kelly was in the joint and I kept hoping he wouldn't reveal that he was gay. It was probably all right. He was always secretive about that. It took me years to know.

Spike was a real short-termer and I was glad when they released him after a couple of months.

Next they moved an ex-marine, Billy Schoener, in with me. He was a strong guy who used to work out sometimes with Paulie and me. We had a real good rapport and used to laugh a lot and philosophize. He was doing ten years for manufacturing crystal meth. He was a solid roommate. Tough but quiet and firm. He looked all-American.

•••

Angela wrote me that *Boxer Rebellion* was a big hit at Sundance. She told me to get ready for reporters to interview me in jail. She was expecting a distribution deal any moment. Nothing happened. I kept looking around the corner of my dormitory building for reporters but they never showed up. All that arrived was snow. It snowed every day in Schuylkill during the winter of '94. Five feet of snow was piled up against the side of the buildings. I slept on the first floor and couldn't see out of my window until April. The guys in landscaping had to shovel the walks throughout the night. I felt like I was in jail in Siberia.

•••

I started writing screenplays every day. I structured my time eagerly. I wrote, read movie scripts, rapped, worked, or lifted weights eighteen hours a day. It was as if I was getting a college degree with a split major in physical education and creative writing. I hit the heavy bag in the hope of getting a fight when I came out. I was always training. I was afraid my opponent would be in better shape than me even when I didn't have an opponent. I scheduled my whole day. I timed everything on a Timex Indiglo Ironman watch I bought at the commissary in prison. I used to wear a Rolex or a Cartier Panther. My Timex was so much better. It was digital and had a stopwatch.

●●●

Jail was a planet inhabited by porno magazines. There were *Hustler Magazines* and *Penthouses* all over the place. I didn't like them. I found the pictures of the vagina too graphic. It made it look that it was independent of the woman, that the cunt was in medias res. I didn't want a cunt. I wanted a woman. I made a vow to myself that I would deal with the total person, not her parts. And where better to start than my wife? I always loved her. My cold acts were expressions of anger towards her. The anger was disappointed love. It was not distance; it was closeness. I was still very much involved with her. The porno pictures disgusted me rather than excited me. I was not interested in the pornographic parts of a woman except in how they related to her personality. Circumstances were maturing me.

In May, Angela wrote me again. Good news. *Boxer Rebellion* made it into the Vienna Film Festival. She wanted me to send her some money so she could travel over there. Didn't she get the picture? I was no longer a rich businessman. I was a broken-down loser in jail. I had given her her shot in the movie business. Couldn't she leave me alone? I couldn't afford to get suckered anymore. It hurt my feelings that she'd think of me that way. Whatever I had left I needed for my future. I was glad we got into another festival. Still, I had nothing left to give.

•••

Lauren phoned the prison psychiatrist, who called me into his office. "Your wife called. She says she could be your psychoanalyst."

"Whatever," I said.

"Anyhow, she says you're manic depressive. I'm going to put you on lithium," the psychiatrist said.

"I don't need lithium. I'm not manic-depressive. She's nuts."

"I think she's right," the psychiatrist said.

"Based on what?" I said. "I want to be put in the Federal Wife Protection Program. She's out to get me."

"Very funny," he said. "I'm prescribing the pills. You do what you want with them."

I picked up the pills the next morning at the medical office. I took them for a month and then quit. They did nothing for me. Or at least nothing dramatic enough for me to notice.

•••

Bad news came in from Angela. She sent me a letter that she was in jail in France for smuggling an ounce of heroin in from Amsterdam. She didn't know how long they'd keep her. Now two of us were in jail. What a bad luck film. It looked like her husband, Jean Marie, would have to represent our movie at the Vienna Film Festival. He was a nice guy but he lacked focus. He'd never be able to negotiate a distribution deal for the film. I would have been really depressed but I was cut off from the outside world. It had nothing to do with me. What mattered to me was what went on inside the jail. My first job there was in landscaping. It sucked and required eight hours a day. My goal was to get a job with minimal hours so that I could spend my time working out and writing. I attended Muslim services twice a week and Jewish services once a week in order to get out of landscaping. Everybody thought I was a religious guy, what with going to services all the time, but when I was transferred to the kitchen to do salad prep I rapidly became an atheist again and dropped out of religious services.

After a few months I was delighted when I moved from my job in salad prep to dish washing. The hours were better. In addition to writing screenplays, I started writing a book of poems about prison. I felt like I was in a writer's workshop.

Every weekend Kelly's freakin' family treked out to Pennsylvania to see him. My parents came every couple of weeks. I didn't want them to come more than that. It was an inconvenience for them to drive three-and-one-half hours each way. My wife only came twice the whole time I was there. In typical style she'd show up ten minutes before the visiting room closed. "Why didn't you bring my son?" I asked.

"You're a felon," she said. "You and your friends are not a good influence on him." Lauren wanted to take control of my son and use him as a weapon against me. I couldn't defend myself from jail.

Lauren looked scornfully around the visiting room at the other prisoners. She hated us. We were failures. She thought she was a success even though she had not yet accomplished anything. She pointed to a scruffy, fat convict near us and said, "How come they don't make him shave?" His wife was hugging him.

"It's not a school for good grooming," I said. "If you dress right you act right," she said. "At least you're wearing khaki. It's big with Ralph Lauren this year. You look better than you did on the outside with your purple hip-hop clothes."

We all looked like boy scouts in our khaki outfits. We were puppets in a children's show. "You're the only wife who doesn't visit," I said. I felt ignored.

"I can't get up that early in the morning. It's a long drive," she said.

"All the other wives do it," I said.

"You left me high and dry," she said. "I can't afford a long distance taxi."

"I left you more than the other wives got," I said. "There are wives here who are on food stamps."

"You need more lithium," she said. She didn't know that I had completely stopped taking it.

"Have you seen my album in any record stores?" I asked. I wondered if Jean was able to get the distributor to do his job.

"If you rap or box when you get out we're finished."

"What do you expect me to do when I get out? Run a bank?" I said. The guard came around and said that the visiting room was closing. My wife had only been there ten minutes but she gave me my first headache in jail. I couldn't wait for her to go. She kissed me on the cheek and I felt like an icicle had stabbed me. I was glad to see her leave. But strangely I had not written her off. I would finesse her. I'd get her to cooperate with me. How? I didn't know. I was in love. I was in hate. I was stupid.

●●●

I called Gleason's from jail every few days to speak to Bruce. He somehow made me feel connected to my old life. The gym was my home.

"When I get out I'm fighting," I said. The thought of returning to the ring helped to keep me optimistic and pass the time.

Tuesday nights I watched *USA Fights* on television in the rec room with the other convicts. All my friends from Gleason's were fighting. I watched Barkley, McGirt, Jake "the Snake" Rodriquez, Curtis Summit, Terry Southerland, and Glenwood "the Real Beast" Brown. I knew all the refs and the cornermen. I saw Hector, Stan Gold, Al Gavin, Pete Jackson, Teddy Atlas, and Joe Cortez. I realized I really was part of the inner circle of boxing. I knew almost everyone on television. I guess it was a lot more than a hobby. It was a lifestyle. I had lived it.

I had come into it from left field and found myself rallying around home plate. The fighters were my family. And now I had another new family. I was related to all the other prisoners who were sharing my degradation. We were made close by our humiliation. I was accomplishing a lot. I had arrived at the bottom of society but I felt like I had reached the top.

●●●

When I called home my father said, "Your mom has ovarian cancer. We won't be visiting for a while." She needed an operation. My mother got on the phone and said, "Don't worry. I'll be all right." I didn't know anything about ovarian cancer. I figured it was curable.

My mother was operated on and spent five days in the hospital recuperating. Then she was sent home. I spoke to her on the phone. "I'm sorry I can't visit you," she said.

My eyes filled with tears. She was thinking of me rather than herself. You can only count on a mother's love.

I called home and asked my wife if she'd visit me with Graham. I was feeling a little soft what with my mother being sick and all. Lauren said, "Jail isn't a place for children."

"It's just a visit. They're not locking him up."

"Perish the thought," she said, and hung up the phone.

Maybe it was better that he didn't come. I didn't want to miss him. I didn't want to be reminded that I was human. I wanted to be hard, a con, a contradiction.

●●●

Boxer Rebellion opened at the Vienna Film Festival. Angela was still in jail. Jean Marie wrote me that we were a hit. He said he'd let me know about a European distributor. A couple of weeks passed and there was no news. In the meantime the Feds came up to visit Kelly in jail and he turned State's Evidence against my brother, me, and some other clients. I wasn't giving him any money so there was no sense in his keeping mum. It's ironic that he used to brag that he'd never snitch and now he ratted out everyone he could think of. He made up crimes. He told them about phony losses and bribing underwriters.

The Feds moved Kelly to the new Federal jail in Brooklyn where he spilled his guts out. It all came down to a pile of peeved bullshit. The Feds already knew most of it. And the rest couldn't be proved. Cramer had already fingered my brother. And they already had me in jail so there was nothing more they could do to me. Still, the Feds loved their snitches. They released Kelly two-and-a-half years early for cooperating with them. Cramer never served a day. My sentence remained at two years. I was a victim, a dupe, a sucker. I did the most time. I lost my business. Kelly and Cramer never owned anything to lose. My brother got stuck with a felony, thanks mostly to Cramer, and had to do three hundred hours community service. They got him on some phony mail fraud charge for sending some inaccurate loss run through the US Postal System. Big deal! It was a throw-in. It had nothing to do with the tax evasion scheme Kelly, Cramer, and I were busted for.

•••

Like I said, my first winter in Schuylkill it snowed everyday for almost four months. I had never seen so much snow. It rose up the side of the buildings so that the first floor windows were covered. I felt like I was tucked into a freezer among the peas and carrots. When I traipsed around in the snow I felt like I was a penguin in the arctic. I expected to get together with my brother penguins and sing Christmas carols. I was a cartoon that was drained of color. I was white borders.

Even the track was closed down. At Christmas some of the other prisoners built a snowman. One night someone knocked the snowman down and shit on it. It wasn't me. I think it was this doof, Ritchie. Everyone hated Ritchie. Except me. Maybe I liked him because everyone else hated him. I felt sorry for him. He was a nerd. He believed in Ayn Rand and was a big libertarian. I didn't know much about libertarianism but it seemed opposite to state authoritarianism where the government locks you up. It was definitely different from fascism, communism, and big government.

I hung around with him to protect him. People knew I was a boxer and I figured they wouldn't want to mess with me so they wouldn't mess with my friend, Ritchie. Then there were those who wanted to mess with me just to see if they could take me. One day a young mafia type screamed at Ritchie in front of me. I didn't do anything. Perhaps if he had hit Ritchie I would have interfered but I just wasn't good at inciting confrontations. I liked to stay out of the fray if I could. I didn't want to get locked up in solitary.

Ritchie was doing two years for selling guns. He believed in our inalienable right to carry guns. He was an intellectual with no college education. He was smarter than most of the prisoners but he was warped. He was gifted with a small brain and he had used most of it up trying to hang onto libertarian theories of free thought. His having pretenses of intellect at least showed he respected the brain. The other guys didn't even know they had brains. They had no sense of introspection. They never looked inside themselves to see what was there. They were too busy shoplifting capers and excuses from the outside world.

Behind the administration building there was a ploughed driveway that led down to the road. It was only a couple hundred yards long. I pretended it was the six-mile loop in Central Park. Every day I ran up and down it for an hour to get my running in while the track was closed for the winter. I had no idea how much distance I did. But I did my hour.

The heavy bag was taken down because of the snow. So I shadowboxed for an hour each morning. I broke it into six-minute rounds and timed them on my Timex. I'd shadowbox in the snowdrifts to give my legs extra exercise. I felt like Rocky Balboa training in the snow to fight Ivan Drago, the Russian, in *Rocky IV.* I sweated buckets even when it was below zero. I once punched myself in the nose so I could drip a little blood onto the snow. I felt like I used to feel at Gleason's when I'd look at the white canvas of the ring and see splotches of blood on it. I bobbed and weaved. I caught snowflakes on my tongue. I laughed.

A lot of my fellow prisoners complained that they couldn't take the snow anymore, that they felt they were imprisoned in Siberia, that they wanted to transfer to a prison camp in Florida. I wasn't one of them.

In April the winter began to disappear. The Poconos were still burdened with substantial patches of snow but the cons would be sitting out in front of their dorms in shorts with sunglasses, sunbathing. It reminded me of spring skiing at Aspen, when all the stunning girls were standing outside of the mid-mountain lodge, sunning themselves and snacking.

This snowy winter in Schuylkill was not the winter of my discontent. It was the content of my self-discovery. I had nothing to complain about. The jail had taken away my freedom but the winter had given it back to me. I was trekking through the endless snowdrifts of my mind. I had the time to look into myself and discover that I was a season unto myself, that I was December, January, February, March and that I could disappear into the daily snowstorms whenever I wanted. That every morning I could wake up to find that the snow was falling again. That every night I could go to sleep with a blanket of snow covering the stars.

●●●

My roommate, Billy Schoener, was transferred to Allenwood. I got a new bunkie, Eddie Nicolace. There was something about cellies that made them relatives. It didn't matter whether they were stupid or not; they were still blood. I felt like we were in summer camp together.

Kelly and I were getting less friendly. I constantly heard rumors about his bad mouthing me. I stayed away from him. If I hit him I'd get slapped with another charge. Also I was afraid one of his mob friends might stab me. I shouldn't have been afraid. That was a weakness. But he hung out mostly with Italians who sat around talking about spaghetti sauces and stealing from the kitchen so they could get fatter.

Prisoners have no character. They don't realize that they've fallen from grace and that they're supposed to be treated like shit. They think they're deserving of some special treatment. They look tough but they're not. I preferred the guards. They did their shitty jobs and didn't complain. They were fair, impartial, and efficient. They were sentenced to life. They worked here with a bunch of losers until they retired. When the blacks said that the guards were racist I couldn't help but laugh. These federal bureaucrats were too afraid to mistreat any race. None of us even existed for them. The only color they saw was the neutral tint of their own indifference.

Looking at the men around me, I was disappointed in my gender. No wonder there were so many lesbians. We were a bunch of farting, belching, cursing slobs. We stank as a sex.

●●●

An alarm sounded throughout the prison camp and we were all called back to our dorms. This was not unusual. It happened about once a week when there was a stabbing next door at the Schuylkill Medium Facility.

I never understood why these guys used to hurt each other. Many of them were doing thirty years. Why would they want to make it any harder on themselves? My friend Pauli, who was doing ten years, said they had nothing to lose. What was the difference if they got a few more years?

I could see why prisoners had such a bad rep. I was embarrassed to be one of these idiots. Because I was so disappointed in the lack of principles around me, I made up my mind to be a model prisoner. I became Alec Guinness in *The Bridge Over The River Kwai*. I identified with the cops. I had no sympathy for the cons.

Eddie came back into our cube. He was my last cellie, a pot dealer from Rhode Island.

Everybody thought Eddie was a dummy. I didn't care. I liked him. He had a funny laugh. Besides, I didn't need a smart cellie. I had enough smarts in my head to occupy a graduate school class. I didn't need any distractions of latent, incipient, budding intelligence.

The main CO, Grady, and his assistant, Joe, came around and told us to strip down to our undershorts. What was this all about? It obviously didn't have anything to do with a stabbing at the Medium.

Had something gone wrong at the camp? That would be unusual. No one here had more than a ten-year sentence and most guys didn't want to mess up and stay longer. You really had to be stupid to screw up a good thing. Then again, most of these guys weren't too bright. A lot of them were taking GED classes to try to get high school diplomas.

They were searching us for scratches and bruises on our bodies. They wanted to see if any of us were involved in a beating. No one in my dorm was bruised up. We were either innocent or careful.

"They beat Juan," Eddie said.

"Who?"

"You know, his friends," he said. "They play cards."

"Why?"

"He cheated."

"How?" I asked.

"I don't know. He probably marked the cards so he could rig the betting and win a can of tuna from another guy's commissary," Eddie said. There was no money at the joint so people gambled with goods from the commissary.

"Serve him right. Cops should be honest," I said. "That's the way of the world."

"He used to rob from drug dealers," Eddie said.

"No integrity. He deserved a beating."

"He might be dead."

"Who cares?" I said. I wanted to be hard. I was a prisoner. I wasn't some liberal lawyer fighting for the rights of criminals I didn't really know and with whom I had a false sense of sympathy. I knew these guys. They were shit. So was I. And what did or didn't happen to Juan made no difference to me one way or the other.

●●●

Juan? What's a Juan? He used to be a cop. I mean an active working cop out on the streets. Even in jail he was still a cop. A cop is always a cop. So walking around in his khaki prison outfit he still thought of himself as a cop, a guy with an edge, a man with a badge. Like all people who were used to setting or enforcing the rules, he was a bit cocky. He had a swagger. He spoke with a deep baritone unlike most of the squeaky-voiced Latinos. His voice had authority. It was an honest voice. A cop's voice. An operatic voice. He could have sung something Wagnerian or done commercials instead of sticking up small time drug dealers. He was muscular like Mr. Clean. But he was dirt like the rest of us. He just didn't know it.

Juan was short and stocky. I guess he was Puerto Rican. There was a halfback on my high school football team who looked just like him. A star at seventeen but too small to ever amount to anything at twenty-one. Juan smiled a lot with that kind of look like his smile didn't mean anything. It was just sitting there on his face like a tattoo. It said, "Don't fuck with me or I'll mess you up."

Most guys in jail didn't take too well to dirty cops. Cops were on the enemy's team. They were the guys who caught us and sent us to jail. It was like our enemies were living with us. And when a cop tried to be a criminal it unbalanced the universal values that floated around somewhere in the Judeo-Christian cosmos or in the collective unconscious of morals. It was wrong. For no particular reason. Like the reason I was in jail. I didn't even remember why.

I myself didn't like Juan. I didn't like his walk. I didn't like the way he talked too loud, like everyone should hear his stupid ticket-giving, juvenile delinquent-arresting voice. And I didn't like the timbre of his voice. It was too deep, rich.

It's not that I didn't like cops in general. I liked them. I thought that they were our fence to keep out the savagery of the criminal element. Kind of like the fence they built in Israel to keep out suicide bombers. The fence that liberal, left wing New Yorkers and weak Europeans protested because they were more worried about inconveniencing terrorist sympathizers than they were about school boys and girls losing their arms, their legs, their heads. The liberal philosophy is like short-term hedonism: be nice to creeps in the short term even if it screws up decent people in the long run. It is short-sighted, self-hatred.

When I walked down a dark, deserted street in a factory district or an alley in a housing project, I was always delighted to see a cop. Cops could save my ass. And if they meted out a little more brutality than necessary to stop someone from killing me, more power to them.

Anyhow, Juan sort of pressed in and out of my consciousness, depending on how loud he was shouting, "I have a full house" or "I fold." I didn't like him but I had little or less to do with him.

●●●

When Grady and Joe finished their inspection of our dorm, Pauli came over to our cube and said, "Come down to the stairwell. Got to show you something."

Eddie and I followed. Pauli opened the door and on the floor there was a large puddle of blood about three feet across, two feet wide and two inches deep. Eddie gagged. I smiled.

There was a bloody dumbbell on the floor. I suppose that was the weapon. There were little pieces of scalp in it. The blood reminded me of the time I broke my nose in the ring and I bled like a pig. I wasn't going to allow myself to feel bad about a little blood in jail. I wanted more of it. I wanted to feel like I was in jail, not summer camp. I hoped the cop was dead. Not for any reason but to be dramatic. I was living in a movie. I would have liked to have some pop-corn for my own drama. That night the sunset was blood red. This was an adventure. Life hurt. It was all good.

●●●

Eventually, sixteen guys were rounded up and thrown into solitary. The Feds questioned everyone even remotely connected with the incident. They grilled the sixteen prime suspects on the beating. They questioned them for hours on end.

After a few days some of the innocent cons that had been questioned started trickling out of solitary back into the camp. A big black guy, Elvis, complained about the treat-ment he got in solitary.

"Most of the guys accused were black or Hispanic," Elvis said. "The system's racist."

I liked Elvis. I used to jog with him. If Elvis weren't my friend I would have said, "Of course they were black or Hispanic. Juan didn't hang out with any whites."

But I didn't want to disabuse him of his self-protective notions. If he wanted to believe certain things to make himself feel better, let him. If racism gave him more ex-cuses for his failures, so much the better.

Ultimately, the Feds narrowed it down to the six re-sponsible ones. They were all so busy ratting on each other, no one knew who was responsible. It didn't matter. The guilty were selected. Case closed as far as the hacks were concerned.

The ex-cop had brain damage. Everybody thought that was a big deal. Six years later I found out that I had brain damage from boxing. So what? Maybe I think better because my thoughts leap around my synapses without the interference of linear logic. I didn't cry any tears for Juan. He didn't know he was a criminal. Juan thought he was still on patrol. When I was in junior high school, I remember a retard riding his bike down my block imitating the sound of a police siren. Maybe that's where they'd find Juan in ten years.

He was shipped to another camp. The six perpetrators were sentenced to a couple of additional years in a penitentiary. Penitentiaries are hard. But I guess you get some street cred for smashing a cop's head in. They'd be all right.

I'm sure they got some pleasure out of almost killing the cop. But was it worth it to do a couple more years? It was kind of like fucking a girl with AIDS. I mean it feels good but you can die.

I was beginning to see that there were consequences to doing careless things. You couldn't get away with everything. I was no longer part of the privileged world where you were innocent until proven guilty. I was in the land of the guilty until proven innocent.

I was surrounded by criminals who said they were innocent when they were all guilty. A presumption of innocence is a creepy idea to protect criminals while throwing victims to the dogs. I never understood the saying that it's better to let a thousand guilty men go free than to punish one innocent man. Did the short-sighted Greeks ever stop to think that the thousand guilty men who go free will punish another thousand innocent victims?

Filmmakers and writers should stop concentrating on the rare criminals who turn out to be innocent and start focusing on soft judges who allow monsters get-out-of-jail-free passes to go back into the world to rape and kill truly innocent people.

I know it makes enlightened fools feel good about themselves to recommend letting a thousand guilty men go free so that one innocent man is not wrongly punished, but they are actually inhumane. A humanist's failure to take the responsibility to mete out punishments where they are necessary is the beginning of chaos and the eventual downfall of society.

The world has changed since George Orwell. We have less to fear from our institutions than from the academic weaklings and the perverts who favor the individual whimsy of criminals and revolutionaries. Big Brother has become Big Protestor or Big Transgender. It is narcissism instead of societal mores that threatens our safety.

Hey, I'm from the sixties. I'm a narcissist too. But it's only in standing outside our narcissism and recognizing that we are worse than the people we criticize that we can find true self-love and complete the circle of narcissism with recognition of our own greatness.

We don't need to clean dirty cops. We need to punish them to give them a chance to recapture their soiled dignity. We need to give up trying to understand enemies who make no attempt to understand us. We must fight to be right, not surrender to be wrong. We need time to think about the whole mess in jail and not pat ourselves on the back for our frivolous, self-justifying humanitarian fantasies.

•••

Just after the cop's brain damage, the warden called me to his office to tell me that Billy Schoener had hung himself at Allenwood. He had no details. He just knew that we had been roommates and that I'd want to know. I did. Billy and I had been close. He was a solid guy in his thirties. He had three kids who used to visit him with his blonde wife. I was jealous of those visits. He was doing ten years for manufacturing meth-amphetamines. Maybe that got to him. I didn't think so. He seemed like a guy who could take it. He used to keep our cube clean so we didn't get demerits. With his money from dealing he owned a deli and a theatrical prop company. I felt bad. He was like a regular friend from the outside world. I never sensed that he was suicidal. Maybe I had kept him alive with my sense of humor and my chatter. I talked a lot. It was hard to feel like you were in jail when you were bunking with me. They never should have transferred him.

•••

There had been next to no snow during the winter of '95, unlike the storms in '94. I was waiting for my release papers to go to a halfway house. It was dragging and dragging. They could come anywhere during the next five months. The system never liked to let you know anything in advance. Then, finally, a hack came over to me and said, "Pack your bags." It was March, 1995. I was going to miss Pauli, Eddie, and Billy's ghost. On the bus heading to the halfway house in New York I was glad that I had been in jail. I had done a lot of writing. I was physically strong. I knew what it was to have no rights and to be humbled. I was an outcast. I was shit in a toilet bowl. I found myself in the muck. I smelled like a wiseman.

David, 2011

35

I MOVED INTO the Hotel Marquis halfway house at Madison and 31st Street. Halfway house required that I have a job. I worked out a deal with Bruce where I gave him two hundred dollars cash a week to work at Gleason's and he gave me back a paycheck minus forty dollars for federal taxes. My mother gave me the cash to give him from a fund she had for me. My job at Gleason's consisted of doing whatever I wanted to do. I boxed. Each week I showed my one hundred and sixty dollar check to the halfway house as proof that I was working. I then gave them fifty dollars for my housing. I also rented an office from Bruce for two hundred and fifty dollars a month. I spent my time in there writing and starting a record company, Renegade Records.

I left halfway house every morning at 7:00 and had to be back by 10:00 p.m. It was beautiful. Except for all the paperwork and forms, the standing on lines to sign in and out. Otherwise I was a free man. No responsibilities. Just hanging out at Gleason's. On weekends I was released to my parents' house on East 72nd Street and First Avenue. Lauren and Graham lived at East 72nd and Madison. I wouldn't dare sign out to her place because she would have told the halfway house I was doing something wrong so she could get me sent back to the joint. When I had dinner with her she'd tell me straight out, "You better behave or I'll call halfway house and have you sent back to jail." She wanted to control me. She didn't think I was capable of handling myself.

I loved passing my days at Gleason's. All my old buddies were there. Chuck had found a job as an asbestos worker but when he heard I was back at the gym he came down to see me. It was my forty-eighth birthday and he gave me an envelope. I opened it and there was a birthday card and fifty dollars. I almost cried. He must have figured I was so broke that I needed it. I had always taken care of Chuck. Now he was taking care of me. He was a better friend than any of the millionaires I knew in business. I took the money so as not to hurt his feelings. I wanted him to be proud.

36

HECTOR HAD ME spar with a heavyweight black woman he was training. A lot more women were boxing since I'd gone to jail. She landed one on my nose. It swelled up. I belted her in the ribs and she fell to the ground. I felt great. She shouldn't have tried to hurt me. Man, woman, or beast: if they took a swing at me I was going to try to kill them.

That weekend my wife saw my swollen nose and said, "If you don't stop boxing, you can't come home when you get out of halfway house."

"Fine. I'll live with my parents," I said. "I'm not giving up boxing. It's all I have left. And rap."

"Rap," she screamed. "If you don't quit that you're never coming home."

"You already said I can't come home," I said.

"Drop dead."

I was desperate. All I had to make me feel like a human being were my hobbies. I wanted to turn them into profitable professions. I knew my wife wanted the best for us. Boxing and rapping were losing choices. Boxing would lead to more injuries and no money. Rapping would suck up my last money as I tried to promote a hopeless cause. But if I listened to my wife I was nothing. I was an ex-con trying to get back into the profession that I had betrayed and gone to jail for.

• • •

I moved in with my parents at 360 East 72nd Street. I lived in their den. It was much smaller than my apartment but after jail it felt immense. I should have been embarrassed living with my parents in my forties. I loved it. I got along better with them than anyone else. They weren't angry at me all the time like Lauren. They didn't resent me. And my mother, who was ill with cancer, stuck up for me all the time when my dad would criticize me for ruining the business. I couldn't blame him. He was reduced to being a wine salesman in his seventies because of me. I was complicit in the ruin of Allied Programs.

I would take care of my mother, bringing her her meals and her medicines. When I was a kid I was never sure if she liked me. Now we forged a bond. While she fought with my dad, I comforted her. I found out how much I loved her while she was dying.

I made a deal with Graham, who was sixteen now, to wake up early and meet me at seven-thirty before school for breakfast at a coffee shop. It was not easy for me be-cause I often stayed up until two in the morning writing. I'd trudge over from First Avenue to Madison just to see him. I wanted some alone time with him. We were two buddies cracking jokes before school. I wasn't much into fathering. I was an older brother. I loved the kid. He was a butterfly. I held him in my palms and encouraged him to fly. I trusted him. He knew where the air currents were.

I had made up my mind not to snuff my son's candle, not to squelch his light. I tried to be the father to him that I would have loved to have had for myself. Not that mine was so far off. When I was younger he was dictatorial. Eventually, he loosened up and let me have my way, but only after he saw a psychiatrist. In my teens my family had group sessions. Imagine how progressive we were. But that's another story.

•••

I called up my record producer, Jean, from Rude Boy and told him I had formed Renegade Records. He was broke, living with his uncle, doing nothing and thrilled that I was back in the business. He came down to Gleason's to work for me. We were going to be the only label to ever operate out of a boxing gym. I found some life insurance policies I had forgotten I had with about $200,000 cash surrender value in them. I was so careless. It was amazing that I thought I was almost broke but had all this money. I cashed the policies in before the government found out about them and threw them into a Renegade Records bank account. The sewer groaned with pleasure. It was going to get fed again.

We got in touch with Rude Boy's old distributor, Mike G. He had done nothing for Rude Boy but we didn't know anyone else to contact. He wanted six hundred dollars a month to distribute us. I never heard of paying a distributor. I had no choice.

We called our first record *Da Masta Plan*. It consisted of four songs. I spent about thirty thousand dollars in the studio recording it. My rhythm was not the greatest; it was weak even for a white man. And I had to keep going over the tracks while the engineer punched me in and out. Sometimes my son would come down to the studio with me. He loved being there and I made him an honorary member of my rap company.

We printed up five thousand CDs, five thousand cassettes and fifteen hundred wax. We were a real record company, an independent label with distribution through Mike Giangrasso. I was a record mogul. Everyone in the rap business pretended they did time. I really had. If I had to invest all my life insurance money in this project, I would do it. In my jumbled mind even two hundred thousand dollars was a detail that rolled over with other items like breakfast, fighting, movies, and the color of the sunset over Central Park. It was ironic that the greedy Feds thought I was a mastermind thief. I was a criminal by accident. I wanted to be a real gangster but my only crime was negligence. The Feds were too corrupt themselves to conceive of someone as pure as myself who didn't really care about money. They didn't know that I was the boy who used to take pennies from his mother's purse to throw down the sewers in the suburbs. They were too busy wallowing in the gutter looking for money to pay their bills for their ugly, fat, suburban families. They were hogs snorting for truffles. Our society needed our hogs. But when they mistook my asshole for mushrooms they were snorting in the wrong place.

•••

Jean and I were having pretty good success in the record pools with *Masta Plan*. In June we were ahead of Snoop Doggy Dogg and Fat Joe on the Rap Charts in the biggest pool in the Midwest —the IRS Rap Pool. This was amazing. But as successful as we were in the pools and clubs, no one was buying our records. We had no radio play. That would have cost us an extra two hundred grand.

•••

Lauren and I were dining at Lenge Japanese Restaurant. She had chicken sukiyaki and I had Sushi B. I was telling her about the songs I was working on in the studio when she said, "If you keep pissing away money in the studio, I'm going to report you to your parole officer."

"Don't you want to do a song again?" I said. I figured I'd bribe her. If I paid for her to do a record, she couldn't be angry at my paying for my own record. What she hated about rap was that I was doing it. That I was spending a fortune on it and unlikely to get anywhere. She, after all, was musical.

"What do you mean?"

"I'll put out your album," I said. Her rap was an afterthought. Before I went to prison I had spent about fifty thousand dollars in studio time recording some of her songs. The whole time she criticized my songs.

"Now you're making sense," she said. "I'm much better than you. I can be a hit."

She actually was better than me. She had a superior sense of rhythm and timing. But she had the wrong image. She never did time. She was a woman who lunched. She wouldn't appeal to an audience of drug dealer teenagers. She put together a record at Unique Studios called *Good Cop/Bad Cop*. I loved it. I spent about fifteen thousand dollars printing up copies of her record and posters. She kept asking me to spend more.

●●●

I took a few days off from my phony job at Gleason's and hooked up with my old friend Crazy Sam. He interviewed me on *Video Music Box* a bunch of times. I was on the show with famous rappers like Das Effex, Fat Joe, Treach, the Bushwackers, and Doug E. Fresh. Sam told me he'd get me on Hot 97 with Funkmaster Flex for two thousand dollars. I gave it to him and sure enough we actually got on the show. Method Man, Redman, and Snoop Doggy Dogg showed up at the studio. I had arrived at the top of the stairs of rap. You couldn't get higher. But my wife didn't want a rapper-boxer living with her, even though I was paying for her rap songs.

●●●

I got another shot to revive my dead boxing career. A 62-year-old man in the gym, Lou Bartfield, the Hebrew Hammer, was looking to turn pro again after a forty year layoff. I agreed to fight him on Dennis Rappaport's card in Old Westbury. We both passed our physicals. What a fight this was going to be—the Hebrew Hammer versus the Renegade Jew. We both trained at Gleason's. One day in the gym Lou said, "I don't really want to hit a Jew."

"That's funny," I said. "I'm more than happy to hit you." I knew I could beat Lou. I had seen him spar in Gleason's and he moved like an old man. I liked him a lot but I really wanted to hurt him. It was nothing personal. It was just that by hurting him I could prove that I was the better man. That I was more hurtful. I think Aristotle said something about the end of a tree is to be most perfectly a tree. I felt that the end of a fighter was to be most destructively and hurtfully a fighter. I should probably look it up. But I won't. Aristotle bores me to death.

About a week before the fight the commission came up with some excuse to turn us down. I went up there to see them and the assistant commissioner said, "You're banned in Massachussetts and we have to follow suit."

"Banned for what?" I asked.

"You'll have to speak to them," the assistant commissioner said.

"What about the Hammer?" I asked.

He looked at me with a sarcastic face and said, "He's too old."

I called the Massachusetts commission and asked the commissioner, "Are you banning me because I was knocked down three times in my last fight there?" I remembered my fiasco in Boston when I fought the guy whose muscles were supposed to be all air.

"They don't allow old fighters in Massachussets. That's why you're banned. Nothing personal," the commissioner said.

The Hammer sued the New York Athletic Commission for age discrimination. Television cameras came up to the gym to interview him. He was becoming quite a celebrity without ever lacing on a glove. The Commission saved his life.

●●●

Lauren was pumped up about her record, *Good Cop/Bad Cop*. She called my old reporter friend, Michael Kaplan, and told him he should do an article about her rapping.

Lauren never wanted to rap. Yet she rapped. Contradiction, thy name is woman.

I guess she hoped for fame. Like me. How superficial.

Michael called me and said, "You're wife wants me to do an article about her rapping. What has she done?"

"She's been in the studio," I said. "Working on some stuff. Not bad."

"That's not exactly newsworthy, David," he said.

"I know that. I got a record out too and I'm making all the charts but it's no big deal," I said.

"You got anything else interesting happening?" he asked.

"Come to think of it, I'm about to box a sumo wrestler, Tiny, at Gleason's Gym. You know Crazy Sam? He set it up as a joke."

"A real sumo wrestler?" he asked.

"The guy's seven hundred and fifty pounds. He even fought in the Ultimate Warrior competition," I said.

"Now that's something I think I can talk an editor into covering," he said.

When Michael called me a few days later he told me that *New York Magazine* wanted him to write a story about my fight and my wife's and my rapping. I was thrilled. I had never been in *New York Magazine* before. "You owe it all to me," my wife said. "I was the one who called Michael."

I didn't waste my time fighting with her. I didn't argue that Michael was my friend, or let her know that *New York Magazine* was interested in my fighting the sumo wrestler.

The day of the big fight arrived. Crazy Sam was there with his camera crew from *Video Music Box*. I figured this was going to be a joke. Tiny weighed five times as much as me. He wouldn't be crazy enough to try to hurt me.

As much as Lauren hated Gleason's, she showed up to make sure that she was covered in the article. She even put her song, "Terrorist Lover" on the boombox, which she set on the apron of the ring. She was bopping around to her own music like she was in a club. It sounded pretty good.

Tiny's hands were so big he couldn't get them into the boxing gloves. They were hanging off his fingers. I kept smiling at Tiny but he wasn't smiling back. He looked like he was talking to himself in his corner. Psyching himself. There was no reason he'd have to make himself angry to fight a little stick like me. I was getting nervous but I figured there was no way such a monster would bother hurting a little guy like me. It would be like swatting a fly. When the bell rang Tiny charged across the ring. He threw a couple of giant slaps at me and then took off his gloves and threw them on the canvas. I was in my boxing stance, bobbing and weaving, sticking out tentative jabs. Next thing I knew I was upside down in the air. He had picked me up in his huge hands. I looked at the ceiling and then felt the wind as he body slammed me onto the canvas. I could feel my whole body getting whiplash. The wind was knocked out of me. He started jumping up and down on top of me. When he threw me, my pants slipped down around my knees. Everybody standing around the ring looked at me like I was going to get killed. Some kids hid their eyes. Tiny was squashing me. Even Crazy Sam realized something was going haywire. He ran over and tried to push Tiny off me but he couldn't get him to budge. A few other fighters ran over and grabbed Tiny but he just ignored them. The bell rang. Tiny stopped instantly like a dog responding to Pavlov's bell. He got off of me and I struggled to my feet. Lauren ran over, "Are you all right?"

"I think so," I said, feeling like I had just been run over by a cement truck.

"You shouldn't fool with these idiots," Hector said.

"You look ridiculous," Lauren said. "Your sweat pants came down and everyone could see your underwear."

"It wasn't a fashion show," I said, pulling my pants back up.

"I'm going to call the police," Lauren said.

"Don't you dare," I said. "Tiny was going easy on me. It's not his fault he's so huge."

"You let everybody take advantage of you," she said. "You're a sucker."

"Leave me alone," I said and went into the locker room to take a hot shower.

Sam suggested that he drive Tiny, Lauren, Michael, and me up to Harlem and give some chicken out to the homeless in order to get publicity for our rap songs. Lauren said, "I have to go home to do the laundry." She had never done the laundry in her life. Michael said, "I have to get back to the office and work up my notes." Tiny and I were the only ones willing to go up to Harlem. When Sam and I got downstairs he led me over to a badly dented car.

"This is Ol' Dirty Bastard's car," Sam said. I was impressed. ODB was the grungiest, craziest rapper in the Wu-Tang Clan. The kids idolized him. Tiny couldn't fit in the car so he followed us in the back of a pick-up truck. A couple of other guys from Sam's posse joined us. Sam took off at about ninety miles per hour. He was the worst driver I had ever seen. He was driving with no hands, singing, weaving in and out of traffic, controlling the steering wheel with his knees. By some miracle we made it up to Harlem.

When we were finished giving away Kentucky Fried Chicken in front of a record store Sam asked me, "You want a lift downtown?"

"I'll take a cab," I said. There was no way I was ever getting into a car with him again.

●●●

I went back into the studio with Jean to work on some new songs. We formed a five person black and white group. Jean brought his cousin Shawn in. Then we added Benny Boy and Joseph who sang reggae and rapped. We called ourselves the Lost Trybe of Hip-Hop. I found a new distributor, Joe Isgro of Raging Bull Records in California. Joe was a powerhouse gangster in the record business and he was willing to print up all the records and distribute my product worldwide through Alliance. He said he'd do radio promotion for my wife for twenty grand and twenty for me. I had already spent a lot of money. I had to think about it. I didn't want to end up broke. Yet this was my chance at the big leagues.

•••

We decided to shoot a video of "Masta Plan." I also paid for my wife to shoot a video for "Terrorist Lover." I got a good deal on both but they still came to about twenty-five thousand dollars combined.

Word got out that *New York Magazine* was doing an article on us. CNN'S *Entertainment Today* contacted Lauren and wanted to do a show on our rapping. CNN was worldwide. It was a big break for us. They came to Lauren's apartment. I was living with my parents. They filmed us in the library. On December 18th it aired. The announcer treated us as serious rappers who were on the way up and called us the Upper East Side Rappers. My dream of making it as a novelty act was coming true. I'd be rich again soon. I'd have money to burn. I thought I might not need fighting anymore, that all I needed was to be famous. But I still went to the gym every day and sparred.

•••

"Oy Word," the *New York Magazine* article about my fight with Tiny, hit the stands. Lauren flipped out. She felt the article mocked her. She was furious about the picture they used of her. "It makes me look ugly," she said. "I'm beautiful. I look nothing like that."

"It's a fish eye lens. It's supposed to be a funny shot," I said. "I don't care how I look."

"You don't care about anything," she said.

David and Lauren in the dining room, 2011

37

WHITE-COLLAR NIGHT was back at Gleason's. Bruce had decided to reinstitute the bouts. I hadn't fought in one since before I went to jail. To get around the commission Bruce made them exhibitions in which there were no winners. It was Friday night and I showed up to fight a thirty-something Russian, Alex. The first round he came after me pretty hard. I showed him some power. But I was very much in control. No wild shit. The second round was more of the same. Back in the corner Hector told me to beat him up a little. In the third round I went out and gave him a good hook to the ribs. This had always been my best shot. He went down like an anchor. When he struggled back to his feet I took it easy on him the rest of the round. We finished friends. I was glad to beat him. I was later thrilled when I heard that he had been on the Russian amateur boxing team.

•••

In the spring of '96 I was sparring mostly with champions. Not that I was good competition for them, but I was one of the few pros there in the morning and I knew how to press them and give them a little work. These were not wars mind you. They were sparring sessions in the true sense of the word.

Arturo Gatti was training with Hector and I got to spar with him a few times. This was before he became the World Junior Lightweight Champion. Even taking it easy on me his punches hurt. I also sparred with the W.B.O. Junior Lightweight Champ, Regilio Tuur, and the Dutch silver medalist from the '92 Olympics, Orhan Delibas. I sometimes did a few rounds with cruiserweight, Don Diego Puede. He later became the cruiserweight champ. I was with the boxing elite. It was as if I was a hitting partner with the tennis players Pete Sampras, Andre Agassi, and Michael Chang.

Most of the time I sparred with Monaco. He was a delightful lightweight Italian who had about thirty pro fights, retired, and then came back to make money as an opponent. Promoters flew him all over the world to fight top ten contenders for a couple of grand. Last year he even fought Paez, the Mexican clown and former world champion. He kept coming back all beaten up claiming that he was robbed. He would challenge everyone, particularly the women. "Woman, you want to fight me," he'd shout. Or he'd challenge a guy, "You a bum. I demolish you."

•••

We finished mixing our album and decided to name it *Lyfestylz*. It cost me about thirty thousand dollars in studio time and another ten thousand dollars to remix. I also remixed Lauren's album for eight grand. I then mastered both albums for five grand. That totaled about fifty-three thousand dollars in recent music expenses. I only had about fifty grand left. I should have hung onto it for dear life. I needed a hit record. I flew out to Ensino, California to Raging Bull Records, the label that was going to do the distribution for me. I met with the owner, Joe Isgro.

"You know the promotions are going to cost on each record," Isgro said.

"I can only afford it on one record," I said.

"Release yours ahead of your wife's," he said. "If yours starts selling I'll advance you money to promote hers."

I went back to the hotel and worked out in the gym. I never missed my workouts. Even if I was on the road.

●●●

When I got home I told Lauren, "I can't release your record until after mine."

"That means it'll never come out," she said.

"If you believe in your project so much why don't you invest the twenty thousand dollars for the promotions?" I asked.

"Are you crazy?" she said. "I wouldn't piss away my money like that."

Boy, did I feel taken advantage of. It was all right for me to spend the money but she didn't believe enough in her music to spend it.

38

IN THE SUMMER and fall of '96 I spent a lot of time sparring again. Terry Southerland, Pedro Saiz, Chinito, the Judah Brothers—the list went on and on. But I wasn't competing. I couldn't get a fight at my age. Everybody was worried about my getting hurt. And for the first time I took the possibility of brain damage a little more seriously. I never worried about it that much when I was running a multi-million dollar business. I mean, a few times. Like that time before jail when I got knocked out on my feet sparring. But that was different. I still had my business to back me up and I didn't need much brains to run it. All I had to do was go out and drink with the guys and bullshit them into placing my insurance. But now that I was an unemployed, ex-con writer, I really needed my wits. I had to keep what gray matter I had left. I had to put sentences together in orderly arrangements like vases of flowers. Every paragraph was a voyage into rocky terrain. Every chapter was a border I clomped over in my Timberland hiking boots. I was more than a handshake and a smile. I had to think, to somehow know what I was doing.

It looked like my rap days were over. The "Masta Plan" single reached thirty-six on the Billboard charts but I wasn't making any money off it. Most of the sales came from promotional discounts. The album was not selling at all. I spoke to a trainer and former Olympian, Reggie Ford, about finding me a fight.

"I can get you one in the Caribbean against Monaco," he said. "It would be like a paid vacation."

I asked my parole officer if I could go. He said, "No." The fight didn't materialize anyhow.

• • •

I had to do something to earn a buck. I was almost out of funds. My wife and son scolded me all the time about not working and not supporting them, even though I gave my son a hundred dollars a week in allowance and my wife was living in my four million dollar apartment. A boxing friend talked me into modeling. I took some professional pictures and landed a few jobs. It wasn't like the old days when you had to be a beauty boy. There was a lot of work for real people. I landed jobs posing as a businessman and construction worker. I appeared in top magazines like *Town & Country* and *Men's Health*. I even landed a job as a bum in a subway poster which ran on almost every train in the five boroughs. Not to mention a television commercial where I dressed in a gorilla outfit and Anna Kournikova hit tennis balls at me in a Coney Island game booth. This got me into Screen Actors Guild and a bonus for leg bruises.

It was a few days before a White-Collar show and I was at Gleason's sparring with my friend Monaco. He kept banging into my right ear with hooks. I looked at his squashed-in nose and got angry. I started wailing straight rights at his face. It escalated into a war and people were crowding around the ring to watch us fight. We were beating the shit out of each other. I felt the adrenalin racing through my system. As I threw my punches they'd speed up and twist at the end. I was trying to knock Monaco out, even though he was my friend. Bruce came out of his office and shouted, "You fight like that anymore I'm going to ban you from the gym."

I was thrilled. I remembered when I was banned years ago for getting hurt too much. Now I was almost fifty years old. I couldn't believe I was repeating history. That I was still brave enough to be considered a threat to myself and others. I remembered what pro boxer Chinito once told me after sparring, *I love my job.* It was amazing that he could think of this bloodletting as a job. It was so much sexier than accounting. It was my poem. My love. I was involved with another human being in a death dance. There was nothing more serious. It was kind of romantic in an asexual way. That's why boxers hug each other after a fight. They have experienced love. All other experiences seem insignificant after that. It's like having survived a plane crash and walking through a green field seeing how green it really is for the first time. It is only by risking all that you can appreciate so little. It's by taking chances that you preserve the quiet dignity of respecting life. Love is death. Death is love. And living through death is the loveliest of all.

●●●

Every time I thought I was going to stop fighting, I started again. It was like my relationship with my wife. I'd fall in and out of love with her on a regular basis. It was like she didn't exist. She was a reflection of my moods. She was an extension of my narcissism. I didn't believe in progress. I didn't believe people changed. All intelligent people stayed the same. I took a screenwriting course where the instructor said, "There has to be a character arc." I quit the course. I didn't believe in arcs or growth. We do not mature. We are attached to dying bodies. We grow more fully ourselves and then we disappear.

I showed up at the gym for the White-Collar Bouts. It was Friday afternoon and I spent the day in my office mailing a single, "Pressure," to record stores. "Pressure" was from *Lifestylez,* the album I had done with Lost Trybe. We were desperately trying to promote the album. Money was running out.

I had no opponent planned but Bruce promised to get me one. Hector was out of town. So YiYo agreed to work my corner. But when fight time came YiYo was gone. He forgot about the fight. He was probably off copping drugs. I didn't care. I didn't need YiYo. Monaco volunteered to work the corner.

I was matched up against Carlos Sanchez. He looked like a Mexican version of Charles Bronson. He was with his trainer and his son. They were all members of the

Kingston Boxing Club. Sanchez was decked out in shorts with his name on them.

"I'm forty-six," he said to me.

He was old but tough. Still, he looked like he was only around thirty. He was lean, mean, and Hispanic. I wasn't afraid. I had some credentials. I was warming up and I noticed Carlos was wearing 12-ounce gloves. Fighters at the White-Collar bouts usually wore 16-ounce gloves so they'd have more padding and wouldn't hurt the other guy too much. I borrowed a pair of twelve-ounce gloves from a girl who had won the Golden Gloves the year before.

The bell rang and Carlos came right after me. He held his hands high and winged straight rights at me. He looked like he had some pro experience. I stayed calm, landing some good body shots, but they didn't seem to be hurting him. The crowd was going wild. Back in my corner Monaco said, "You're losing."

"You can't lose in an exhibition," I said. I was completely in control.

The bell rang and the fight was over. Carlos and I hugged each other. The audience applauded wildly. I banged my gloves together for Carlos. I respected Carlos and he respected me. We knew we put on a great fight. We gave it our all. Tried to kill each other. Yet we both had the skills to survive with no major injuries.

The next fight at Gleason's was a rematch. It went down the same way. Our fights were the hits of the night. Every time I thought of retiring I remembered my fights with Carlos and felt we should go on tour fighting each other in every city throughout the country. We'd prove that two middle-age guys could still get it on. We'd beat up all

the young men and steal their girlfriends. We'd be primi-
tive. Or not. It was just a thought. I was excited. I shot myself up with youth.

●●●

Later I met Lauren for dinner. There were no marks on
my face so she had no idea that I'd been fighting. But at
one point during the meal my sleeve rolled up to my elbow
and she saw a bunch of bruises there.

"Where'd you get those?" Lauren asked.

"Sparring in the gym," I said.

"When are you going to outgrow that stupid sport?"
she asked.

"Soon. You don't think I'm going to be boxing in my
fifties, do you?" I said.

I was going to be fifty in a few weeks and I wasn't
thinking of stopping.

●●●

I didn't quit fighting. I was true to my obsessions. On December 28, 1999 my mother died. She had had numerous
operations since the onset of her ovarian cancer. Her last
four months she spent in a hospice, Calvary Hospital. She
shouldn't have left me. I visited her every day and I fell in
love with her. It was the saddest-happiest time of my life. I
wanted to protect her like a child. We reversed roles. I was
her parent. I was the ferryman from the Inferno who trans-
ported her across the river to death. I helped her on her
journey. I was Virgil. I am still waving to her, stranded back

on my own bank. I sometimes throw silent kisses to the bus on 72nd Street that used to take me to Calvary Hospital in Morris Park.

●●●

In the year 2000 I was fifty-three years old. I'd had twenty-four fights since I got out of jail. One of them was yet another war with Sanchez. He was becoming an obsession.

Some of my fights were simply sparring sessions with people I was teaching to box. I fought a judge, Phil, three times. He moved fast, circular, and had a quick jab. We hung out. We became good friends. He still trains with me today.

I was training people to pick up a few extra bucks. Who would have predicted that when I first showed up at Gleason's in my Rolls Royce that I would have ended up training people there for twenty dollars an hour? Back then I could have bought the gym with my pocket change. Now I was a boxing coach. Not very glamorous. I was no longer even rapping. I couldn't afford the studio fees. I was nothing. Just a piece of my old image, a bit of myself. Yet I enjoyed my job. I no longer felt I had to prove anything.

I lived with my father. I dated my wife several times a week. We were close but we weren't having sex. I didn't want to be touched by any other human being. I was afraid of them. I didn't trust them. My wife was like a sister to me. I respected her too much to make love to her. But I loved her too much to even look at another woman.

Sex was pussy stuff, if you know what I mean. Ironically, I felt like fucking was soft and feminine, not manly. It might bring me to tears. I didn't want to cry. I didn't want to moan. I didn't want to lose control.

I had become more pure about my sport. It was a religion to me. I was a white sheet on a vestal virgin. I didn't think about the future. It would tell me about itself when it arrived. As for the past I didn't remember it too well. Too many punches to the head or too much stress. The past was an obsession for jerk-offs. History taught no lessons. I lived in the present: writing, boxing, and enjoying my life. I think the careless crime I committed when I allowed Kelly to commandeer a gay money laundering ring behind my back gave me a second lease on life. It allowed me to dump everything I no longer respected. I am glad to no longer be part of the business world. I have returned to my origins in art and bloodshed.

A friend of mine told me that Social Security was giving out money for insanity. I went to their office in Brooklyn and told a nice Puerto Rican lady that I was bipolar. She sent me to a psychiatrist who looked like Rosa Klebb. She agreed that I was bipolar. So did the psychiatrist at Schuylkill. So did one in New York. Maybe the fact that I didn't think that I was crazy proved to them I was crazy. I had chopped down the luxuriant forest of my life with a mad ax. Social Security provided me fourteen hundred dollars a month in benefits. I used to earn that in an hour. I really needed it now. It was a fortune to me.

AFTERMATH

A hot day in June, 2001, a pharmaceutical company came into Gleason's Gym to check boxers for brain damage. Since I got out of jail the New York commission wouldn't let me fight pro anymore. I applied to the commission in Boston but they wouldn't let me fight either. In the hope of one day being allowed a comeback, I sparred thousands of sessions and fought in thirty white-collar fights. I loved sparring but I was beginning to notice holes in my memory. I was taking some acting classes and found that my memory was failing me. One page of dialogue would take me about three days to memorize. I landed a few small parts in independent films. When a Russian film company offered me a thousand dollars to play the role of a detective I said, "Yes." Two days later, after seeing a ten page script, I told them, "No." I said I had decided to quit acting. I was in a panic. I didn't tell them that I didn't think I could remember the part.

I decided to volunteer for the pharmaceutical company brain test. Better to be cautious. I told myself that there was nothing really wrong but when I took the test my short-term memory was terrible. The examiner would recite a list of four words, come back to them five minutes later and expect me to repeat them in sequence. I couldn't remember one word. I asked him if I had brain damage and he just smiled. He was there to get information for his studies, not to help me figure out if I had problems. I usually laughed things off, but I became worried. I felt like I had an iron plate in my head that was separating me from my past.

At least I could still write poetry. I didn't need a memory for that. I couldn't understand other people's poems. But mine I loved. I knew what I was getting at. I wanted holes in my logic. I wanted my brain to leap across black spaces. To bang against its own ineptitude in a flurry of images. To be a fireworks occasion in a jar.

Still, my poor results on the brain test at Gleason's worried me. Not that I was really worried. I almost wanted to do badly. It would enable me to feel sorry for myself. I decided to get a complete battery of brain tests. I went to see Dr. Joel Redfield, who gave me a four-hour version of the Gleason's mini-test. While I was taking it I sensed that something was wrong. I felt I should be doing better. Dr. Redfield told me that my short-term memory was damaged, my ability to discern spatial relationships was off, and that I had no sense of smell. I asked him the magic question, "Am I brain damaged?" No one wants to answer that question head on. He said, "You're not functioning as well as you should for a person with a Ph.D."

"Can I still box?" I asked. I hoped he'd say yes. I had nothing else to feel proud about. Except maybe my poetry. I could do that again. Unlike rapping in the studio it wouldn't cost me anything. I wouldn't need the same linear imagination that I would for prose. I wouldn't have to put ideas together. I could put the words out there and let them stand up and sing.

All I'd need is a computer. Actually, I had never really quit poetry. I was always doing it in drips and drabs, here and there. But ever since college I hadn't really concerned myself with making a name as a poet. Maybe I could do that now. After all, it was always my major talent, what came most naturally to me. Even if I didn't like the sensitive posturing of poets, their walking around in black outfits and oohing and aahing at each other's effeminate readings.

"Boxing's too dangerous," he said.

He didn't say it but I knew he thought I was brain damaged. Who was he to think that of me? He didn't know what great thoughts were going on in my head; I was beginning to feel defensively manic. I was the greatest literary genius who ever lived. He had to be kidding. I had a tough brain. I had a boxer's head. It was thick like a Mexican's, like Chavez's. I was on his undercard in Vegas. That made me proud. The Mexicans can take punches. I never beat a Mexican in the ring. I was knocked out by one at my pro debut in Denver. Still, I was no pussy. Sure, I was a Jewish poet. But I was also a Jewish boxer. Jewish had nothing to do with it, I thought. My brain cells had calluses. They were wrapped in punches.

Many people had told me not to box over the years. I always resented them. But this was no joke. I felt helpless like my hands were falling off my wrists. I was all stumpy. My grace in living was gone. I was smashed into depression. I was usually manic and joyous. But without boxing? I was a blood clot.

●●●

After a few days I decided that Dr. Redfield was wrong. He was trying to fool me. Maybe he was in cahoots with my wife to get me to quit because my wife was jealous of my skills and didn't want me showing off to girls in the audience. Anyhow, what could Redfield tell from a verbal test? Words could mean anything. I was a poet. I was too brilliant for simple sentences. My mind was not an open book. No one was smart enough to see what was in there.

I had to find another route to seeing if I had brain damage. I wanted a test to see if there was structural damage. That was the key. If my brain was misshapen or if the waves were out of joint, then I'd know that something was wrong.

●●●

I was seeing a psychopharmacologist, Jesse Rosenfeld, for bipolar disorder. Not that I thought I was manic-depressive. It's just I didn't have much to say to contradict Lauren when she pointed out that my behavior was manic: I had bankrupted a multimillion dollar business; I used to go to work in the conservative insurance business wearing diamond studs, gold chains, and purple baggy hip-hop clothes; I fought professionally in my forties; I thought I was a great rapper even though I was tone deaf and had no sense of rhythm; I threatened to win the Academy Award for my movie *Boxer Rebellion* which played at Sundance Film Festival; and I kept telling my wife over and over again that I was going to win the Nobel Prize for poetry.

Rosenfeld suggested I go see a neurologist, Dr. Jonathan Charney. I went to his Park Avenue office. When Charney told me that he used to be a fighter, I felt right at home. We talked about boxing. He said that fighters got most of the damage sparring. He gave me an MRI and an EEG. I waited eagerly for the results. I was hoping I'd be all right and that I could continue boxing. I was also hoping I'd be brain damaged because I wanted to feel sorry for myself. I don't know what I was hoping. A little of this and a little of that. To me there were no such things as contradictions. Opposites merely existed side by side. They didn't clash. I was large enough to encompass them all. Maybe I'd know what I was feeling when I got the results from the tests.

I called Dr. Charney every day but he was too busy to get on the phone. Finally, one of the nurses told me that Dr. Charney hadn't read the EEG yet but the MRI had come out OK. That was a relief. See, I wasn't a masochist. I was happy that I was all right. It took me another four days to get through to Dr. Charney to get the results of the EEG.

"Why'd it take you so long to talk to me?" I asked. "I might have brain damage here. Don't you think you could pick up the phone?" Not that I thought that I really had brain damage. All the clues pointed that way. But they were footsteps on wet sand, erased as the ocean flopped on the shoreline. I usually wasn't forceful or testy with doctors. Women were like that. My wife. But not me. I prided myself in being stoic and cool. But I was angry that Charney had ignored me.

"I'm sorry," Dr. Charney said. "I had to go over the test several times."

Uh-oh. That didn't sound good. Or it did. Depending on what I wanted. "What do you mean?"

"Your waves are slower on the lower right side of your brain. Did you ever get hit in the head?" he asked.

"I told you I was a boxer," I said. I couldn't believe he didn't remember discussing that.

"That's it," he said. "The boxing has slowed up your brain waves. There's an underlying structural abnormality."

I had visions of becoming an old brain-dead fighter biting my tongue as it hung out over my lip, dribbling on my chin, remembering nothing, imagining I was champ.

"Will it get worse?" I asked.

"It shouldn't get worse. What's damaged is damaged. Just don't get hit again," he said.

"What do I do?"

"Come back in a month for another test."

I was both sad and relieved. I didn't want to give up boxing. Yet the idea of not getting hit anymore wasn't all that bad. I was getting on in years, way on, and the idea of getting belted by twenty-year-olds was becoming a little intimidating. If only I could deal with the anger. What would I use for a catharsis? Maybe I'd take up alligator wrestling or bull fighting; or maybe I'd slip back into the gym and get hit in the head, die in a blaze of glory.

A month later I took the test again. The results were the same. Now I knew it was time to quit. I didn't want to become Muhammad Ali. I didn't want to be trundled around as a boxing casualty. I didn't want to be a poster boy for brain damage. I went back to the gym and told my friends about my head injury.

I was depressed that I couldn't spar anymore but as usual I figured out a way around this. I sparred with everyone but we just hit to the body. It wasn't as good as hitting to the head. But at least it was something. I was still a sort-of, kind-of boxer. I was still in the game.

I went to visit my wife Lauren. I told her about the

brain damage. She was proud that she had been right. She said, "I told you so." She was radiant, happy. She'd be able to control me now. I was her patient. I wanted her as my nurse. She was sexy.

Later I went into the bathroom and laughed in the mirror. She sneaked up behind me and started wagging her finger at me. Was she admiring me or scolding me?

"What am I going to do with you?" she asked.

"The same thing I'm going to do with you," I said. "Be beautiful companions."

I wanted to get to know her again, to be with her. Through the disagreements and problems we had gotten closer. She was my sister, my mother, my girlfriend, my wife.

We went for a walk in Central Park. I realized that Lauren was the most important person in the world to me. That's the way things were, for no reason. She was still there. Maybe she was my mind. Maybe she didn't pick on me to pick on me but because she cared about me; maybe all the years of our relationship still existed in the present in some sort of time warp. I was still the original me, alive and brainy, in the tension of our marriage.

I wanted to move back in with her and start over for the hundredth time. I would get up on a surfboard and ride the brain damage wave back to her. She was the shore. I'd plant a beach umbrella over us and sip daiquiris with her. Everything was so beautiful. The day was suntanning itself. The sky was one step beyond blue.

"Can I move back?" I asked.

"You must," she said. "You're brain damaged. You need my help."

I didn't need her help. But I appreciated it. And no matter what the neurologist said, my brain was as sweet as ever. I was poetry. The synapses in my brain were blank. There were lyrics being born in the spaces. I jumped between ideas like I was weightless. I was no longer linear. I had no ambitions. We walked sideways through the park.

"I want to rake up all the leaves and start a fire in your reluctance," I said. I liked that. I didn't know if it made sense.

"What are you talking about?" she said and laughed.

And I kissed her. Not like I was kissing myself or my narcissism. She was another person. I wanted to recognize her for her integrity. I would no longer see her through the eyes of a child who was hurt by the mother he loved but through the clear eyes of a man who allowed her to stand up as an entity on her own, unalloyed by my significant chemical imbalances. If I was a vial of confusion, she was a pharmacy of intellectual balances. I needed her good medicine. Even when her dosages were wrong, she calmed me.

She had stayed with me through more than half of my life. Maybe she had criticized me so much because I meant too much to her. We were separate yet we were pieces of each other.

I felt like we had been slugging it out through a three-decade bout. Our marriage had been a hard fight. I respected her fortitude. We were both bloodied with cheap shots and sucker punches. I walked over to her corner and hugged her like I used to hug my opponents after a hard fight. I raised her hands. We were both champions. I respected her, the way she fought and the way she made up. There'd be other fights. Perhaps they'd be shorter. The changes and growth would be swifter. But I knew we loved each other too much to ever be enemies. There would be no winners. Being part of the game was good enough.

David's current office in Gleason's gym

ANOTHER TEN YEARS

It's May 2011 and I am sixty-four years old. I have been living back with my wife since 2001. We are comfortable again. We look young but we are seniors. We are almost wise. The last decade has sprinted by quickly based on the ratio of years elapsed to those that are upcoming. I don't have that much time left now that I've already completed about three quarters of my life. Back when I was twenty years old, a decade amounted to one half of what I had lived. Ten years is long or short depending on how long you have been around. Now it represents about fifteen per cent of my life.

I can't say that I have accomplished anything startling in the last ten years. I have had a lot of fun teaching students to box at Gleason's. I befriended them. They became my buddies. If I weren't broke I might have taught them for free just to hang out with them during the lessons.

I work out every day at the gym. I want to be the world's strongest old man. I can do curls with one hundred and ten pounds and can do forty-five chins. I only weigh one hundred and fifty-seven pounds. When I'm on the chin-up bar the professional fighters come around and applaud. I get a kick out of it. I have this fantasy of moving to Florida and beating up any old man on the golf course who is rude to me. But I'm not confrontational.

I have written thousands of poems, hundreds of which have been published. In 2007 Four Way Books published my book *Lane Changes*. It got a few good reviews and comments but didn't rise into the consciousness of the miniscule poetry reading public. This despite that Four

Way Books is a well-reputed publisher and that I have a highly vaulted opinion of myself as one of the best, most masculine, talented poets living.

I am different from the other whiners. I don't write for money even though I used to be a big earner. But then again, if you wrote poetry for money you'd have to be insane. Not mildly crazy like me.

I have no interest in defining the petals of a rose or the sadness of being dumped by another person. I don't write nature poems. I write about the nature of man. Primarily, myself.

Not that I particularly care if other people realize the uniqueness of my poems. I somehow feel that my works will live after me. As I told a psychiatrist at the Social Security Office when I received my disability stipend, "They should send my poems in a rocket into outer space so that after the world is destroyed future generations will be able to read my work."

I mean it. It sounds idiotic but opinions are merely opinions are merely opinions. My greatness is unopinionated. Just ask me. If I don't celebrate myself, who will?

My wife and I have become a darling aging couple. The anger, the disappointment, the selfishness have all gelled into acceptance and forgiveness. I no longer have the energy to do anything wrong. I no longer fight. A calm eye opens up in the hurricane of forgotten, demanding youth. I pop lithium twice a day and see myself behaving in startlingly normal ways. We still look young, especially her, but we are waddling around in the last fourth of our life spans. We become closer and closer. We will die together like two shadows. I am glad I have someone to be close too. I am glad that the absent God made something as wonderful and chemically magnificent as love. It is completely baffling. It is what anchors manics like myself to the solidity of tomorrow's wharf. It is what has always been beautiful in society. It is something worth dying for. It is why Caesar, upon looking at Cleopatra, asked, "Is this the face that launched a thousand ships?" The physicality of boxing, of love and of poetry. All bring me closer to myself. I embrace their purity and hug my separation from the trivia of life's minutiae as I fight on a dramatic, artificial stage. I am not lonely when I am punched, when I am kissing, or when I am writing poems. I have turned inside myself like a sock.

CODA

Narcissism is hungry for itself. So I have ignored my wife's development over the last decade. I can't see beyond my face. Then again this isn't her book. But she is part of me so that it is her book.

Ever since I went away to jail my wife became worried about earning a living. Rightly so. I wasn't bringing anything home. I didn't even have a desire to work.

Lauren has a Masters in Psychology and in Theatre. She decided to write some scientific papers in the hopes that it might give her a career. I don't know how she learned to do it. But she miraculously ended up publishing a bunch of them in top journals such as *The American Journal of Psychoanalysis* and *The Journal of Mind and Behavior.*

Lauren always had an interest in dreams and one day she woke up and decided to write books on dream analysis. From 1999–2011 she published five books, including a rather famous one, *Private Dreams of Public People,* for which Harry Winston's threw a book party catered by Le Cirque.

In addition she got a column in the *Daily News* and magazines such as *George* and *Swing.* She ended up on radio and television numerous times and has been written about in dozens of newspapers. She now moderates her own television series, *Celebrity Nightmares Decoded,* on the Biography Channel.

In other words, she is a hit and her résumé keeps growing. When I review her accomplishments I feel like writing a book about her instead of me.

But for better or worse I only really know myself. I can write about her accomplishments from a distance and with pride but they are not my own. As a self-involved person I can't get too involved with what she's done. I can only stare at her from a distance and fall into the well of her accomplishments and my own self-obsessions.

I'm looking at her. She's looking at me. We are happily drowning in life's pool. We are splashing. We are growing up to be children again. We are permanent. We have worked out a kind of mature love coming from a hippy generation where everything was free and meaningless.

David and Lauren, 2011